FIGHTING
TUSCARORA

A YORK STATE BOOK

FIGHTING
TUSCARORA

The Autobiography of
Chief Clinton Rickard

EDITED BY

**BARBARA
GRAYMONT**

SYRACUSE UNIVERSITY PRESS   1973

First Edition

Library of Congress Cataloging in Publication Data

Rickard, Clinton, 1882–1971.
  Fighting Tuscarora.

  (A York State book)
  Includes bibliographical references.
  1. Rickard, Clinton, 1882–1971. 2. Tuscarora
Indians. I. Graymont, Barbara, II. Title
E99.T9R53 1973   970.3 [B]   73-8208
ISBN 0-8156-0092-5

BARBARA GRAYMONT, an honorary member of the Indian Defense League of America, is the author of *The Iroquois in the American Revolution* (1972). She is Head of the Department of History and Economics at Nyack College, Nyack, New York, and holds a Ph.D. from Columbia University.

Manufactured in the United States of America

Contents

Foreword by BEULAH RICKARD   ix

EDITOR'S PREFACE   xi

EDITOR'S INTRODUCTION   xvii

1 Early Years   1

2 Army Life   14

3 Marriage and Family   37

4 Indian Leadership   49

5 The Border Crossing   69

6 Tragedy and Turmoil   90

7 Legalized Treachery   102

8 Depression and Oppression   115

9 The State Power Authority   138

10 Undefeated   153

EDITOR'S AFTERWORD   163

NOTES   169

INDEX   179

Illustrations

FOLLOWING PAGE 34

Lucy Rickard / Tuscarora school boys / Delia and Elizabeth Patterson / William Garlow / Rickard brothers / Private Clinton Rickard / Football team / Cavalry officers / Clinton and Ivy Rickard / Edith and Herald Rickard / Patterson family / Tuscarora school picnic / Clinton Rickard / Boiling sap / Elizabeth Patterson / Elizabeth, Clinton, and Clark Rickard / Marcus Peters / Edward A. Everett and Cayuga chiefs / Julia, Melvin W., and Dr. Sarah Dolan Patterson / William H. Patterson / Basketball team / Chief Rickard and group / Chief Deskaheh

FOLLOWING PAGE 98

Sophie Martin / David Hill / Frank Meness / Algonquins and wampum belts / John N. B. Hewitt / Alvis and Silas Hewitt / Chief Rickard and W. W. Husband / William and Clark Rickard / Border Crossing Celebration / Presenting Cayuga Claim / Chief Rickard and mayors / Lila Jimerson / Nancy Bowen / Tuscaroras at Maniwaki / George D. Rickard / Charles Rickard / Ox team / IDLA picnic / Fred Shipston and Chief Rickard / Chief Rickard and Cub Scouts / Indians at the UN / Chief Rickard and Andrei Vishinsky / Peace pipe at the UN

FOLLOWING PAGE 154

Indian Masons / Beulah Rickard / IDLA officials / Chief Rickard / William Rickard / Melvin W. Patterson / William Rickard / IDLA flag / The old soldier / Clinton Rickard and David Hill / Teresa Meness

Maps

Iroquois Indian Reservations   2
Luzon in 1902   18
Tuscarora Reservation   38
Algonquian and Iroquoian Indian Reserves   58

Foreword

As the wife of Chief Clinton Rickard, I should like to say a few words about this book which you will be reading. It was put together by our good friend, Barbara Graymont, who urged my husband to dictate his life story to her. I consider this book to be a great honor to him. Every word of it is true. I hope it will make as deep and lasting an impression on those who read it in the future as it has made on me. I cannot help but feel that way because I shared my life with him and know that his work—first, last, and always—was for the Indians. I can wish only that he had lived long enough to see the book in print, because this project had become very important to him.

After having read over the Preface and Introduction, I can say that every bit of the material is accurate. I fully appreciate all the years of effort that went into this work and am glad that this much of our Tuscarora history will now be preserved.

My husband and our friend worked together many years, not only on this book, but on recording Tuscarora language and history and in fighting for Indian rights. He often used to say to me, "Barbara's doing a great work. Nobody realizes what a great work she's doing." I am in full agreement and, in our own language, want to say, *Nyaweh!*

Tuscarora Reservation   Beulah Rickard
Spring 1973

Editor's Preface

THIS BOOK was many years in the making. Chief Clinton Rickard, the Tuscarora leader in the Indian rights movement, founder of the Indian Defense League of America, and self-taught expert on Indian-American legal history, had long been encouraged by his friends to gather and record his memoirs. But because the chief led a very busy life until well into his eighties, this autobiographical project did not get under way until the 1960s.

I first became acquainted with Clinton Rickard in November of 1959, when I was invited to attend the annual banquet of the Indian Defense League of America, an organization which had originally dealt with the United States–Canadian border crossing problems faced by Indians in both countries. The following day I was asked to the Rickard home for Sunday dinner. It was the beginning of a long friendship during which I worked closely with Chief Rickard and his son William on Indian affairs as well as the preservation of Indian history and culture. Both on that visit and later I was fascinated as I sat at the table and listened to the older man recount traditional Indian history and folklore and also tell of his own experiences throughout his many years of work for his people. I longed for a tape recorder so that I might take these tales down exactly as he told them.

In 1960, I began working with William Rickard on a study of the Tuscarora language. We both had a concern to preserve as much knowledge as possible of a language that was fast dying. After William's premature death at the age of forty-six in 1964, I continued my work on the language with his father. By 1965, I had a tape recorder, which would make the cultural and linguistic study much easier.

My schedule permitted me to spend only a few days with Clinton Rickard during the summer of 1965; so, I used the time to fulfill my longstanding desire to record the stories I had heard him tell. We began with the history of the founding of the Indian Defense League of America and then proceeded to the later work of the league. After this, he recorded some traditional Tuscarora history. Each tale was recorded first in English and then again in Tuscarora. We also taped several lists of vocabulary.

Clinton Rickard made a perfect informant. He was more than eager to be of use in this way, to preserve the culture of his people. Also, the loss of his son had left him desolate, and he felt that this work gave him a new purpose in life. During the summer of 1928, the Flemish linguist Frans Olbrechts and his wife had lived in the Rickard home while he studied the Tuscarora language. The chief's wife, Elizabeth Rickard, eventually became Olbrechts' major informant. The Rickards were thus carrying on a longstanding interest in linguistic work with me.

When I arrived at the Rickards' early on a June morning in 1966 to begin my summer's stay, I discovered that the chief had been taken to Veterans Administration Hospital in Buffalo the night before. Visiting him in Buffalo that afternoon, I found him much recovered. He greeted me with enthusiasm and said: "Why, I believe if you had come sooner, I wouldn't be here!" I smiled at his assurance of the therapeutic power of my presence and replied that I was ready to go ahead with the recording sessions as soon as he came home. He told me how happy he was to have me at his house for the summer and emphasized: "That is your home!" It was a sincere expression of his esteem and affection and made a great impression on me.

One of the first few days he was home from the hospital, as we were sitting on the porch talking, he politely but frankly asked me where my money was coming from. Since I had never up to that time, or subsequently, received any financial grant for the ethnological and linguistic work I did on the Tuscarora Reservation, I told him truthfully that I was living on money I had saved from my salary. He himself declined to accept any remuneration from me for our work together. Also, he was adamant that I should "not pay a cent" for my room and board. This decision put me in somewhat of an embarrassing dilemma. I knew that his income was very limited, and I did not wish to put any further financial strain on the family. Later in the summer, when he discovered that I was paying his wife for my keep, he emphatically reiterated: "No, no! Not you! You should not pay a penny! Not a penny!"

Early observers of the Iroquois had often remarked that the chiefs were often the poorest men in the village because they were always giving away what they had. Clinton Rickard grew to manhood in the nineteenth century and so was much closer to the old Indian way and philosophy of cooperation—a spirit that is rapidly dying out among many Indians today under the impact of the surrounding aggressive and competitive white culture. His son William had once particularly called my attention to this extremely generous trait in his father's nature and attributed it to the fact that he was "an old-time Indian."

When we were not busy recording, the chief sat and showed me his extensive collection of photographs, many of which concerned events pertaining to his long career in Indian affairs. I was most impressed with the historic significance of this collection.

At other times, I did secretarial work for him, typing the letters he dictated on the old battered machine that William had once used. In sorting through some of the boxes that contained his extensive correspondence, I came across much material of great ethnological and historic interest. With a wave of his hand at the cardboard boxes containing his correspondence, he said: "There are letters from all over the world in those boxes!" And so there were. He had an enormous number of friends.

These many letters and documents so carefully preserved were the record of his life's work. It was quite clear that Clinton Rickard had a deep sense of history. He knew the importance of his own work as well as the significance of his people's history and traditions. He was as scrupulous in preserving these materials as any trained archivist.

One afternoon while we were sitting on the screened porch looking through his old documents and photographs, he commented: "Some people have urged me to write this up, but—" He shrugged.

As I learned later, Glenn B. Coykendall, an Episcopal minister who had known him for over thirty years, was one of the most persistent in urging him to write his memoirs. The clergyman was well aware of the significance of Rickard's activities over the years. Now I felt that an opportunity had presented itself to me, and I immediately offered to be his amanuensis.

In subsequent months, I spent a certain part of every vacation period with the Rickards, simultaneously continuing my study of the Tuscarora language and taping more and more incidents from the chief's life story. It was obvious during these sessions that the two areas of activity that impressed him most and that he talked about most freely and completely were his struggles in the field of Indian rights and his army service in the Philippines. The story of his incarceration at Hull also came forth spontaneously and in great detail. Sometimes I would have to prod him to fill certain gaps in the story. In some instances he would respond readily and with great humor, but at other times, he was stubbornly silent or else protested that we had better not deal with that particular topic. For instance, it was only with the utmost difficulty that I could get him to talk about either of his first two wives—both of whom had died very young.

During the preparation of the manuscript, I found it necessary to go to others who had known and worked with the chief in years past to get details and confirm dates that he was not sure of. His wife Beulah Rickard was very helpful in providing information. Ivy Rickard's aunt, May Reed of Waverly, Ohio, also gave me some information about her niece, who had been Rickard's first wife. After the death of his eldest daughter Edith, Bettye Clement of Amarillo, Texas, a niece of Edith's husband Tom Hill, sent me Edith's newspaper clippings and pictures relating to Ivy and Clinton. Nellie Gansworth, sister of his second wife Elizabeth Rickard, reminisced with me about past events and provided some of the pictures for this book. Mrs. Jean M. Walker, deputy registrar of the Town of Lewiston, rendered much valuable service in searching for birth and death dates. Glenn B. Coykendall of Angola, New York, a long-standing friend of the Seneca Indians, reviewed for me his association of many years with Clinton Rickard, particularly during the Marchand murder trial. Sophie Martin, a charter member of the Indian Defense League of America, discussed some of the incidents leading to the founding of the league and added some names and details that Chief Rickard had forgotten. Teresa Meness of Maniwaki Indian Reserve, Quebec, also provided information on the early years of the border struggle. David Hill, the chief's closest friend and associate, came over to the Rickard home one evening and spent a long time recording his memories of the early days of the Indian Defense League of America. Chief Rickard kept prodding him to add details that he was leaving out and urged him to tell about their first meeting. The two old friends had a good laugh over the latter story. Later I was able to refresh the chief's memory with much of this information and have him tell the stories in his own words. Also of inestimable help in composing the entire biography were the innumerable newspaper clippings, letters, and other documents that comprise the personal papers of Clinton Rickard.

The chapter on Rickard's army years is particularly significant for the description it gives of soldier life in the Philippines during this period. Such first-hand accounts are rare in the literature of the Philippine Insurrection—or the Philippine Revolution, as the Filipino people prefer to call it. In addition to the chief's own vigorous narrative of his army experiences, several other persons were helpful in providing background material. Morton J. Netzorg of Detroit, Michigan, a specialist in Filipiniana, suggested and provided a number of important sources for the period. The National Historical Commission of the Republic of the Philippines gave very prompt attention to my inquiries. Charles J. Helenbrook, a comrade of the Eleventh Cavalry, gave many sidelights on his and Rickard's army service and also filled in the words to the old cavalry song, "Vinegar Bill," which Rickard had given me only in bare outline. John Albright of the Office of the Chief of Military History, United States Army, kindly permitted me to consult his research materials on the Eleventh Cavalry. These were very useful in establishing the chronology of some of the engagements described by Chief Rickard.

Much of the material that I had collected throughout the years was episodic and needed to be woven into a chronological and topical pattern. I tried as much as possible to keep Clinton Rickard's wording in doing this. It was necessary, of course, to do some editing to make a smooth narrative, for material spoken spontaneously is frequently marked by unfinished sentences, interrupted chronology, and grammatical lapses. Each chapter I put together was, however, read back to the chief for his approval, revision, and correction.

During the completion of the last part of the manuscript in the summer of 1969, Chief Rickard was seriously ill in Veterans Hospital in Buffalo. I had to proceed on my own but was much assisted by the tape recordings made earlier and also by the very carefully preserved collection of private manuscripts in the Rickard household. His large file of newspaper clippings dating from the early 1920s also saved me many a trip to the library. The last chapter was finished after his discharge from the hospital.

I was able to place the completed typescript of Rickard's autobiography in his hands in early 1970 and to read to him the new chapters that we had not checked previously.

The first typed draft was read by William N. Fenton of the State University of New York at Albany and Melvin W. Patterson and Beulah Rickard of the Tuscarora Reservation—each of whom made helpful comments. The chief's daughter, Karen Jacobson, also read the manuscript and brought to my attention certain significant incidents that her father had neglected to mention to me. A tape that she and her father had recorded several years previously also provided many details not covered in my own tapes.

The last item to be inserted, early in 1971, was the border-crossing problem on which Senator Walter F. Mondale gave assistance. By the time Senator Mondale's letter of March 23 arrived, enclosing the Immigration Commissioner's favorable ruling of March 17, 1971, Chief Rickard was again in the hospital and too critically ill to reply. I have therefore taken the liberty of inserting a brief paragraph in my own words in the last chapter describing the commissioner's letter. Following this paragraph, I have quoted the entire letter, since it will be a document of major importance to Indians in future years in crossing the United States–Canadian border.

Besides Clinton Rickard and his family, the following individuals very kindly provided photographs to be used in this book: Nellie Gansworth, Harry Patterson, Elsie Schimmelman, and Sallie Thomas, daughter of Chief Marcus Peters—all of the Tuscarora Reservation; Ray Fadden, Six Nations Indian Museum, Onchiota, New York; Theodore B. Hetzel, Haverford, Pennsylvania; Teresa Meness, Maniwaki, Quebec; and Raymond V. Putt, Toronto, Ontario. Thomas E. Zimmerman drew the maps.

To Chief Clinton Rickard, kindest of men and greatest of friends, I owe my most profound thanks for the privilege of working with him over the years and for the joy of experiencing the hospitality of his home and of learning the traditions of his people.

Nyack, New York   BARBARA GRAYMONT
Spring 1973

Editor's Introduction

THE TUSCARORA NATION—always least in importance among the tribes of the Six Nations Confederacy, always classed by them as a nation of secondary status in the League of the Iroquois, whose chiefs are restricted in speaking in the Grand Council—has, despite its subordinate role, raised up in its midst a man whose name and work will long be remembered wherever Indians gather to discuss the virtues of courage and justice. Clinton Rickard, born on May 19, 1882, and reared on the Tuscarora Reservation in western New York and largely self-educated, accomplished far more in his long career than many others with greater advantages and higher academic attainments. The United States Congress has been forced to recognize the Indian provisions of the Jay Treaty of 1794 and the Treaty of Ghent of 1814; many Indians falsely arrested and jailed have been set free; Indian civil liberties have been upheld; high schools in New York State have been opened to Indians; and tribesmen have been inspired to take pride in their own culture—all because of the work of this very remarkable and very gifted twentieth-century Tuscarora leader, who died on June 14, 1971.

This book joins the small but growing corpus of Indian autobiographies. It is unique in that it is the first autobiography of a Tuscarora Indian. The famous Sauk leader Black Hawk and the Cheyenne warrior Wooden Leg were participants in some of the great events of nineteenth-century Indian history, and their memoirs are accordingly important chronicles of the Indian past. The autobiographies of the two Winnebago Indians, Crashing Thunder and Mountain Wolf Woman, reveal the often shattering impact of white contact on Indian culture and personality in the late nineteenth and early twentieth centuries.[1]

This is the story of a modern Indian who yet had deep roots in his own cultural tradition. Although he far preferred "the Indian way," he moved easily in the white world and even became a leader and educator of whites. Every bit as much a patriot as Black Hawk and Wooden Leg

xvii

in defending Indian rights, Clinton Rickard was a new type of warrior in fighting for his people. Sure of his role in society, he possessed an inner security that Crashing Thunder lacked. His self-assurance enabled him to succeed in whatever form of employment he was engaged and to gather about him a large circle of both Indian and white friends as allies in the struggle for justice for the Indians. It also fortified him in meeting the threats of an Indian "establishment" that was often hostile to him.

Clinton Rickard lived a long life and was a part of great events. He lived the formative part of his life in the late nineteenth century, when the Tuscarora Reservation was far more isolated from the surrounding white community than it is today. The fact is a significant one, both for the development of his personality and his philosophy and for the deep knowledge of his own cultural traditions which this early environment gave him.

He was long an advocate of Indian nationalism and intertribal co-operation and, as founder of the Indian Defense League of America, a fighter for Indian rights. Even when he first became involved in Indian affairs in the 1920s and his field of political activity was confined mainly to helping Iroquois and Algonquin people, he never lost sight of the larger issues facing all Indians. His best friend and closest associate, David Hill, once related how "Chief trained me to watch the news-papers"—i.e., check the newspapers regularly for any material pertaining to Indians that might require Indian Defense League action. In later years, Rickard broadened his activities and fought against such government policies as enforced assimilation of Indians, suppression of traditional tribal methods of governing, intensified governmental relocation of reservation Indians to cities, and unilateral termination of federal responsibility for Indian affairs and placing Indians under the jurisdiction of states. He saw that the end result of the termination policy would be the eventual destruction of the Indian land base and the suppression of tribal sovereignty.[2] As he became better known throughout the country, Indians from many distant tribes made regular pilgrimages to his home on the Tuscarora Reservation. Among the most steady of these visitors were Hopi traditionalists from Arizona; but, there were also visits from Pit River Indians living in California, the Shoshone of Nevada, Potawatomie of Michigan, Stockbridge and Menominee of Wisconsin, and Carib from Dominica, British West Indies.

Despite his keen awareness of the problems facing tribes other than his own and his promotion of the concept that all Indians everywhere are brothers, he never forgot and never downgraded his own tribal affiliation. His Tuscarora heritage was always a source of much pride with him.

The Tuscaroras, who are perhaps less known to history than their other Iroquoian neighbors, are part of the famed Six Nations Confederacy that was organized about A.D. 1451. It was composed originally of the Five Nations: Mohawks, Oneidas, Onondagas, Cayugas, and Senecas. This was an early United Nations or League of Peace among the five tribes. Their union made these Iroquoian tribes the most powerful group in the Northeast, whose alliance was later eagerly sought by the contending European colonial powers in America. In the early eighteenth century, the Five Nations opened their door to their Tuscarora kinsmen from North Carolina who had been overcome in their conflict with the white settlers of that region. Then followed the long Tuscarora "Trail of Tears" northward, through Virginia, Maryland, and Pennsylvania, and into Five Nations country in what is presently New York State. The Oneidas gave them land, the confederacy accepted them as the sixth member nation, and they settled down to a few years of peaceful existence. The confederacy, however, never accepted them as full members in the same manner as the original five tribes and never gave their chiefs an equal voice in confederacy affairs. Even to this day, members of the other five tribes continue to remind the Tuscaroras of their subordinate status within the confederacy.

The American Revolution split the Six Nations Confederacy as each of the tribes chose to support either the British or the American side in the war. Most of the Tuscaroras and Oneidas chose loyalty to the Americans and sent their warriors to fight on the side of liberty and independence for the Thirteen States.

After the war, the citizens of New York, heedless of the welfare of the tribes who had supported their cause, placed the utmost pressure upon the impoverished Oneidas to sell their lands to the state.

The Tuscaroras, who held their lands only on sufferance from the Oneidas, once again found themselves homeless as a result of land sales by their Oneida protectors. They then moved westward and settled down on a mile square, or 640 acres, of land given by the Senecas. By grant from Robert Morris in 1797 and by purchase from the Holland Land Company in 1804, they later added more land to their reservation to comprise the present tract of 6,249 acres. The Tuscarora Reservation today is located within the geographical boundaries of the Town of Lewiston, Niagara County, New York.

At the conclusion of the Revolutionary War, most of the Iroquois partisans of the British, under the leadership of the famous Mohawk Captain Joseph Brant, moved to Upper Canada, now called Ontario, and settled along the Grand River. This tract, known as the Six Nations Reserve, is today the most populous of all the Iroquois reservations. The Fort Hunter Mohawks from the Lower Mohawk Castle along the Mohawk River refused to follow Joseph Brant and went with their own war captain, John Deserontyon, to the Bay of Quinté, which is now known as Deseronto or Tyendinaga Reserve. The émigré Oneidas who left the United States in 1849 settled along the Thames River, just south of present-day London, Ontario, rather than on the Six Nations Reserve.

For a number of years after the Revolution, the Six Nations Indians on both sides of the Canadian–United States border kept the confederacy strong and united. The council fire was moved from the ancient seat at Onondaga to Buffalo Creek—the largest of the Seneca reservations and now a more central location for the Iroquois than Onondaga.[3] Gradually, however, those who lived on each side of the border drifted apart and set up two Six Nations Confederacies, with council fires at both Grand River and Onondaga. There were now two complete sets of confederacy chiefs. Each confederacy went its separate way, each following the traditions and rituals as they had been handed down from the ancients.

The structure of the Six Nations Confederacy is that of an extended family, organized along clan lines. Each of the six tribes has its own clans or kinship units. Each member of a tribe belongs to one of these clans according to the affiliation of his or her mother, for Iroquoian descent is matrilineal. The Mohawks and Oneidas have only three clans: Turtle, Wolf, and Bear. The other four tribes have these three clans in addition to others, which vary from tribe to tribe. The remaining Iroquoian clans are Hawk, Snipe, Eel, Beaver, Deer, Heron, and Ball. Some persons identify this latter clan as the Ball Playing clan. Others say it is in reality a bird clan, which takes its name from a small bird that rolls up like a ball. Still another interpretation, and the one officially accepted by the chiefs at Six Nations Reserve, is that this is a Deer clan, named after a "rock" deer, which rolls itself into a ball when at rest.[4]

The Tuscaroras have seven clans, which at one time were divided into two groups, or moieties, to use the technical term. The First Moiety contained Bear, Eel, Turtle, and Beaver. The Second Moiety contained Wolf, Snipe, and Deer/Sand Turtle. There is today an ongoing controversy among members of this latter clan whether it should be called Deer or Sand Turtle. The Tuscarora Eel clan became extinct in recent years with the passing of Chief Tom Isaac, who was its last living member. During his later years he had no clan mother, and when he died, there was no woman left in the Eel clan to carry on the line. The Eel clan people on the Tuscarora Reservation today are the approximately sixty Onondaga Eels, descendants of the four Chew sisters—Leah, Charlotte, Diana, and Elizabeth. Since descent follows the mother's side, these Onondagas, though they and their maternal ancestors were born and raised on the Tuscarora Reservation, are technically outsiders and are carried on the Onondaga enrollment record rather than on the Tuscarora roll. They do, however, receive their treaty cloth annuity at the Tuscarora Reservation, rather than going to Onondaga for it, and are listed separately by the Tuscarora chiefs for annuity purposes.

Since everyone within a clan is related, marriage within a clan is forbidden by Iroquois traditional law. This prohibition also holds for in-clan marriage across tribal lines. A Tuscarora Turtle clan member, for instance, is related to the Turtle clan members of the other five tribes and is not permitted to marry into his clan, no matter what the tribal affiliation. Such in-clan marriages are considered incestuous; when they do sometimes occur, the offspring are barred from any tribal office, such as chief. It is said of such people: "They have their heads cut off."

Marriage within moieties was also anciently forbidden. A member of a clan belonging to the First Moiety was not permitted to marry a person from any of the clans that belonged to that moiety, but rather had to pick a marriage partner from the Second Moiety. The division of clans into moieties seems to have had mainly a ritual function. With the decline of the old traditional rituals among the Tuscaroras, the concept of moiety has also declined and become largely forgotten. The former moiety marriage prohibition is therefore no longer followed among the Tuscaroras, and in-moiety marriage has been practiced for about a hundred years. The Tuscaroras are still generally careful about not marrying into their own clans, however.

The clans form the political basis of the Six Nations Confederacy.

Each clan within a tribe is entitled to a certain number of chiefs, according to ancient tradition. These chiefs are picked by the leading woman
or clan mother of each clan and confirmed by the clan and Chiefs'
Council of the tribe. These village chiefs then become confederacy chiefs
upon approval of the Confederacy Council. Once installed in office, a
man is chief for life unless he voluntarily resigns or is deposed by his
clan mother.

Although Tuscarora chiefs usually go through the confederacy installation or condolence ceremony, they are not recognized as confederacy chiefs along with the holders of the original fifty—some say forty-
nine—chiefly titles of the former Five Nations. As Lewis Henry Morgan
explained the situation, according to information he received from his
Seneca informant, Chief Ely S. Parker, the Tuscaroras "were never
allowed to have a sachem [chief], who could sit as an equal in the
council of sachems [Confederacy Council]. The five nations were unwill-
ing to enlarge the number of sachemships founded at the institution of
the League."[5]

There have been many changes on the Tuscarora Reservation since
Clinton Rickard's younger days. As with any community, progress has
been a mixed blessing to the Tuscaroras. A modern, spacious brick
building and well-trained teachers have now replaced the old one-room
schoolhouse and haphazard educational system of Rickard's boyhood.
In his day, all the children grew up speaking Tuscarora and learned
English at school and in their associations with their white neighbors.
Today no one under the age of twenty speaks Tuscarora fluently.

In the early years of the twentieth century, only two or three men
who were permanent residents of the reservation worked off the reservation. Most of the Tuscarora men in those early years were very efficient
farmers. The New York State Indian agents, in their annual reports to
the Bureau of Indian Affairs throughout the nineteenth and early twentieth centuries, always mentioned especially the fine farms of the Tuscaroras.

With the coming of World War I, there was a great demand for labor
in the Niagara Falls factories. Some of the younger Tuscarora men began leaving the farms at that time for employment in the nearby factories. A few women from the reservation also began working in the
city of Niagara Falls as domestics. The Great Depression of 1929–39
was disastrous to Indian farming and entirely changed the economic base

of the reservation. Today a large majority of the men and many of the women are full-time wage workers, no longer self-employed but working off the reservation for a variety of white employers.

The coming of electricity to the reservation, and with it television, has guaranteed that the Tuscaroras will not only have a daily link with the white world but will be subjected to a steady barrage of white American culture and white ideas. The automobile has not only provided convenience in transportation for Indians but, as among whites, has contributed to a population dislocation and weakening of ties of home and community.

Clinton Rickard grew up under the old way, when the community was more closely knit. His lack of formal education was perhaps more of an asset than one would first suspect, for it meant that he was not taught to be ashamed of his culture by a series of misguided teachers all too eager to encourage Indian children to adopt white ways. Such has been the fate of very many young Indians. Rickard's roots in the community gave him a steady self-assurance. With a firm persistence and a quiet dignity, he began wearing Indian regalia on all ceremonial occasions and whenever he was to give a speech before either Indian or white groups. In the face of continued ridicule from his own tribesmen, who accused him of "going back to the blanket," he gradually educated both his own people and whites on the values of Indian traditions and culture.

His Indian regalia represented several cultural traditions. The fringed moose-hide suit, tanned in the traditional Indian manner, was made by an Algonquin woman. The beadwork on the jacket was sewn according to Chief Rickard's direction to depict the ancient Six Nations alliance of friendship with their white neighbors. Although he occasionally wore the regular Iroquois feathered cap, or gostoweh, he much preferred the splendid eagle-feather Plains headdress. The Plains bonnet, popularized by Wild West shows around the turn of the century, has now been adopted by many, if not almost all, non-Plains tribes.

As an Iroquois and a member of the Six Nations, Chief Rickard was always strongly traditional in his leadership in Indian affairs and in his attitudes. He was anti-assimilation, anti-citizenship, and pro-tribal sovereignty. This meant that he considered his own Tuscarora Nation to be a sovereign nation, capable of governing itself as a political entity without interference from the government of the European immigrants who surrounded his tribal territory. He believed that, since the Six Nations Confederacy had existed for many centuries before the establishment of either the United States or Canada, the integrity of this ancient confederacy should not be destroyed by attempts at political and cultural suppression from these newer nations located on what was formerly Indian soil. He advocated the same sovereignty for all other Indian nations that he did for his own. His ideal was one of cooperation between races and nations rather than dominance of one over the other.

As a young man, Rickard enlisted in the United States Army and fought for the United States government. He saw no contradiction in these actions, for he was merely following the traditions of his Tuscarora ancestors who had always come to the aid of the United States in all its wars. Among themselves the Iroquois had formed a League of Peace, and its protection extended to all who chose to adhere to it. But against those who threatened the confederacy and its friends, war was considered justified.

Rickard was devoted to several veterans' organizations in later years, responding to them as a newer version of the old traditional warrior societies—he found a camaraderie with men who had lived through a common danger and displayed their bravery and who had experiences to share. That this good will worked both ways is evident when considering Rickard's success in calling on his friends in these veterans' organizations to exert pressure at various times on the United States government to help Indians in their struggles.

Unlike many men who join the Masonic Lodge for business reasons or for prestigious social contacts, Rickard took Masonry, and especially its religious teachings, very seriously. Masonry has been quite attractive to many Indians over the years. Ely S. Parker, Arthur C. Parker, Henry Roe Cloud, Charles Eastman, and Carlos Montezuma were but a few noted Indians who were Freemasons. Arthur Parker particularly equated Masonry with the ancient Indian secret societies.[6] Here again Rickard continually called upon his lodge brothers, and with much success, for help in the fight for Indian rights. He never ceased to educate his white brethren to the values of Indian culture and to the injustices the Indian people suffered.

The Indian Defense League of America (IDLA) was originally founded by Rickard to combat the restrictive provisions of the United States Immigration Act of 1924 and to open the border between the

United States and Canada freely to Indians. Once this aim had been achieved, he and the members continued the organization to carry on the fight for Indian rights in general and to educate both Indians and whites on the values of Indian culture. The annual Border Crossing Celebration serves admirably as an educational medium, teaching the public the value and dignity of Indian ways.

Membership of the IDLA has been heavily Iroquois and Algonquin, but for a brief time there was also a chapter among the Stockbridges in Wisconsin. Activities by the IDLA on behalf of Indians have therefore frequently concerned either Iroquois or Algonquins, but not exclusively so. The Indian Defense League, and particularly its Wisconsin branch, were also active in the unsuccessful fight to keep the federal government from terminating its responsibilities for the Menominee tribe. After termination of the Menominees had taken place, the IDLA continually publicized its disastrous effects on the Menominee people in the effort to reverse the government's short-sighted policy.

In addition to its political and cultural activities, the IDLA supports a continuing social program to bring Indians together in close fellowship and to give aid to any of the members in personal need. The several "socials" that are held during the year serve both to raise funds and to bring members together for good times. Corn soup suppers, strawberry socials, and a free Christmas party for all are regular IDLA events. Members who are sick are regularly visited and also helped with financial donations if they must go to the hospital. The organization has also assisted Indians, whether members or not, to find jobs, pursue their education, and secure pensions due them.

The IDLA has had its roots among both reservation and urban Indians and has thus been unique in the history of Indian organizations. It has shown great success in bridging what are often sharp differences in outlook between reservation and urban Indians.[7] Problems faced by Indians in an urban environment often cause these city dwellers to ignore or downgrade the problems of their reservation brethren, such as treaty rights and issues of tribal sovereignty. Part of the success of the IDLA in unifying both its urban and reservation membership is no doubt a result of the fact that its urban members still maintain close ties to their reservations and return frequently for visits.

There has always been a certain amount of tension between the IDLA and other Indian organizations, such as the National Congress of

American Indians, that advocate either Canadian or United States citizenship for Indians and assimilation of Indians into the dominant society. Chief Rickard was continually adamant in urging Indians not to vote in the white man's elections, for to do so would transfer allegiance from the Indian nations of their birth to the nations of the white man. European immigrants, he felt, have no right to try to confer citizenship on the American Indian in his own country. Accepting the white man's citizenship and voting in his political system, according to such traditionalists as Rickard, jeopardize the sovereignty of Indian nations and undermine their treaties. As Rickard noted, "How can a government make a treaty with its own citizens?"

Clinton Rickard became very knowledgeable in the areas of Indian law and treaties. In his great desire to help his Indian people, he secured a copy of the *United States Code* and studied thoroughly the section dealing with Indians. He also had in his library a large book of Indian treaties whose pages are now quite ragged from extensive use by both him and his son William. The training in leadership he received in his veterans' and Masonic organizations and the experience in working with whites in these groups, as well as his work in the Tuscarora Chiefs' Council, were valuable for his own role as leader and interpreter of his culture to whites.

He was a person of commanding presence in whom others had confidence. He could take humble people—both Indians and whites—and so inspire them to dedicate themselves to a cause that they became not only active workers but remarkably well informed on both the more general and the technical aspects of Indian affairs. Most of these friends remained steadfast over the years. Some of his associates, however, playing upon his good nature and trust, used his friendship and knowledge of Indian affairs in order to exploit the movement. On occasion, Rickard trusted some of these people too long, and he frankly admits in Chapter Eight the consequences of this unguarded trust in describing his unfortunate relations with one of these opportunists. Such betrayers angered him but never made him cynical, since he found too many positive goals to work for to spend time brooding over disappointments.

One of the projects that concerned Rickard most deeply was the protection and preservation of the Indian land base. The typical Indian love of the land can be seen in Clinton Rickard's great pride in his farm.

He viewed the land as the heritage from his ancestors, never to be alienated. It is the foundation of the community.

This attachment to the land is still present in the Tuscarora Indians, even though most of them no longer support themselves entirely by farming. The majority, however, have kitchen gardens to supply a large amount of their food, and all of them feel a closeness to the land that is often incomprehensible to many modern urbanized Americans. Indian feeling was most dramatically revealed in the determined Tuscarora resistance to the New York State Power Authority's efforts to seize a large portion of their reservation for a reservoir.

It was during the State Power Authority struggle that William Rickard, Clinton's eldest son, first began to emerge as a tribal leader. He had previously received training in Indian affairs under his father's tutelage in the Indian Defense League of America. When the crisis in the community came, he took a leadership role in holding out for traditional Indian values that he had learned from his elders.

William and his father were always very close and in many ways very similar. They were alike in their interest in Indian rights, in their Indian conservatism, and in their personalities. Both were men of brilliance and native genius, easygoing nature, selfless devotion to others, and tenacious belief in the rightness of their own actions. Both were deeply religious men but revealed this trait in different ways. Clinton always preferred the church. William, though he had been voluntarily baptized as an adult and had passed through the "Christian degrees" of Masonry, came to be a devoted follower of the Longhouse religion, much preferring it to Christianity.

Clinton, remembering how the Longhouse chiefs had used him ill in the past by ridiculing him and blocking him at every turn, was much hurt by his son's inclinations and often argued with him on matters of religion. William would not be moved. He felt that the newer chiefs of the nearby Tonawanda Reservation were more upright and dependable men than the older chiefs who had opposed his father, and he wanted to learn more of the religion they followed. In truth, Clinton had a high regard for some of these newer Tonawanda chiefs, but he also had a strong attachment to his own religious faith. He always believed that a person could be a good church member and a good traditionalist Indian, too, devoted to the culture and values of the Indian people. But he could also accept those of differing faiths, for there was never any religious discrimination within the Indian Defense League of America. Within his organization, both Longhouse followers and Christians joined together in working amicably for Indian welfare.

One of the traits that his Indian friends admired most about Clinton Rickard was his courage despite much personal misfortune and his refusal to be cowed by whites. As his wife Beulah Rickard expressed it: "He always stood up to the white man." Although he was well aware of the injustices suffered by Indians and continually fought against the oppression of his people, he never preached hatred of whites. He always believed in converting them where possible. Throughout the years, he came into contact with many whites with whom he had close and affectionate relations. Some of them had a very important formative influence on his young life—the three Masons who used to visit his father when Clinton was a boy, his army captain, and his first wife. And those whites who became his followers were dedicated to him. Many of them joined wholeheartedly in the Indian rights movement and made continued valuable contributions over the years.

It was one of the unique achievements of Chief Clinton Rickard that he was able to be a mediator between two worlds. He considered it his aim not only to contend against injustice but to bring reconciliation. He was a warrior who was also a man of peace and who remained throughout his life a fighter for the rights of his people.

FIGHTING
TUSCARORA

1

Early Years

MANY YEARS AGO, our Tuscarora people lived in the region that the white people later called North Carolina. How long they lived there, nobody knows. They had separated from the other tribes known as Five Nations and had gone south to find better hunting lands. When the Europeans came to our land and settled near the Tuscaroras, there was controversy. The whites wanted our land, and they kidnapped our children for slavery. This caused war. As a result of these wars, my people moved back north again where the Oneidas kindly received them. Our people followed the white roots of peace to the source.[1] The Five Nations then became the Six Nations.

When the American Revolutionary War came, many Tuscaroras supported the American army. One of my ancestors was a lieutenant in this war and did good service for the Americans.

After the war, my people again moved westward, almost to the Niagara River, and settled on land given them by the Senecas. Later, they bought more land next to this tract, and here they have lived ever since.

I was born on the Tuscarora Reservation on May 19, 1882, the third son of George and Lucy Rickard. My two elder brothers were Edgar and Frederick. Chester was the youngest. We were all very close in age. Edgar was born on October 11, 1878; Fred on February 1, 1880; and Chester on January 12, 1883.

Among my people, it has always been the custom that the children take the nationality and clan of the mother. Both my parents were Tuscaroras, and we boys were all members of the Beaver clan because our mother was of that clan. My father always claimed to be Deer clan. He had been made a chief in 1885 and was the sachem, or peace chief, of his clan. His nephew, Dr. Philip T. Johnson, was the chief warrior, or sub-chief. Chief Luther Jack used to keep a personal notebook on tribal affairs, and in a notation for the year 1915 he has a list of all the Tuscarora chiefs, the years they became chiefs, and their clans. He has

1

my father listed as Sand Turtle clan. For many years there has been a disagreement among our people about these two clans. Some claim there is no Deer clan, and others claim there is no Sand Turtle clan. My father once made a joke about it. He said: "Some people say we're Deer clan and some say we're Sand Turtle. I guess we're half and half!"

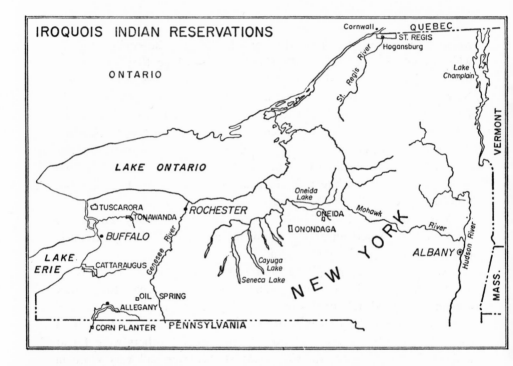

My father's mother was originally named Rihsakwad Patterson.[2] Her first name is the Indian form of Elizabeth. When her first husband, whose name was Isaac Jack, died, she married a German from Pennsylvania. This was my father's father. I never knew this grandfather because he soon left my grandmother and the children and moved on to Canada. He settled on the Six Nations Reserve at Grand River and raised families there. Grandmother Rihsakwad was a good and kindly woman whom I loved very much and who was always very affectionate with us boys.

My grandmother traveled from place to place on the reservation, taking turns living with one of her daughters or sons. Her traveling in

this way came about for the following reason. Among our people, it is
the custom and tradition that, should we lose a family member by death,
we should stay at home for ten days and not go anywhere in public. This
is because the spirit of the departed might want company during those
ten days, before its final departure. Then, after the ten days are up, it
is all right to go abroad. My grandmother had lost an eighteen-year-old
son, but she was not able to stay at home ten days, according to custom.
The result was that from then on she continued to travel here and there,
staying a while with a son or daughter, then going on to the next one of
her children.

She owned cows, and wherever she went she drove her cows before
here when she came to live at one of her children's homes. My brothers
and I always appreciated having this good woman come and live with
us. For one thing, we were so poor that we often had practically nothing
to eat. Whenever we boys saw grandmother coming to our house with
her cows, we knew we would have some good milk to drink. We were
always so happy to see her with her cows, and we appreciated her visits
so much, that we would run to her, laugh, and jump up and down
around her.

My mother's father was also a goodly man. This was William Garlow, who lived to be over ninety years old.[3] He lived with my parents
for many years and he taught me much history about our Tuscarora
people. William Garlow's father had left North Carolina after the wars
with the white settlers there and had passed on the story of this dispute
to my grandfather. Grandfather Garlow told me all this history just as
he had it from his father.

In 1846 William Garlow was one of a number of Six Nations
Indians who went to Kansas at the insistence of the government. During
that period, the government was trying to move all Indians west of the
Mississippi River. A white man came and told our people that fine
houses and farms would be waiting for them in Kansas. Many believed
him and set off on this long trip. My grandfather was a young man of
about nineteen at the time. When they arrived in Kansas, they found
nothing but emptiness for miles and miles. Without food and without
medicine, these poor people sickened and died off in great numbers
until there were only a very few left out of the whole emigration party.

My grandfather was fortunate enough to escape. The Mexican War
was on at the time and he got a job driving cattle for the United States

Army. After the war, he came back to the reservation to live. He had no claim here now, for he had given up everything when he and the others left. He begged to be allowed to build a small house in the fence corner—that corner of the field, next to a rail fence, which is not plowed and not in use. This permission was given him by the council, and he settled down on this reservation again, married, and raised his family.

The house where I was born is no longer standing. It was a frame house situated on the left-hand side of a lane running south from Upper Mountain Road, just across from the place where my son Clark now lives. We lived here for several years while my brothers and I were small.

One of the earliest memories I have is of the four of us boys riding on one of my father's hogs. All four of us were on that hog together when my mother's brother-in-law, Jeremiah Peters, came by, saw us, and called out: "There goes the whiskey gang!" He said this because my father was quite a drinker and Jeremiah Peters thought that we boys would turn out the same way. He was wrong. As it eventually happened, only one of my brothers ever took to drink.

This Jeremiah Peters had been a drummer in the Union army during the Civil War. He was captured by the Confederates and sent to Libby Prison in Richmond, Virginia. There, he said, the guards fed them just like hogs, throwing dried corn in their pen. He made his escape by going to the camp toilet, which was over a river, and slipping through the hole into the water beneath. He followed the river to freedom before the guard realized he was gone. Then, not knowing any other regulation of the army whatever, he made his way directly back to the Tuscarora Reservation without trying to find his unit again. As a result, after the war, he could not collect a pension for his war service, even though he was greatly weakened as a result of serious sickness while in the army. This shows how our people often do not know the white man's ways. If Jeremiah had known, he would have gone back to the army when he left prison and would have had everything that happened to him listed on his record. In later years, my father helped him to get his pension. Just after he received it, he died at age fifty-eight on March 10, 1900, of what Doc Huggins called malarial conditions.

When I was about four years old, my father took up with another woman and left us. He joined a Wild West show and traveled to England. During all the time he was gone, he never wrote to my mother and never sent her a penny. Those were hard times with us. My mother did washing for white people who lived on the ridge. They would bring their clothes to her and she would haul water, heat it, and work at the washboard all day long for fifty cents. My mother made out the best she could, but it was not always possible for her to get us enough to eat. One day a white farmer paid her with a small sack of flour and we were overjoyed at the thought of the big meal we were going to have. After mother baked the bread and we had started to eat it, we discovered that the flour was half sand. We had to go hungry that time.

I remember many times in my childhood, even when my father was home, that food was scarce. Often we lived only on Indian corn bread with no meat to eat. My mother would also cook a green which grew wild in the yard and which we called pig weed. But it was tasty, and even today I long for it.

My father had a sister who had married Ely Patterson. Their daughter had a little boy named Eddie whom I used to play with. They lived at the back of our place at the time. Eddie had broken his back and was therefore not able to get about like the other children. His mother used to call me over to keep him amused. I had a sleigh bell tied on a string that I used to give him. He enjoyed dragging the bell around his chair and listening to the jingling noise it made. One night during the time my father had left home, when we four brothers were asleep in bed with our mother, I was awakened by a strange noise. I looked out into the dark and saw something in the middle of the floor going round and round and I heard a bell jingling. I was so scared that I was afraid to move. Finally I crawled underneath the covers and kept well hidden. The next morning, Eddie's mother came over and told us that her boy was dead. I always thought it must have been his spirit that had come over to us that night.

One day we boys saw a man with a suitcase coming to our place. We thought it was a peddler and we all ran up to him and begged him to open his case so that we might see his wares. We had a surprise coming for it was no peddler at all, but our father. He had been away nine months and my brothers and I did not recognize him.

Although it had been hard for us while my father was away, it was also hard after he returned. All his life he had a problem with alcohol. When he was drunk, he was mean to all of us. My mother was a big woman and my father was small and slight for a man. In spite of the difference in their size, he used to beat her brutally when he had been drinking. His behavior in this regard made a very deep impression on me, especially so since my mother was a very good woman and in no way deserving of this treatment. My father would also take his feelings out on us boys when he was in a bad mood. One winter night he came home drunk and went on a rampage, threatening to shoot us. We boys ran outside and hid in the outhouse, lying flat on our stomachs inside and never daring to move. Father had also come outside and was shooting in all directions. We then slipped out of the outhouse and hid in the bushes, where we thought he would have less chance of finding us. Before long, we could not stand the bitter cold and so went to a neighbor's house and hid under the bed. We returned home the next morning and stopped to examine the outhouse where we had been hiding. The boards were full of bullet holes.

When I was about seven years old, I took my brother Chester with me and went out into the woods. I made an appeal to the Great Spirit for three things. I asked that He keep me always from the temptation to drink alcohol. I prayed also that He would keep me from ever harming a woman. And then I asked that He would allow me to grow big and strong so that in the future I could protect women and other helpless people who were being harmed. The Great Spirit heard my prayer and granted every one of my requests.

My father continued in his usual abusive manner until we boys grew old enough and strong enough to put a stop to it. Once when he had been drinking and went after our mother, we caught him and put him down on the floor. My brother Fred held him there while he fumed and squirmed, trying to get loose. Father tried his best to bite Fred, but Fred just turned father's face to the floor and said, "Now, bite that!" After this incident, our father never troubled our mother again.

When we boys were still quite small, our parents moved to another house on the north side of Upper Mountain Road. It was here we lived until we were grown. The house and grounds now belong to my son Clark, who lives there with his family.

It was a custom in the old days for people to let their livestock roam loose and root or graze for themselves. In the evening, my father used to send us boys to round up the cows. I would usually find them grazing down by Black Nose Spring. This area down by the spring was one that I always admired, and in later years, it was the place I would pick out to build my home.

We lived next to Luther Jack, who was sachem chief of the Wolf clan. Luther Jack used to complain about our pigs coming over to his place. One day he poisoned our sow; so, we were not able to have any more pigs. There was nothing we could do about this killing, but we never forgot it.

My father used to do business with some white men down in Ransomville, selling them chickens. They and my father became very good friends, and they would frequently come to our house for Sunday dinner. My mother had the reputation of being a very good cook. These men treated me very kindly. They would bring presents, such as candy or sometimes a nickel, and always had a good word for us boys. I asked my father who they were and he said they were Freemasons. I remember their names were Burmaster, Curtiss, and Ransom.⁴ These Sunday visits were events that I always looked forward to. I was about seven when these fellows first started coming to our place. They were constant visitors for many years and were such good men that I began to form in my mind the hope that I would grow up to be like them. I thought what a great thing it would be if I could also be a Mason. This was my dream for many years.

One time, when I was still a small boy, my grandmother took me up on her lap and read my palm. She said she saw me going far away. I would pass between a gateway that had lions on each side. She then saw me going into battle. There were two flags—one of which was an American flag and the other of which she could not recognize. She said I would pass between two lines of fire, and would be fired upon first by one side and then by another and would almost lose my life. "But," she said, "you are going to go through this line of fire and come back home to your people. You will come back as a young man, and your lifetime will be devoted to helping your people. And you will live a long life."

I put this prophecy in the back of my mind and never thought of it again until years later when certain events in my life would call it forth.

There were many important traditions of our tribe that the chlidren learned from their elders. When the children grew up, they in turn passed these traditions down to their children. In this way, our history was never forgotten.

I was taught when I was a boy that if I should ever discover gold while digging on our land that I should cover it up again and keep my mouth shut about it forever. The old folks on our reservation never wanted to find gold because they knew from experience the white man's greed for wealth. The white people kill each other for gold, and if ever they found that we had any on our land, they would kill our people, take our land, and leave us with nothing. This warning has been handed down among my people for about two hundred years.

There were two churches on our reservation—Presbyterian and Baptist. The Presbyterian was the older and was the original Christian mission among our people.[5] The building used to be situated on Upper Mountain Road next to the cemetery, which was the old Presbyterian burying ground. This building was moved to its present location on Walmore Road in the spring of 1893. The Baptist church was up on Mount Hope Road, and Frank Mt. Pleasant was the preacher there.

My parents attended the Presbyterian church. My mother was a good singer and a good piano player, and I always enjoyed listening to church music. My grandmother Rihsakwad would frequently take me to church with her. Sometimes she and I would be the only attenders. Nicholas Cusick was our preacher. He was the father of Simon Cusick and a direct descendant of Lieutenant Nicholas Cusick, the Revolutionary War veteran.

My grandfather Garlow, who was living with us, was a kindly man and a great lover of music. He had the reputation on our reservation of being a noted fiddle player, and he frequently used to perform at the Tuscarora National Picnic. I remember how he could really make that fiddle talk. One day when some visitors came to our house, Grandfather got out his fiddle to entertain them. In those days, church people were very strict about dancing; so, when Mother saw he was about to play some music for the guests, she said: "All right, Father, just so long as it doesn't raise the foot."

Grandfather started out very sweetly, but the music began to get faster and faster. Suddenly he swung into *Turkey in the Straw,* and everybody started feeling very gay. Just then, Mother called out to him: "Father! That's enough!"

We had a good laugh for years over how Mother kept Grandfather from leading the family astray.

When I was a boy, there were two schools on the reservation.

School Number One was located near the Baptist church on Mount Hope Road. It was the closer one to our house and the one we boys attended. My brother Chester and I had a difficult time at this school. The boys did a lot of fighting, and the teacher could not maintain order. She was particularly lenient with some of the bigger boys who, we discovered later, were her nephews. With some of the rest of us, she was very strict.

We had one big fellow in our school who was an expert skater. One day while we were playing hockey on the ice, I skated over and took the puck away from him. He came up behind me and cracked me over the head. I walked back to the school house and waited by the entrance. When this big boy came by, I hit him. He hit back and I grabbed his head and held on, all the while punching and scratching him. He kept gnawing at my wrist and every time he did so, the blood spurted out, but he could not make me quit. This fight went on for a long time while the teacher stood ringing and ringing the bell. I would not let go of the boy because I knew he would give me a beating if I did. Finally he gave up and we went back into the school house and took our seats. I looked over at him and saw that he was all black and blue with lumps and bruises.

One day at school my brother Chester asked permission to leave the room but was refused by the teacher. The little fellow just had to sit and relieve himself right there in his seat. When I saw this, I did not bother to ask permission when I had to leave the room, but just walked out. The teacher made us both stay after school for this. The next day, she called me up to her desk and had me hold out my hand so she could hit it. I did so, but just as she was about to hit me, I quickly pulled my hand back. She came down with a whack on her own hand. Seeing how angry she was, I turned and ran out the door with her after me. She grabbed for my frock but slipped and fell. I gave a whoop and was off. My brother Chester thereupon got the whipping that she had intended for me. When we returned home that day, we told our father that we would never go back to that school again.

From that time on, Chester and I attended School Number Two, which was situated in the western part of the reservation and quite a distance from our home. Tamar Johnson was the teacher there and was very good to us. She was the daughter of Elias Johnson, who had written a history of the Tuscaroras and Six Nations. Her mother was my father's half-sister. In later years, when I was about sixteen, I had a white teacher who was only a year or two older than I.

In my childhood days, I remember how our family was poorer than poor. We boys would walk two or three miles back and forth to school, through the snowbanks and in all kinds of weather. The only lunches we had were the salt pork sandwiches that we carried in our little buckets.

We did not have Christmas parties and presents such as the children today do. Some teachers were always good to us, and at Christmas time they gave us presents of one orange apiece and maybe little bags containing a half dozen pieces of candy each. These were great pleasures when I was a boy.

The educational system on our researvation was very inadequate. It was not necessary for the teacher to have much training. Nor was it required that the children attend school regularly. Girls and boys both helped out at home and on the farm and their school attendance was often irregular. I myself began working for a neighboring farmer when I was seven years old and received a dollar a week. Also, of course, I helped out at home. Children always worked in those days.

We did not have schools equal to those of the white children. Our education was limited first to six grades, and later to eight grades. There was never any high school for Indians. Any Indian child who wanted a higher education than that which was provided on the reservation had to go outside to a white school and pay extra. Not many Indian parents could afford to send their children to boarding schools or to the white public high schools. Some Tuscarora children went to Tunesassa, the Quaker boarding school which was situated next to the Allegany Seneca Reservation. Some stayed at this school only a year or two and then came back to our reservation to finish their schooling. Others stayed a longer time and got a far better education than what they could in our Tuscarora schools. Some others went to Hampton Institute in Virginia, a school that educated both Negroes and Indians, and others went to Carlisle in Pennsylvania or Lincoln Institute in Philadelphia. Most of us, however, stayed right on the reservation and got what education we could from our own schools. Our children frequently went to school only off and on and did not have anything like a steady education. I went to school until I was about sixteen and I finished the Third Reader. My brother Chester finished the Second Reader. Edgar, my eldest brother, went away to Carlisle Indian School and received the best education of any of our family.

Tuscarora boys learn to hunt when they are still very young. Hunting and fishing are great pleasures to all Indian boys, and they were to me. This is not just recreation for us. A good hunter can be a good provider for his family. This is true even today, despite the fact that our reservation is surrounded by cleared land and increasing white population. On the little more than six thousand acres of our reservation, there are still woods, brush, and swamp where both deer and small animals live.

When I was eleven years old, I had a hunting experience that I shall never forget. My father had an old muzzle-loading shotgun that I used to use for hunting. I took this gun with me into the woods one day to do some shooting. I aimed at a patridge and pulled the trigger, but the shot went only a short way. It annoyed me so much to miss my game that I poured an extra generous handful of powder down the muzzle for the next try. Then I aimed at a squirrel in a tree and fired. The shot hit the squirrel with such force that he flew way up into the air and the gun went over my head backwards and stuck into the ground, muzzle first. I pulled the gun out, cleaned it off, and loaded up again. Very shortly, I noticed a pain in my right shoulder. Suddenly I could not use my arm. When I went back home, I was afraid to tell my father what had happened.

For the next few days, I kept my secret to myself. Whenever my father asked me to harness the horses or yoke the oxen, I ran as fast as I could to the barn to do the chore, all with my left hand, before my father could come and see that I could not use my right arm. Once I was in the field with the oxen rolling the ground and my father told me to hurry up. With that, I whipped the oxen, using my left hand. My father told me: "You're not left handed! Use your right hand!"

It was then that he discovered that I did not have the use of my right arm and I had to explain to him what had happened. He examined my shoulder, found that the collar bone had been broken, and told me to go to Doc Huggins in Sanborn.

I walked the five miles to Sanborn to see the doctor but found that he was out when I got there. Then I walked back home again and told my father that the doctor was out when I called. I never did get to see the doctor for this injury. My collar bone eventually healed but left a small lump where the bone knit together. I have this small memento of my early hunting escapade with me yet.

Above all, I loved to fish. When I was very young, I used a rod which I made myself from a hickory pole. For bait I used worms or small crabs that I caught by hand in the creek. When I grew a little bigger, then I used a spear for fishing. My brothers and I would take our spears, walk all the way to Wilson, fifteen miles away, and there we would fish all day and all night long in the creek, lighting our way with a kerosene lantern after dark. The next day we would come home with our catch. There was good fishing right on our reservation, too, with northern pike and suckers being the most common fish.

These were some of the ways in which we passed our time as boys and learned how to do the things that boys and men should do.

When the Spanish-American War broke out, I was still in school. I tried to enlist in the army, but was turned down because of my age, since I was only sixteen.

Sometime after this, when I had left school, my parents and my brothers and I went to Kane, Pennsylvania, to seek employment in the lumber works. While we were there, my mother went to Carlisle where my brother Edgar had finished school and took him money because he wanted to study further to be a minister. When she came back, we were done cutting wood and all returned home to the reservation.

While my brother Edgar was away at school, he frequently wrote letters home saying that even though all his brothers would become drunkards, he would be steady and would become a minister. He said he wanted to study at Dickinson College and under D. L. Moody in Chicago.[6] My father, mother, and grandmother, therefore, did their utmost to send him all the money they could. The unfortunate result was that Edgar never carried through with his ambition to be a minister and was the only one of us boys who ever turned to liquor. When he married, his family always suffered much hardship and sadness because of his drinking.

After we had come home from the lumber works, I took the money I had earned and bought some work clothes, a team of horses, and a few other things. I also had a job working for a white farmer named Jim Hewitt who lived next to our reservation. It was an ancestor of this James Hewitt who gave his name to our Tuscarora Hewitts. The original Indian Hewitt changed his last name to please his white friend and also to get a new broadcloth suit of clothes that his friend offered him to make this change. In my work, I was beginning to make out well and was very encouraged.

My father was a chief and had the job of collector for the Chiefs' Council. This meant that he had to collect the wood tax of $12 a year from each of the white people and other non-Tuscaroras who lived on our reservation.[7] This tax covered the cost of letting these people pick up dead wood and fallen trees for use as firewood. They were not permitted to cut standing trees. My father had used up this money that he had collected. He therefore took what was left over of the money I had saved from my lumber job to make up his deficiency when he turned the taxes over to the council. This very much discouraged me, and I determined to strike out on my own.

The year was 1901. The Spanish-American War was over in Cuba but still going on in the Philippines. Because of the Philippine Insurrection, the United States Army was calling for more volunteers and had increased the cavalry from ten to fifteen regiments. A way to a new life had opened to me.

My old school chum, Nelson Mt. Pleasant, and I went to Fort Niagara to enlist in the army. We were given a ride in a horse and buggy part of the way and were let off not far from the fort. We decided to run the rest of the way. When we reported for enlistment, the army doctor told us to take off our shirts so he could examine us. My friend was still out of breath and his heart was beating hard. The doctor told him to put his shirt back on and dismissed him. I tried to intercede, explaining to the doctor that we had been running, but he just shook his head. He then examined me and pronounced me the best physical specimen he had ever seen. I was only nineteen but weighed about 200 pounds and was very powerful. The prospect looked very favorable for me. It was so important to me not to be rejected this time because of my age that I added on two years to bring my age to within one month of twenty-one. In the United States Army records I am therefore listed as having been born May 19, 1880.

My desire came to pass. I was accepted and I enlisted in the army at Fort Niagara on April 20, 1901. At that moment, when I first became a soldier, I determined to do the best possible job I could during all the time that I served in the army. It was a great opportunity and I felt very excited.

2

Army Life

No DOUBT women everywhere feel the same when their sons and grandsons go off to war. My grandmother Rihsakwad loved me; she therefore berated my father greatly because it was his treatment of me that caused me to enlist in the army. For me, however, the army was a new beginning in life. Even though I would be leaving those I loved, I felt this step was necessary for me.

Many of my ancestors were soldiers and warriors. I was following in this tradition. My great great grandfather was Lieutenant Nicholas Cusick of the Revolutionary War. He took part in the Battle of Saratoga and also served as an interpreter and as bodyguard to General Lafayette. He was one among many of our Indian people who helped these United States achieve their independence. My grandfather's half-brother, Captain Cornelius Cusick, was a professional army man and fought in the Civil War. Also, my father's eldest brother was on guard at the White House the night Lincoln was shot.

I was assigned to Troop G, Eleventh Cavalry, and trained at Fort Niagara, Fort Porter, Fort Myer in Virginia, and Fort Ethan Allen in Vermont.

I was stationed at Fort Ethan Allen in September of 1901 when we received the news that President McKinley had been shot in Buffalo. Vice-President Theodore Roosevelt was on vacation in Vermont at the time and immediately prepared to go to the president's side. I was one of ten soldiers from Fort Ethan Allen detailed to guard the vice-president when he came to Burlington to take the train to Buffalo.

Our squadron left Fort Ethan Allen on December 4, 1901, bound for New London and New York, to take ship for the Philippine Islands. I was on guard that last night when the weather was 40° below zero. We were not able to sleep on the train because the steam heating had frozen. The men had to wrap themselves in their blankets and walk back and forth most of the night to stay warm.

We arrived at Pier 13 in New York City on December 5 and prepared to embark on the transport *Crook*. The story had circulated that the rats had left the ship, and this made us all rather nervous, because we knew the old tradition that rats will leave a sinking ship. The ship did make it across the ocean, but the old sailors told us that our crossing was the roughest they had ever experienced. I was nearly dead with seasickness for nine days. Two men from the 27th Infantry died from seasickness on that voyage. Their caskets lay beside our mess hall and the boys used to sit and eat on them.

We had a colonel named Hennisee in our regiment whom the men heartily disliked and whom they had nicknamed "Vinegar Bill." On the transport going over the ocean they made up a song about him: "There's a Red Light on the Track for Vinegar Bill." The red light, of course, meant danger and was a warning about what they would do to Vinegar Bill when they got into battle. This was the song we sang, but never in his hearing:

> There's a red light on the track,
> There's a red light on the track,
> There's a red light on the track for Vinegar Bill!
> There's a red light on the track,
> It'll be there when we get back.
> There's a red light on the track for Vinegar Bill!
> As we go marching,
> And the band begins to play,
> As we go marching,
> Tra le le la le la le la le lay!
> There's a red light on the track,
> It'll be there when we get back.
> There's a red light on the track for Vinegar Bill!

Our ship arrived at Gibraltar fourteen days after leaving New York. There we took on coal, fresh water, and provisions. Our next stop was Malta. We had four days in port there. Our soldiers went ashore and were paraded with the British soldiers, who were commanded by General Lord Roberts.

While on leave in Malta, some of my comrades and I visited the Chapel of the Bones. Nearly a hundred years before that time, we were told, the French army had killed many thousands of Maltese people. Later, the people of Malta gathered the bones of their slain brethren and built this chapel to house them. So that this sacrifice would never be forgotten, the bones lined the walls. When the door to the chapel is closed, you cannot see where you entered, for the bones are affixed everywhere. The Maltese women also wore the hood of shame because the French soldiers had abused the women of Malta long ago. They vowed to wear this hood for one hundred years, but I suppose now they no longer wear it since the hundred years are up.

After we were one day out of Malta on our way to the Suez Canal, the British soldiers who had deserted and stowed away on our transport came out of hiding. There were around twenty or more of them. Some of them had even crawled into the coal bunkers and came out just as black as Negroes.

Our next port was Alexandria. There we saw an ancient ruin, a huge pile of rocks. When we inquired about it, we were told that it was the remains of the Tower of Babel.

From Alexandria, we sailed on to Port Said and then through the Suez Canal. It was so narrow through the canal that you could jump out of the ship onto dry land. Some of us crossed the desert by camel and met the transport at Bitter Lakes. Along the way, we had encountered many poor people who came to us begging for food and clothing. The poverty of these people was the most severe that many of us had ever seen.

From Suez City, our transport proceeded on through the Red Sea, past the Twelve Apostle Rocks, and docked at Aden and Colombo.

The South African War was on at the time and there at Colombo I saw five thousand Boer prisoners in a concentration camp. I asked them what caused the war. They told me that when the biggest diamond in the world was discovered in South Africa, the British moved in and started big mining operations. They paid their British workmen twice as much a day as their Boer workmen, and that was what started the war. Now here these poor people were imprisoned far from their homes.

Great Britain was a great colonial power in those days. It has been said: "Nations shall rise and nations shall fall." We have seen the downfall of the British Empire and the decline of England in our day. This will happen whenever a nation oppresses people. It will happen to the United States if it continues to wrong my Indian people. A nation cannot build its future on a foundation of oppression.

From Colombo we went by way of Singapore and Borneo to the Philippine Islands. We arrived in Manila February 3, 1902.[1]

The insurgent General Emilio Aguinaldo had been captured several months before our arrival, had taken the oath of allegiance to the United States, and was now confined in a private house in Manila. The leadership of the insurgent forces then fell to General Miguel Malvar, and he continued the guerrilla warfare throughout the archipelago. Malvar's followers were especially strong in the provinces of Batangas, Cavite, Tayabas, and Laguna on Luzon. Major General A. R. Chaffee had replaced General Arthur MacArthur as military governor of the Philippines by this time and was determined to stamp out the resistance.

We had many garrisons throughout the islands, but they were generally small, often only twenty-five or a dozen men. It was not safe for an American to travel alone anywhere in these provinces, not even for short distances.

Even though many Filipinos sided with the Americans and even joined our army, particularly as scouts, we could not always be sure who our friends were.[2] Many villagers would claim to be firm *amigos* to the Americans, then, at the first chance, would slip into the jungle with their rifles or bolos, attack an American unit, and then return to their villages and become *amigos* again. Our soldiers always had to be on on the alert against the enemy's many ruses.

The insurgents were very hard to track down. They had their camps in the most out-of-the-way places—the forest, ravines, mountains, and old volcano craters. They had large supplies of food hidden away— enough supposedly to keep the war going for many months and even years. The American army was being worn down trying to cope with this situation.

Just shortly before our arrival, Brigadier General J. Franklin Bell had begun a new strategy to conquer the insurgents. He ordered all Filipinos in the region that he commanded to concentrate in what he called zones of protection and to bring all their foodstuffs in from the countryside with them. Once the people were in the towns or the protected zones, the American soldiers could watch over them and their supplies. This cut down on the rebel strength, because anyone outside these zones was presumed to be an enemy. Also, it meant that the inhabitants' food supply was no longer freely available to the insurgents.

Along with this policy of concentration of the population, General

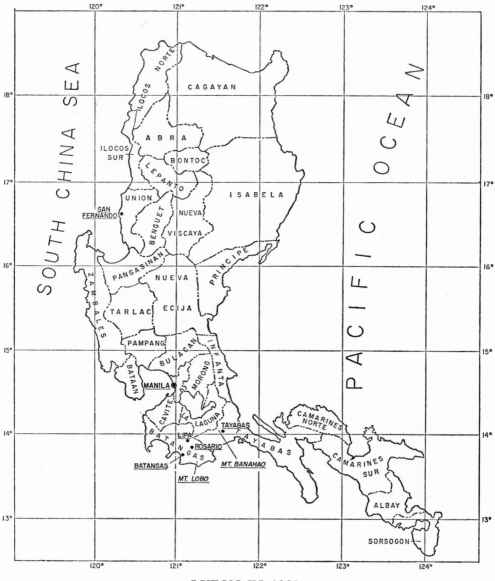

LUZON IN 1902

Bell constantly ordered American soldiers out to search for the enemy, to destroy their camps and all food supplies, and to give them battle. Every mountain and every stretch of forest would be searched. The plan was not to give the enemy any rest, to run them down constantly until they were worn out and had nothing left to fight with.

We arrived in Manila right in the midst of these operations and almost immediately became a part of them. The First Squadron of our 11th Cavalry was sent to the Island of Samar. Our Second Squadron, of which I was a member, would see service in Batangas and Tayabas Provinces on Luzon during the war. The Third Squadron, which arrived in the Philippines a little later, was stationed in Ilocos Sur in northern Luzon.

We left Manila on February 9 on a transport bound for Batangas in Batangas Province, where we made camp.

Very soon after our arrival in Batangas, our Colonel Hennisee—the hated "Vinegar Bill"—was determined to rush us into battle. We as yet were without horses, but he had three which he rode alternately. We marched after him through the jungle at a very fast pace. When one horse got tired, he would exchange it for a fresh horse, and continued in this manner throughout the march. If he had had to walk along with the rest of us, he would have kept a slower pace. He pushed us so hard that we became separated from the pack train to our rear. The Filipino guerrillas were quick to take advantage of our colonel's blunder and cut off and captured the whole pack train—men, mules, ammunition, and food. We turned back and searched for our comrades and our supplies, but they were gone just as if the earth had swallowed them up. The boys were determined that when we got into battle, Vinegar Bill would be the first to be shot. The soldiers never had the opportunity to carry out this threat, for shortly thereafter Vinegar Bill was relieved of his command and, as we heard, was transferred back to the United States because of his incompetence.[3]

When we were stationed in Tayabas Province during February, we heard that a call had gone out for volunteers to conquer Mt. Banahao, which is near the northernmost border of that province. In a crater atop this dead volcano, the insurgents had a stronghold that could not be dislodged. Many of our soldiers had attempted before but had failed. The intense cold, rough terrain, and continuous rain on the mountain had proven too much for the American soldiers. Since our 11th Cavalry had trained in a cold northern climate in Vermont, Captain Frank Tompkins of Troop G volunteered his own services, believing that he and his men could perform that feat. He picked fifty of the strongest men out of the troop, and I was among them. The captain explained the mission to us and requested volunteers from among the fifty for that service. He warned that many had tried before and failed and told us frankly that not all of us would come back. Now a regular army man follows the orders of his officers without question, but our captain was giving us a choice whether to volunteer or not. He requested those who declined the mission to fall out one pace forward. Not one of us moved. I know that I myself would have gone through fire for our captain, and I am sure the rest of the men felt the same toward him. He was a first-rate officer, an excellent soldier, and always fair to the men. We all knew he cared about his soldiers and would never ask us to do anything he was not willing to do or not capable of doing himself. I personally admired him for his honesty and high character and thought he was one of the finest men I ever had the privilege to meet. Captain Tompkins kept exhorting us and warning us of the danger ahead, but no one made a move to decline the service. When the captain saw that we all intended to undertake this mission with him, he stood there and applauded and then made a speech complimenting us on our courage and determination to carry out this assignment.

We started climbing Mt. Banahao February 26, 1902, at 4:00 A.M. There were fifty American soldiers and about fifty Filipino pack carriers. By noon we were crawling up the mountainside on our hands and knees and using scaling ropes. The sides were nearly straight up. We went along like this all day. When darkness fell, we were still climbing and proceeded on until midnight when we reached the top of the mountain— a distance of 7,670 feet from the starting point. There we rested until daylight.

The water we got to drink was squeezed from the foot-thick moss. Our food was one spoonful of salmon and one hardtack for a meal.

At the top, it was raining incessantly and was bitter cold. We had the most uncomfortable night there that we spent through the entire war.

At the first sign of daylight, we were ordered down into the crater. We reached the Filipino fort about noon and found that the enemy had deserted it. We were so angry that we burned everything to the ground at once, never thinking that this fort should have served as our shelter for that night.

We spied a little stream in this crater, clear as crystal, with many boulders and brimstones lying about. We rushed to fill our canteens with water but were ordered to dump them out again. This was a strong sulphur water that would have eaten through our canteens in a very short time.

In this crater, it was continually raining. We could look up and see the clouds hanging overhead. Our shoes and clothing were saturated with water and our flesh was like a wet dishrag.

That night, we were forced to camp in the open again, unprotected against the elements. We all suffered in the extreme from cold, wetness, and exposure.

Early the next morning, we began our ascent from the crater. We were forced most of the time to inch forward on our hands and knees, clinging closely to the inside wall of the mountain. The cold water poured over our hands and faces and down our necks, making the climb most difficult and dangerous. We had strict orders not to look back lest we become dizzy and fall two or three thousand feet to our death. When we got near the top, the sun shone through the clouds and down into the depths of the crater. Then we disobeyed our orders and looked back. There was the most beautiful sight we had ever seen. The rays of the sun played upon the mist, forming hundreds of rainbows, crisscrossed and piled upon another like huge stacks of hay, entirely filling up the huge crater.

It was the middle of the afternoon before we wearily pulled ourselves over the top of the mountain. I was on the rear guard and was the last one to arrive at the top at 3:00 P.M. We began our descent and finally reached the bottom of the cloud line. There the sun was shining and provided a welcome warmth for us. We were ordered to rest for half an hour there before continuing on down. Our officers had great difficulty in arousing us at the end of our rest period and so had to prolong our stay about an hour more. By that time the hot sun had dried our shoes, causing the leather to shrink and draw up tight. For the rest of the trip down, we were in the utmost pain and could hardly walk.

We reached the bottom without the loss of a man and made our way back to camp. We all looked forward to the big beefsteak dinner that had been promised us at the conclusion of our mission. Unfortunately, that was not to be. About twenty-five of the soldiers who came down the mountain were sent to the general hospital, suffering from exhaustion and severe exposure, and from there were returned to the United States. As for the rest of us, we were ordered out into the battlefield again the next night after our return from Mt. Banahao.

I was stationed as night guard inside the walls of the large prison where we had many insurgent captives. While I was standing in the dark beside the wall, I saw a light thrown inside the prison. Immediately I reported the incident and the troops turned out. They discovered a number of armed rebels crawling up the walls, no doubt with the intent of freeing the prisoners. Our soldiers went out at once and gave battle to the enemy.

From February 26 to March 4, 1902, our Troop G campaigned throughout Tayabas Province, destroying insurgent strongholds and supplies. Then we went into camp at Tiaong in western Tayabas Province and continually sent out scouting parties.

Our soldiers had stockaded the town, in accordance with the concentration orders, and left only one entrance. Here we placed guards at all times. The soldiers were stationed inside with the friendly Filipino villagers, and our patrols would go out constantly, searching for the enemy and protecting the town. We also provided food for the villagers out of our own supplies.

We were not to allow anyone in or out without proper authorization, but we had strict orders not to disturb the funerals. The cemetery was a distance outside the village and the mourning processions would go back and forth from the church to the cemetery. They had only one casket, which looked like a long basket. They would go out to the grave, bury the corpse, and come back with the empty casket. In this manner, they would continue with their funerals every day. Every time there was a funeral, they would ring the three church bells. A young boy sat up in the bell tower and pulled the bells, and then the procession came out on its way to the cemetery.

One day when a comrade and I were on duty at the gate and a funeral procession was coming out, my companion said: "Let's take a look at this corpse."

"Well," I said, "you know what the orders are. But I won't tell on you. Let's do!"

With that we stopped the procession and looked into the casket.

There instead of a corpse we discovered food from the American commissary. I made a report right away and the officers ordered an immediate investigation. It was found that these supposedly peaceful Filipinos whom we had been feeding had been taking food out to the cemetery for the insurgents and had been bringing back guns hidden in the casket. They had quite a large cache of arms in the church.

What we had uncovered was a plot that would probably have meant the death of all the soldiers stationed at that town. These Filipinos had been waiting for the day that a large number of our soldiers should leave the stockade to go into the field so that they could rise up and massacre those who stayed behind. Then they would do the same to the unsuspecting soldiers who were returning from duty to a supposedly friendly town. If we had not discovered this scheme in time, the same thing would have happened to us that happened to General Smith's Ninth Infantry at Balangiga on Samar. There nearly the whole of Company C was wiped out by supposedly friendly Filipinos. The massacre occurred at breakfast time, and most of the American soldiers were cut to pieces by Filipino bolomen or mowed down with their own rifles, which the rebels had seized. A remnant of the company, firing on the insurgents, finally drove them off.

We regular soldiers were armed with Krag-Jorgensen rifles and carbines, which used smokeless powder and could be fired rapidly. American volunteers were armed with Springfields, but they always tried to get a Krag if they could. The insurgents had the Spanish Mauser, which was a very good gun. As the war went on, we captured more and more rebel arms, so that the enemy was frequently desperate for guns and had to rely primarily on bolos. But the bolo was a deadly sharp weapon and most effective. With a flick of the wrist, a boloman could take an opponent's head off.[4] Sometimes rebels would creep up to an American camp at night, strip off their clothes and grease their bodies, and then slip into the barracks to steal the rifles. American soldiers generally could not hold onto these thieves with the greasy skins and the lucky insurgents often got away with a few highly prized Krags. We heard about these incidents, but they never happened in our barracks.

From March 24 to April 20, 1902, we were fighting under Brigadier General J. Franklin Bell on an expedition over the Lobo Mountains into Batangas Province for a campaign against Rosario. These mountains, which are on the southernmost coast of Luzon, resemble a vast field of huge haystacks. Our orders were to kill the enemy, capture prisoners, and destroy all foodstuffs.

Throughout my experience in the war, we much preferred to capture rather than to kill so that we could get information. We treated prisoners kindly, fed them, and played with them. Every so often we would send a few of the prisoners back to the insurgent army. When their companions heard that we treated prisoners well, then more would come in and surrender to us.

There were about twenty-five hundred of us in this army, and we stretched out on a skirmish line twenty-five miles long to cut off a peninsula. While we were pressing through a series of great rice fields in a valley, some of our men set fire to the fields. The flames roared up in the dried grass and rushed toward a group of us. We dashed toward the mountain and up into the bushes to escape. Though we saved ourselves, we were now lost.

Our little group wandered around for four days and four nights looking for the army. We ran out of rations and water. Finally we reached the ocean. One of the Filipino scouts with us made a wild dash for the water only to discover that it was salt water and undrinkable. He had never in his life seen the ocean before.

Then I said: "Well, I'm a scout, too, and I'll see what we can do. We'll follow a lower trail."

We ended up at a mud hole where the wild animals came to wallow. We could not be particular, but got down and drank this stuff that was halfway between water and mud. All the while we were drinking, there was a carabao wallowing in the mud with just his nose out of the water.

One of the scouts went out to find a fresh trail. Suddenly we heard a great commotion and shooting over in the bushes. We all jumped up and pointed our guns in the direction of the shooting. Then we saw that a huge wild boar was chasing our comrade, who was running for his life. He then turned and fired again, this time killing the boar. We were standing around remarking on the incident when we were suddenly surrounded by soldiers, who came running from every direction. To our surprise, we saw that these were Americans. We had been only five hundred feet from where our army was camped. That was a most happy moment for us, for we had nearly starved during the time we were lost.

We received intelligence of where the insurgents were holding some our men captive. These were the men who were captured when we lost our pack train because of Colonel Hennisee's blundering. The officers ordered us to prepare for a forced march to attack this Filipino camp.

During our many campaigns in the Philippines, we were continually on the move, giving the enemy no rest and getting none ourselves. Our men were constantly exhausted. Often I would carry two and three guns for my comrades on these marches, because they were too weary even to bear their own equipment. Now once more we were off on an exhausting expedition. This time, as usual, I was asked again and again by some of my weary comrades to help lighten their loads by carrying their carbines.

While we were on the forced march, Captain Tompkins told his troop to break for lunch. He then proceeded to open up his food and eat. We just stood around and looked at him.

"Why aren't you boys eating your lunch?" he asked us.

"What lunch?" we answered. "We don't have any food to eat!"

With that, Captain Tompkins folded up his lunch and put it away. He refused to eat when his men had no food.

We finally approached the Filipino camp in the mountains. We proceeded cautiously along the mountainside under cover of the tall weeds. Ahead of us was our Filipino guide riding on a carabao so that just his head projected over the weeds. The 13th Cavalry was stationed on the upper mountain, and they spotted our guide and shot him. Then they began firing on us also. We got down right away and began to skirmish. Then we saw that our own men were shooting at us, and we sent them a signal to cease firing.

When this shooting started, we saw a big fire come up on the side of the mountain, and smoke rising. The Filipino camp was right above us, and we gave battle and defeated them. From the captives we took, we learned what this big fire was. They had held our pack train men captive all the while, and had tied them beside an ant hill and let the ants eat them. When they heard our firing and saw us approaching, they built a big brush fire and threw our soldiers onto it and cremated them alive. When we entered their camp, all we found was the charred bones of our comrades. These we very sadly buried.

Upon one occasion when we were stationed in a valley, we were engaged in a battle with the insurgents and captured a number of them, including a colonel and a captain. We also captured a very valuable bolo mounted in gold, with a purple grip. After we had had these men in captivity a while, we looked up and saw sparks coming from one side of the mountain. Then sparks came up from the opposite mountain. Soon, these sparks began spurting fire until the two sides of the mountains facing each other looked like two Niagara Falls of shooting fire. This was their method of signaling each other.

Our captive colonel explained: "That's my lieutenant who got away. I'll go over there and ask him to surrender to you."

We thereupon took the colonel over as far as he requested. He wrote a note and left it on the trail with a stone on top of it. Then we returned to camp and waited for the results.

The next morning, we returned to the same spot and found an answer there. The lieutenant had said: "I will surrender to those men who captured you."

Our men then followed the guides through the jungle to the rebel hideaway, which was situated in a large cave. These insurgents came out and surrendered exactly the same as any organized military body. They had the white flag of truce, and they marched forward smartly and stacked their guns in front of us.

The lieutenant spoke good English and told us about the recent battle. He said that when our soldiers had been firing at him, if he had stood against a wall, his figure would have been cut out in bullet holes. The miracle was that, of all those bullets flying around him, none ever touched him.

Word came to us one day that an insurgent army was preparing for an attack against us. We waited until nightfall, and then began a forced march to surprise the enemy. At one point we had to cross a river on foot. The water was up to my neck. I was in the rear guard and was the last one over. Despite the darkness, I found the trail on the other side and followed along behind. We were going uphill, and the water that dripped off the soldiers' clothing was streaming down the trail, making the footing very uncertain. I had proceeded about forty or fifty feet when I slipped and fell all the way back into the river. When I finally made my way to the shore again, the army was far on ahead. It was dungeon dark, and I was not able to find the trail. I suddenly had an idea. I knelt down and felt all along the ground and past a bush trail. Everywhere I felt, the ground was dry. Finally I came to the spot where the water that streamed off the soldiers' clothing was coming along the ground in little rivulets, and I knew then that I had found the right trail. I hurried along it and soon caught up with the army and took my proper position again in the rear guard.

At daybreak, we were formed into three attack groups. Flanking troops were sent in advance over the mountains on the left and the right of the ravine, where we knew the enemy was situated. The middle group of troops followed a little to the rear along the bottom of the ravine. I was in the group that went over the mountain on the left.

The troops on the right flank came over the mountain first and spotted our scouts on the left, and began firing on them. We quickly formed skirmish lines and went over the top, where we saw that our own soldiers were shooting at us. The commander of the scouts called out: "Hold on, Captain Hardiman! You're killing all my men!"

We were right under the insurgent camp. The enemy began firing into our ranks, and the bullets tore around us from every direction. We were right in the middle of a cross fire. The man next to me was shot, and I saw others getting killed around me. Then a bullet whizzed close to my scalp and clipped a small branch over my head. At that instant, I thought of my grandmother's prophecy of many years before, that I would go into battle, would be caught between two lines of fire, and would nearly lose my life. Everything was coming to pass just as she had said.

After this bullet had barely missed me, one of my comrades called to me: "Chief, they're trying to kill you, ain't they?"

"It looks like it!" I answered.

"I'll fix that!" he said. He aimed his carbine up and shot the sniper out of a tree ahead of us.

I was able to save Captain Tompkins' life on the battlefield. A Filipino soldier was going to kill him with a bolo. I rushed in between them, blocked the blow with my gun, and knocked the man down.

We defeated the enemy in that engagement, which was to be the last battle of the war. Our campaign in Batangas Province resulted in the surrender of insurgent General Miguel Malvar and practically ended the insurrection in the archipelago.[5] There was some spotty guerrilla activity after that, but it never amounted to much. There was also a Moslem revolt on Mindanao, but this had nothing to do with the insurrection.

We were in the field when we received the report that the war was over. Orders then came for us to march to our post. While on our line of march, every once in a while one of the men would drop as though shot. All during the war, not one of us ever took sick in our troop. Now the boys were dropping everywhere from sickness and exhaustion. We would strap them onto a native pony and keep on going. Later, I myself began to see the world rock.

We stopped by a little bamboo field hospital and the doctor came along the line taking our temperatures. When he came to me, he asked: "Well, how do you feel, Rickard?"

"All right," I said.

"Do you think you can march twelve miles?"

"Yes, sir."

He told me to step one pace forward. Just then it happened that the world was rocking and I was forced to take three or four steps.

Then he went on by me and asked the corpsman to come back and take my temperature. The corpsman did so and reported back to the doctor: "The man's got a hundred and four fever."

The doctor came back and said to me: "You say you think you can march twelve miles?"

"Yes, sir."

He pointed to the field hospital one hundred yards away and said: "If you can march to that little hospital over there, you'll do well."

I walked over to the hospital as I was directed and the corpsmen put me to bed. Then I got much worse. For six days and six nights, I battled a fever of 106 degrees. Most of the time I was delirious. Everything that had ever happened on all the battlefields passed before me. I imagined that I was going into battle without my gun. I cannot describe what a distressing feeling that was. I got out of bed and demanded my gun. The corpsmen rushed up to put me back into bed, and I knocked every one of them down. I kept calling for my gun.

One of the corpsmen ran and got my carbine and put it in my hands. Then I partially came to my senses and realized where I was. My knees gave way and I fell to the floor. The men picked me up and put me back into bed.

The doctor sent fifty miles with a carabao cart for some ice. There was not much of the ice left when the driver returned, but what remained they cut up into little pieces. Then they put me in a rubber stretcher and packed me in ice. They placed me in the shade and took turns fanning me. The next morning, I felt much better.

The doctor came by checking and he stopped by my bed and asked me: "How do you feel this morning, Rickard?"

"Good! I feel good!" I said.

"Do you know what you have?" he asked.

"No, sir."

"You have one of the worst attacks of malaria fever. And if it hadn't been for that good ox heart of yours, you'd have gone over the river sure."

When the doctor saw that I was steadily improving, he ordered a Filipino with a carabao cart to take me twelve miles forward to join my troop. Every once in a while after that, I would have to return to the hospital for treatment.

From May 1902 to February 1904 we were in La Union Province on Luzon. We took station first at San Fernando de la Union until we built our quarters. These were constructed, in the Filipino style, of bamboo, thatch, and planks. This was Camp Wallace, about two miles outside San Fernando, where our Second Squadron stayed for the remainder of our duty in the Philippine Islands.

We had different recreations to amuse ourselves when we were not on duty. One of the favorites was a mounted tug of war. This was always great fun to the contestants and spectators alike. Another pastime was to try to pull a seated man off a chair by using just one finger. You would hook your finger around the finger of the seated man and pull him up, if you could. We also had a number of favorite soldier songs we sang to while away the time. Soldiering was hard work, but we made light of it.

One of the pastimes the boys liked was boxing. We used to practice down behind the stables. I had never engaged in this sport before going into the army and was not very expert at it, but I did join in some of the sparring. Those who had fought with me told me: "Chief, you hit like a mule!" I was always called "Chief" because I was the only Indian in Troop G.

We had a sergeant named McManus who was always mean to the men. This man had been a professional boxer in civilian life. The men therefore hatched a plot whereby the sergeant and I would be matched against each other. I was somewhat of a coward in those days and the last thing in the world I wanted was to get into the ring with a professional boxer. We were watching the sergeant work out one day in a little hut where he had his own private gym set up. He had a special cot in there to rest between workouts, and only he was supposed to use it. The men very cleverly maneuvered both of us into a fight. They had me sit down on the sergeant's bed. When the sergeant saw this, he, of course, bawled me out. The men, even one of the officers—a lieutenant —suggested we settle the argument in the ring. Neither one of us could get out of it, especially when we were told that a ring was already set up. There was, by this time, a big audience urging us on. There was nothing left for us to do but to get into the ring.

We walked out toward the ring in a leisurely fashion. As we got near it, I broke into a trot and jumped into the ring. Everybody went down to the ocean and sat down for a ringside seat. The news had spread, and practically the whole camp was there. I think there must have been close to a thousand men gathered to watch this match.

Both my opponent and I were very evenly matched in height and weight, but I lacked confidence. The men were sure I would knock the sergeant's head off, and I was just as sure he would knock mine off. For three rounds, I kept out of his way, bobbing, weaving, and dodging his fists. He was never able to lay a hand on me, and I had no intention of getting close to him.

Suddenly he swung hard at me and grazed my forehead. It was a sharp blow and it hurt. I got mad and came back fighting. I threw my left at him, caught him on the chin, and sent him through the ropes. He was out cold for a long while and the men had great difficulty reviving him. He just lay there stretched out and his whole body quivered. I believe if I had hit him with my right hand, I might have killed him.

When he came to, he looked up at me and said: "You were trying to kill me, weren't you, Chief?"

"No," I said, "I wasn't trying to do any such thing, because we're both comrades. But one think I ask of you from now on is to lay off the boys and treat them right."

"All right, Chief," he said. And he kept his promise.

It was as a result of that fight that I lost my cowardice.[6]

One night when I had come off guard duty, I lay down on my cot just inside the door of our barracks. As I lay there, my grandmother appeared by my bed and smiled, but never said a word. I got up and went toward her but lost sight of her. I went out and all around that hundred-foot-long barracks looking for her. Then I said to myself: "What a fool I am! Here I am ten thousand miles away from my grandmother and I'm out looking for her!"

A month later, I received a letter from my father telling me that my grandmother had just died. She had gone outside and had lain down under a tree to take a nap in the shade. A rain came up, and the family forgot that grandmother was outside. No one went to waken her, and as a result of being out in that rain, she was chilled through and caught a cold which later turned into pneumonia. She was eighty years old and was not able to pull through this attack. From the date on the letter and from the information my father gave me, I could see that my grandmother had died at that very time when she had appeared to me a month previously—May 9, 1903. The letter had taken a month to reach me.[7]

Our regiment was stationed in the Philippines as an army of occupation for about two years after the war was over. It was our duty to keep the peace. There were numerous bands of *ladrones,* or highway robbers, who preyed upon the people. The Filipinos looked to the United States Army for protection against these gangs of bandits.

American soldiers were frequently assigned as guards for Filipino workers who were cutting timber out in the mountains, far from a settled area. It was necessary to protect these men from the *ladrones.*

I had been assigned with a squad of twelve soldiers on one such project. We had trenches dug around our area for protection and we drilled regularly to be ready for any surprise attack. The *ladrones* would send a message to us to get out of their country or they would wipe us out. We would send a message back telling them to come ahead any time they felt like it. They had one hundred bolo men and one hundred rifle men and we were only twelve, but we had a large store of ammunition in our trenches and felt confident of our ability to stand them off.

While we were stationed there, I saw a Filipino going through the bushes carrying a bowl in his hands. I thought he was one of the *ladrones,* so I halted him. He took off his hat, came over to me, and offered me the bowl. I looked into it and there I saw fish and rice with fly blow all over it and large-sized maggots crawling through. The odor was enough to knock you down. He said: "Bueno!" meaning that the food was good to eat. I let him go on his way in a hurry.

One evening, we spied a Filipino on a pony racing down the trail toward us. I ordered the men into the trenches and I jumped behind a tree. As the horseman appeared, I leveled my gun at him and stepped out, ordering him to halt.

The man jumped down from his pony, took off his hat, and said: "Americano, mucho amigo," indicating that he was a friend. He then handed me a message from the American schoolteacher in a nearby town, which gave information about an attack of *ladrones* intended for that night. The teacher appealed for our help.

We then prepared to move on the town that evening. We took off our shoes and marched three or four miles to the town and lay all night behind the barricades that the people had erected for protection. Nothing happened that night, and we therefore returned to our post the next day.

Later, we received a message that the battle was on at the town. We hurried back there and formed a skirmish line to pursue the *ladrones*. They turned and ran when we approached and just disappeared. We were not able to find a trace of them. There were quite a number of people killed in this battle, including the American teacher, who had five bullet holes in him. There was thus not much difference between peacetime and wartime in the Philippines in those days.

One of the assignments I had after the war was to transfer prisoners different places in the islands. I had both American and Filipino prisoners in my charge. Any of those who had more than a year to serve, whether Filipino or American, were sent to Malahi Island prison in Laguna Province, thirty-one miles from Manila.[8] I was detailed one day to take a man to this Malahi Island prison. When our transport arrived at Manila, I transferred the man into a Manila prison. There behind the bars I was surprised to see a soldier I knew. We talked a little while, and then he told me: "I got scared because I thought you were coming in here, too." Then I went out and bought him a large basket of fruit to cheer him up.

When I went up to the main office of the prison to make my report, I saw a room full of clerks—so many that they were nearly falling over each other. The captain took one look at me, and came over to where I stood. Then he called out: "For heaven's sake! Come over here and pacify this wild Indian!"

Our presence in the Philippines was meant to bring peace to the country and assure order. When this was done, then our job was finished.

A soldier is a fighter, but he also loves peace as much as any man. It was therefore good news when we heard that the 11th Cavalry was to be shipped home to the United States, or God's Country, as we always called it.

We were ordered to wade out to a flatboat which would take us to a transport bound for Manila. The soldiers took the officers on their backs so they would not get wet. Captain Tompkins refused this service. He said he was no different from anyone else and plunged into the water just like the enlisted men. He never asked us to do anything that he was not willing to do also.

Before we leave the Philippines completely, I want to say a few words about the insurgent leader Aguinaldo. Our soldiers had a lot of respect for him, even though he had been an enemy. He was a captive in Manila and was at first confined but was finally allowed to walk about freely. I had seen him there in the city upon several occasions. For my part, I always thought he was a good man.

Our transport set sail from Manila March 15, 1904, bound for Japan. On the way, we were challenged by a Japanese battleship, but showed our colors and were allowed to pass. The reason for the Japanese caution was that the Russo-Japanese War was in progress at the time.

We had a four-day stop in Nagasaki, where we took in all the sights. One very strange and unpleasant thing we saw was a Japanese battleship unloading the frozen corpses of soldiers brought back from the Russian war. The soldiers were stacking them up on the beach just like cordwood. I asked what they were going to do with them, and a Japanese soldier told me they were going to pour oil on them and burn them.

We took a rickshaw ride for only 10 cents an hour to see all the various wonders. When we wanted our drivers to hurry up, we would say: "Ooy! Ooy! Ooy!" Then they would run all the faster in carting us around the city. We visited the many temples and saw all the large images of horses and many other unusual things. We also had a big feed of very good Japanese food, which was a great relief from eating the army slum, as we called it. We could visit all civilian places but not anything military. The guards would not let us anywhere near the fort. Many years later, when I heard of the dropping of the atomic bomb on Nagasaki during World War II, I was much saddened at the news of the destruction of this most beautiful city.

Our next stop was Hawaii, and here again we had our leave in port, but only one day this time. We therefore made it a point to visit as much of the countryside as we could. The scenery there was the most beautiful of any I have ever seen. Also most enjoyable were the pineapples picked fresh right off the stalk, and we ate as many as we could.

Just before we reached San Francisco, one of our officers was asking another if he thought the Golden Gate would be open when we arrived. We sailed into the harbor, but we did not see any golden gates. Our trip had taken just one month from the time we left the Philippines.

We were now stationed temporarily at Camp Presidio in San Francisco. My enlistment would be up in a few days, but I fully intended to reenlist.

I was discharged from the army at San Francisco April 19, 1904, after completing my three-year enlistment. The remarks on my discharge were: "Qualified Marksman. Character: Excellent. Service: Honest and Faithful." I immediately reenlisted for another three years and was shipped with my squadron to Fort Des Moines, Iowa.

During August 1904, while I was stationed at Fort Des Moines, I was granted a one-month leave. This gave me an opportunity to go home to the reservation to visit my family and friends.

On my way east to spend my leave, our train stopped at a town in Ohio where about a hundred young ladies got on. They had just come from a party in the park. They spotted me sitting there in my uniform, the only soldier on the train, and suddenly they descended on me in a mob, trying to snatch my buttons and any other souvenirs they could. It was all I could do to keep my uniform from being torn off.

When I arrived in Buffalo, I saw the place where President McKinley had been shot in 1901. I thought back to that day at Fort Ethan Allen when we had first heard this sad news.

When I got to Niagara Falls, I hired the driver of a horse cab to take me out to the reservation. As the old familiar places came into view, I began to feel much anticipation.

We stopped in front of the old homestead, and I paid the driver and started up the walk. My mother came out into the yard and was crying. Then the rest of the family came out to greet me. It was a good feeling to be able to see everyone again after such a long time and to realize how fortunate I was to be there alive after all my army experiences.

During the time I was home on leave, I met a girl named Ivy

Lucy Rickard, wife of
Chief George D. Rickard
and mother of Edgar,
Frederick, Clinton, and
Chester. *Courtesy of
Clinton Rickard family*

Tuscarora school boys around 1890. Seated, Chester Rickard and teacher Tamar
Johnson. Standing, left to right, Webster Cusick, Clinton Rickard, Nelson Mt.
Pleasant, Albert Williams, William Mt. Pleasant. *Courtesy of Clinton Rickard
family*

Delia Patterson and her half-sister Elizabeth (Rihsakwad), paternal grandmother of Clinton Rickard. The women are displaying the beadwork which they regularly sold to tourists at Niagara Falls. During the War of 1812, Tuscarora warriors performed meritorious service for the United States and protected the life of General Peter B. Porter. As a reward, the Porter family permitted the Indian women of the Tuscarora Reservation to sell their crafts in perpetuity on what was then Porter property, next to Niagara Falls. This area, Prospect Park, was later sold to New York State by the Porters, but a few Indian women still sell their crafts there. *Courtesy of Clinton Rickard family*

William Garlow, maternal grandfather of Clinton Rickard. He was one of the few fortunate members of the Six Nations who survived the hazardous migration to Kansas in 1846. Photograph around 1915. *Courtesy of Clinton Rickard family*

The four Rickard brothers. Seated, left to right, Edgar and Chester. Standing, Clinton and Frederick. The picture was taken in 1901, shortly after Clinton's enlistment in the army. *Courtesy of Clinton Rickard family*

Private Clinton Rickard in late 1901 when he was stationed at Fort Ethan Allen, Vermont. *Courtesy of Clinton Rickard family*

Some of the members of Troop G's football team at Fort Des Moines, Iowa, in November of 1904. Rickard, who played center, sits over the ball. Seated front row far left is Sgt. William M. Kartzmark of Lockport, New York. *Courtesy of Clinton Rickard family*

Officers of the Eleventh Cavalry in the Philippines. Captain Frank Tompkins of Troop G is seated second from right, holding the swagger stick. Tompkins, who was highly respected by his men, was idolized by the young Private Rickard. *Courtesy of Clinton Rickard family*

Clinton and Ivy Rickard
after their marriage
in December of 1904.
Courtesy of
Clinton Rickard family

Edith Leona Rickard and
Herald Rickard,
children of Ivy and
Clinton, about 1910.
Courtesy of
Clinton Rickard family

The Patterson family. Left to right, Titus Patterson (father), Harry Patterson, John Wesley Patterson, Julia Garlow Patterson (mother), Willard Gansworth (with a kitten in each pocket), Nellie May Gansworth, and Elizabeth Patterson. Titus was the eldest son of William H. Patterson by the latter's first wife, the former Leah Chew. *Courtesy of Clinton Rickard family*

A Tuscarora school picnic on Goat Island in the Niagara River, about 1903. Elizabeth Patterson is seated third from left in the front row, in striped dress. Her two brothers, John Wesley and Harry, are seated directly behind and to the right of her. Nellie May Patterson, eldest child of Titus and Julia Patterson, was attending school at Lincoln Institute in Philadelphia at the time. Children of the Tuscarora Reservation dressed in the same very proper style for an outing as did white children of the period. *Courtesy of Clinton Rickard family*

Clinton Rickard
during the time he
worked as foreman
at the Empire
Limestone Quarry.
*Courtesy of
Clinton Rickard
family*

Boiling sap in the sugar bush behind the Rickard farm. Left to right, William, Clinton, Clark, and George Nash. *Courtesy of Clinton Rickard family*

Elizabeth Patterson as a young woman, before her marriage to Clinton Rickard.
Courtesy of Clinton Rickard family

Elizabeth, Clinton, and Clark in the summer of 1921. *Courtesy of Clinton Rickard family*

A tintype portrait of the young Chief Marcus Peters, sachem of the Tuscarora Beaver clan. He became a chief in 1873 and thereupon assumed the chiefly title of Loud Voice, which belonged to the sachemship of his clan. In later years, when he became too infirm to carry on the duties of his office, he went before the Chief's Council and surrendered his chieftainship and his chiefly name to Clinton Rickard, who had been chosen as his successor by the matron of the Beaver clan.
Courtesy of Sallie Thomas, Tuscarora Reservation

The Honorable Edward A. Everett and his secretary, Mrs. Lulu G. Stillman, two longstanding friends of the Indian people, pose with Cayuga chiefs on the steps of the capitol building in Albany, New York, in 1922. Left to right, Alexander John, Ernest Spring, Edward A. Everett, Edwin Spring, Lulu G. Stillman. The picture was probably taken at the time Assemblyman Everett, who was chairman of the New York State Legislature's Indian Commission, presented his report on Indian affairs to the legislature. The "Everett Report," which the legislature rejected, was the stenographic report of the hearings held on various Iroquois reservations in 1920, and concluded with Chairman Everett's strong statement in favor of Indian land claims in New York State. In 1945 Mrs. Stillman was given authority by the Mohawk Nation to speak for them as a representative at any time and at any place.
Courstesy of Ray Fadden, Six Nations Indian Museum, Onchiota, New York

Julia Patterson (left), wife of Titus; Dr. Sarah Dolan Patterson, wife of William Moses Patterson, and her son, Melvin W. Patterson. It was Sarah who gave Titus Patterson the idea to build the gymnasium. She was both an M.D. and a registered pharmacist, and had been cured of tuberculosis by the famous Tuscarora medicine man, William H. Patterson, whose son she married. Her husband, "Mose" Patterson, was also a medicine man, trained by his father. *Courtesy of Clinton Rickard family*

William H. Patterson ready to set off on his morning rounds to deliver his herbal medicines to his patients. *Courtesy of Elsie Schimmelman, Tuscarora Reservation*

The Tuscarora All Stars basketball team in 1916. Seated, Harry Patterson. Standing left to right, manager Willard Gansworth, Alvin Printup, David Sylvester, John Wesley Patterson, Noah Henry, Orsamus (Ray) Gansworth, brother of Willard, and Titus Patterson. *Courtesy of Harry Patterson, Tuscarora Reservation*

This picture was taken at the height of the controversy with Chief Grant Mt. Pleasant in 1923. The group had just returned in triumph from taking possession of Emmeline Garlow's estate on behalf of her sister, Julia Patterson. Left to right, Clark Rickard (partially obscured), Chief Clinton Rickard, Willard Gansworth, William Rickard (in front of Willard), Chief George D. Rickard, Chester Rickard, Harry Patterson, and John Green. *Courtesy of Nellie Gansworth, Tuscarora Reservation*

Chief Deskaheh, or Levi General. *Courtesy of Ray Fadden, Six Nations Indian Museum, Onchiota, New York*

Onstott who was living on the reservation with her mother. She was a friend of my family's, and we soon came to know and like each other very well. This new development in my life made it much harder to leave when it came time for me to return to my post.

I hired a man to take me to the station where I could catch a train for Des Moines. Ivy came along with me and she cried all the way there. As I learned later, she also cried all the way home from the station.

We had promised to write to each other, and this we did do. One of my great pleasures was to receive letters from her. It made me realize that the nearly three years I had left to serve was a very long time.

While I was stationed at Fort Des Moines, it became possible for soldiers to purchase their discharges. It cost a good sum of money—about $75, if I remember correctly. Now I proceeded to make this payment and put in a request for a discharge, for I was determined to return home and marry Ivy.

I was mustered out of the army December 9, 1904. When Captain Tompkins was about to hand me my discharge, he grasped my hand in farewell and then talked to me for about half an hour, giving me much good advice—more so than my father ever had. He told me that if I ever enlisted in the army again, he would be very hurt if I did not come back to serve under him. Then he wished me well and we parted, but in later years we kept up a correspondence. My second discharge listed me as a sharpshooter and carried the same high recommendation from my captain that my first discharge had.

It was most hard to leave the captain, because I thought the world of him, and it was also hard to leave all my good comrades. The boys gathered around me to say good-bye, and as always they called me "Chief." Then those who were off duty escorted me to the station. There they took me into the saloon. Many times during my army days I had gone to the saloon with the soldiers, even though I never drank. When they got drunk, I was the one who helped them back to the barracks. Now these fellows insisted that I have a drink for the occasion.

"We have been with you nearly four years now and have never seen you take a drop of liquor," they told me.

Just then they grabbed me and got a bottle of beer and put it in my mouth. When they thought I took a swallow, they let me go. Then I turned my head and spit the beer out. That is the most alcohol I had ever tasted up to that time, or ever wanted to taste.

The boys had a laugh over that, but they did not try to force me again.

All during the train ride home, I had deep regrets about leaving the army and all my good friends. This was the career I had chosen for myself and now I was abandoning it. It was almost as though I was being pulled two ways, but right then, Ivy had a stronger hold on me than the army did.

3

Marriage and Family

JUST A FEW DAYS after I had returned from the army, on December 18, 1904, Ivy and I were married. We had a small wedding at my parents' home, with a few friends and relatives in attendance. I had been out of the army only a little more than a week and was married in my full-dress cavalry uniform with saber.

We lived with my parents for about two years and then moved to a log cabin on what is now called Printup Road, but which most of our people call Dead Man's Road because a white man once committed suicide in a field beside that road. Ivy was very anxious to have a home of her own and, of course, so was I. It was one of the things we worked and saved for and looked forward to the day when we could own our own place.

My first job after coming back from the army was with Junior Nichols, a white farmer who lived near the reservation. He and his family had always had good relations with Indians and always gave us employment, which not all white farmers would do. He also boarded all the people who worked for him, which was the old custom.

One day as we were sitting at our noon meal at Junior Nichols' place, two of his white workers who were drifters or tramps were just about to fight in a quarrel over bananas. One of them said bananas grow up on the stalk and the other said they grow down. And one was telling how good it was to eat bananas right off the stalk, while the other was protesting that bananas do not ripen on the stalk.

Just as they were about to come to blows, Junior Nichols said to me: "Rickard, you've been in the tropical climate. You know how they grow. You tell them how it is."

"Well," I said, "maybe they both know what they're talking about and I can't tell them anything."

"No," the boss insisted, "they can't both be right. You tell them!"

So the men both sat down and listened while I told them that I had

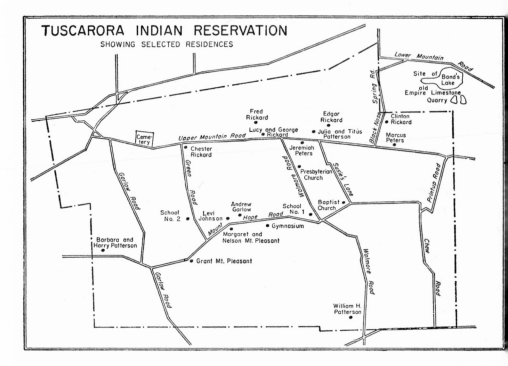

seen bananas grown and harvested many times and the fruit grows
pointing upward on the stalk. Also, the farmers pick the stalks while
the bananas are still green, put them in a dark place, and let them ripen
there. With what I had learned in my army travels, I was thereby able
to settle that controversy.

I later went to work for the Empire Limestone Quarry just northeast
of the reservation. The quarry was operated by the Lackawanna Steel
Company. My wife and I were both pleased with my new job, for this
company treated me well. After a year's work there, I was chosen as
one of the foremen in the quarry, and the only Indian foreman.

In 1906 the members of our Tuscarora Nation received $100 each
as partial payment on our Kansas claim. This award was directed by
the court of claims May 18, 1905, and payment was begun the following
year. The award was paid to all Six Nations Indians within the borders
of New York State. It was meant to reimburse us for the Kansas lands
our people gave up when they returned home from their enforced migration to that territory in 1846. Only a very few of our people had sur-

vived that ordeal in Kansas. Most of the migrants had died of disease and sickness very shortly after they arrived there. An additional small sum was to be paid us later when the government straightened out the claims of certain mixed-blood Indians. This money gave a great boost to my finances just at a time when we needed it most.[1]

Also in 1906, at the insistence of Doc Huggins, who was secretary of the pension board, I applied for an army veteran's disability pension. I was very sick for a while after coming out of the army and had lost a lot of weight. Doc Huggins told me: "I brought you into this world; I have known you all your life; and I know you were in perfect physical condition when you went into the army. I urge you to apply for a pension because of what has happened to you."

The government approved my application and granted me $8.00 a month. This was compensation for my chronic attacks of malaria and the rheumatism I had contracted in the Philippines. All my life I continued to have constant pain as a result of these two illnesses dating from my army days. The pension was small but it was a great help to us.

Before I got the job at the stone quarry, I used to walk several miles every day to work for the fruit farmers who lived just to the north of our reservation. I took a little trail down the hill past Chief Marcus Peters' place and past Black Nose Spring. This spring was named after Chief Black Nose, one of our Beaver clan chiefs, who used to live there long ago. He was called so because of a black spot on his nose.

Across from the spring was a rise of land all covered with thorn bushes and wild grapes, so overgrown that anyone would think it was useless land. But as I went back and forth to work, I sighted this spot and thought it would make a wonderful place for a home. From my boyhood days I had always admired this area by the spring. In December 1906 I therefore bought this plot of land from its owner, Chief Marcus Peters. As soon as weather permitted, I set to work clearing this land for our homestead.[2]

Now it would soon be possible for us to begin building our house and at last to have our own place. We put up a four-room house and moved in as soon as we could. I also had an Indian carpenter, Homer Patterson, build a good, sturdy barn for me. Gradually, now, I was able to start farming.

Despite the fact that we now had our own farm, it was still necessary for me to work off the reservation. It takes much money to establish a farm. Also, I still had the debts to pay off that we owed from building our house and barn and starting farming. I accordingly continued with my job at the quarry and did the farming early in the morning and late in the evening. We both looked forward to the day when we would be debt-free and independent.

We had two children born to our marriage. The elder was a girl whom we named Edith. The younger child was a boy named Herald.

My wife and I were both very happy together, and we both worked for each other and for our home. It was thus a great blow when my wife took sick. She had what we called in those days galloping consumption. Her mother, who by that time was living in Oklahoma, prevailed upon us to let Ivy go live there in a drier climate. In the fall of 1912, then, Ivy and the children went to live in Oklahoma. My mother-in-law took them to stay with her eldest sister in Shawnee. This left me very much alone and downhearted.

We corresponded often, and the letters made the absence a little more tolerable. Ivy's letters were always tender and cheerful. Even my little boy, who was not old enough to write, would see his mother writing to me and would imitate her by scribbling on a piece of paper. This was a letter for his Papa, he would say, and Ivy would send it along to me. I was so lonesome that I wanted to leave our home and go there to be with them, but Ivy encouraged me to stay on for there was no work to be had in Shawnee.

Ivy was optimistic that she would soon be cured and that we would be back together again. She had found a woman who claimed to have some skill in treating consumption. This woman charged $5.00 a week. Ivy believed these treatments were doing her a lot of good, and I kept sending her the money for them, as she requested.

My wife did not recover. I received word that she had died of her illness on February 25, 1913, just about three months after she had left home. The day of her death, she seemed much stronger and more cheerful than usual. She woke up before dawn and began reading until late morning, which was unusual, because throughout her sick days at her aunt and uncle's house she always asked some one to read to her. She said if only I would come, she believed she would recover. Her aunt and uncle therefore sent a telegram to me immediately. By late afternoon, however, it was evident that she was in her last moments. She passed away at 4:10 P.M., just three months after her twenty-third birthday. When I received notice of her death, I borrowed a suitcase from Nellie and Willard Gansworth and left immediately for Shawnee, Oklahoma. This was the saddest day in my whole life.

I knew that it would probably be best to leave my two little children with their grandmother, at least temporarily, for without their mother I was in no position to take care of them. It was distressing to have my family broken up so suddenly. It would be very hard to face an empty house when I returned home, but I could see no better way. At least the children would be with people they knew and would receive good care.

My little boy Herald was sick with a bad cough while I was in Shawnee for the funeral. The doctor assured me he would be all right. With this assurance, I left Shawnee and began my journey homeward. In Waverly, Ohio, I stopped off to see my wife's Aunt May, her mother's sister. While I was there, word came that Herald had also died, March 25, 1913, exactly one month after his mother. The doctor had been treating him for a cold, whereas he had actually had whooping cough. Thus in a short time I had lost nearly my whole family. My wife and I had been married only eight years. My little boy was not yet four. What was worse, the great 1913 flood suddenly came upon us in Waverly. I lost all my possessions and was not able to leave to go home or to Oklahoma City, where my mother-in-law was living, until the waters had subsided and the roads and rails had been cleared. I felt that I was held captive there by those waters, and I was overwhelmed with grief. There was not a thing that I could do to help my family or to relieve my sorrow.

It was not an easy thing for me to go back to my empty house and be reminded of the family I had lost, but I did have an obligation. I still had a little girl to think about and I had the farm. There was also the community work I had begun to do. The Great Spirit gave me strength to continue.

In the fall of 1913, just eight months after I had lost my wife and little boy, I realized my great boyhood ambition. The superintendent of the quarry where I worked called the four of us foremen in one day to tell us that he was going to join the Freemasons. He asked if we wanted to join the lodge with him. We all accepted and secured our petitions for membership. I was raised November 19, 1913, in Ransomville Lodge No. 551. Since that time, I have gone through all the degrees of Masonry up to the Thirty-second degree and Shrine. This stroke of good fortune showed me that the old saying is certainly true that every dark cloud has a silver lining. My very deep sorrow was lessened somewhat by the knowledge that there were still good things in this life.

Not long after my wife's death, I had an opportunity to remarry, but I turned down this offer which had come from the girl's parents, who were prominent members of our tribe. I felt that the time was not right, even though I would have come into much land by the match. There would perhaps come a day in the future when I would marry again, but that day was not now.

I had begun to be active in community affairs which in many ways helped me to forget my sorrows and also to be useful to others. When I had first come home from the army, my parents had tried to prevail upon me to become a chief. My mother was clan mother of our Beaver clan, to which I also belonged, following the custom of descent among Indians. As clan mother, she could designate the chiefs for our clan. My father was also a chief in his clan. I was compelled to refuse this offer of a leadership role. Since I had come back to the reservation after a long absence, I could see the situation as it was more clearly than my parents could.

There were two individuals on our reservation who had the greatest power and influence and who were not using their power properly. They were our head chief, Grant Mt. Pleasant, who led the whole council by their noses, and his brother, the Baptist minister, Frank Mt. Pleasant.

When I had first come home from the army, Frank Mt. Pleasant came to see me and persuaded me to join the Baptist church. We had always been Presbyterians, but now I became persuaded by Frank and agreed. It was January and they had to break the ice for me to be baptized.

After I learned some of the things that went on at the Baptist church, I began to lose interest in it. We had a very fine, upright Christian man on our reservation named William Patterson, and he had been secretary of the Baptist church. He told me a number of things that were very disturbing to me. One time, he said, the women sewed a trunk full of beadwork, and Frank Mt. Pleasant and Holland Patterson, one of the deacons, went out to the white people selling it and trying to raise money for building a new meeting house. When they came back, they brought $50 with them as a result of their trip. Later, William Patterson went out to the white Baptist churches soliciting money from them for the building fund. The people at these various churches said that Frank Mt. Pleasant had been there already and that they had donated $150, $200, $50, and other similar sums to him for the Tuscarora Baptist Church. When Frank came back from his trip, he turned over only $50 to the church and then bought a lot of land for himself. William Patterson said to me: "Remember, all that land that he bought will never be of any use to anyone." This prediction came true, for all that land went back to bush and became completely useless.

Also, with Frank's full knowledge, one of the deacons had two women—his rightful wife and another woman on the side. He even had a child by the second woman. While all this was going on, he continued to serve as a deacon in the church. When William Patterson found out what the situation was, he would never accept communion from the hands of this deacon.

William Patterson went one time to the conference of the New York State Baptist Convention as a delegate representing our church. Frank Mt. Pleasant refused to recognize him as a church member, so he could not be seated as a delegate. This was because William Patterson had protested to Frank about all these wrongful activities. Then one of the white delegates befriended William Patterson and learned the whole story. This white man was incensed and brought the matter up to the officials of the convention. They then called up Frank Mt. Pleasant and questioned him and made him admit that one of his deacons had two women. After that, the Tuscarora Baptist Church was disfellowshipped by the other Baptist churches and remained in this status for many years thereafter.

Grant Mt. Pleasant was chief warrior, or sub-chief, of the Turtle clan and was president of the Chiefs' Council. He had accumulated a large portion of the land on the reserve, frequently through very questionable means. He would, for instance, lend money to a widow in distress in exchange for a mortgage on her land. When she could not pay her debt, he would take her land and put her off. He used many harsh methods such as this to add to his property holdings. One time, my mother's aunt mortgaged her two acres of land to Grant in exchange for a dollar's worth of groceries. When the mortgage fell due and she was not able to pay, Grant took possession of her land and put a fence around the spring so that she could not continue to use it. My mother went over and paid him two dollars and got the mortgage back. Then she told Grant never to bother the poor woman again. These were just examples of the ways in which this man enriched himself at the expense of helpless people.

White visitors and officials who came and spent only an hour or so on our reservation always admired Grant because he had the biggest farm and was the most prosperous member of the tribe. To them, he was the greatest example of a civilized Indian. They never stayed long enough to discover his methods or the distresses he caused by his greediness. It is not the true Indian way to become successful by stepping on others. I could see how these two brothers had the whole reservation under their thumbs. There was no one in a position of power to protest these injustices. I told my parents that if I were chief, the first thing that I would do would be to tangle with Grant Mt. Pleasant in council. The whole council did as he directed. I would never go along with him. My father did not quite see my reasoning at the time, and I thought it would be pointless for me to become a chief.

There were other things I could do in the community, and I did become active and take an interest in our reservation affairs. Also, I was active in veterans' affairs off the reservation. I had joined the Army and Navy Union upon my discharge from the army and eventually worked my way up to various high offices in the state organization. In addition, in 1912 I began working on securing a pension for Spanish-American War veterans. There is always work to be done in society for a person who has the interest.

I had been a widower for about three years when another opportunity of marriage presented itself. In those days, many people still followed the old custom of arranging marriages. Titus and Julia Patterson had a marriageable daughter named Elizabeth. The Pattersons came to see my parents and let it be known that they thought I would be a good man for their daughter. My parents thought well of the Pattersons and of Elizabeth, so they came and suggested to me that I should go and call on the young lady. This was agreeable to me, and I started to become better acquainted with Elizabeth.

I had always liked the Pattersons. I was particularly fond of their older daughter Nellie and her husband Willard Gansworth. Nellie and Willard had always been good to me, particularly when my wife died. The Patterson family also had a good reputation for uprightness. Julia

Patterson was a Tuscarora and a member of the Bear clan. Titus was a member of the Onondaga Eel clan, even though he was born and raised on our reservation and spoke the Tuscarora language. His father, who was William Patterson, had married an Onondaga woman named Leah Chew, who was of this clan. Since children take the descent of their mother, Titus was not on our Tuscarora roll. He was an industrious farmer and always interested in progress and betterment on our reserve.

Elizabeth and I were married at the Patterson homestead. The marriage was performed by a Methodist minister, J. H. Underhill. Nellie and Willard, who were living in Niagara Falls at the time, did not come, for we had a measles epidemic raging on our reservation, and they had a baby whom they did not wish to be exposed to this sickness. My wedding turned out to be rather eventful in an unusual way, for my bride came down with measles on her wedding day.

Our family began to grow. We had a son William born to our marriage and, a little later, another son, Clark. Also, my daughter Edith came back to live with us after I was married. Later, Edith went to stay with her grandmother. They had moved to Forth Smith, Arkansas, and it was there that Edtih met and married a man named Tom Hill. Edith and Tom came back to visit us for a while after their marriage and then later went to Amarillo, Texas, to set up their home.

Sorrow struck our family again in November 1918. My brother Fred became a victim of the influenza epidemic that was then sweeping the country. When Fred first became sick, my father insisted that he be taken to the hospital. The doctors were unable to save him. He was only thirty-eight when he died. He had been suffering from a heart condition prior to the epidemic and his body was therefore less able to resist this disease. He left a widow and several young children to mourn for him. We had always known him to be a good husband and father.

In 1923, Elizabeth and I had a little boy named Ralph. The poor fellow was born with a harelip and cleft palate, which made it difficult for him to take food. We did everything we could for him and even took him to Children's Hospital in Buffalo for care. Despite all these efforts, the doctors could give him no permanent help. He lived only nine months, dying February 20, 1924.

I was now farming full time since my marriage to Elizabeth. I raised a variety of vegetables and grain, including the authentic Indian corn, and had several orchards and a small vineyard. For heavy work on the farm, such as plowing and rolling the ground and hauling heavy loads, I used an ox team. The team was also used to break a passage through the snow in the winter time. For cultivating, I used horses. I bought a second-hand tractor about 1925, but it broke down after a brief use, and I therefore returned it and stopped payment. We also had some milk cows, chickens, and ducks. The farm supplied almost everything we needed.

Every spring, I tapped the trees back in my sugar bush and boiled sap for syrup and sugar. There is only a short time in the spring when we can do this. When the weather first begins to thaw, freezes, and thaws again, then the sap begins to run. The spiles, which we make from sumac bush, are readied beforehand. The whole family works making these. Then I gash the trees and insert the spiles so that the sap can run off into buckets. This is hard, steady work, all day long and even all night long while the sap runs. It is much effort for very little return, for it takes many gallons of sap boiled down to make a quart of syrup or a pound of sugar.

Everyone on our reserve used to boil sap in the old days. I was one of the last ones to continue this practice. We used as much of the sugar and syrup as we needed and sold the rest or else gave small amounts away to friends as gifts.

It was an incident that happened early in World War II that brought my sugar-making to an end. When we are finished using the buckets after the boiling is over, we clean them and pile them up in our bush and leave them there until next year. No one ever bothers them. One time just after the war had started, one of the rough fellows on our reserve came by my bush and used my buckets for target practice. He filled all 140 of them full of holes. During the war it was nearly impossible to get metal buckets or anything else metal. After the war, pails that had once cost 10 cents were then selling for $1.00 apiece. Since I could not afford the $140 outlay for buckets, and I would probably never make up the cost by selling syrup and sugar even if I had bought them, I never used the sugar bush again. This is one way our old customs come to an end.

I hunted and fished also, both for pleasure and to provide food for my family. Fishing was my favorite pastime. There was plenty of good fishing on our reserve, with pike, bullheads, and suckers being the most common. I would also take my flybeard spear and go down the Niagara

River to fish. This spear is about twelve feet long. The head is of metal with three tines and barbs which lock when thrust into the fish. Ellis Mackey, a blacksmith who lived over on the North Ridge, was the first man in our neighborhood to make this kind of spear. I once caught a 115-pound sturgeon in the Niagara River with my flybeard. We used to spear blue pike, but that fish is all gone from our area now. When we fished all night, we set a kerosene lamp by the shore so we could see to spear the fish. Fishing season starts in March and continues nearly all summer.

Years ago, the state passed a law forbidding the use of a spear for fishing. Then we began using a bow and arrow to catch fish. The arrow is special and is really a small harpoon. After much protest from us and white fishermen on this restriction against spear fishing, the state relented but required a special license for using the spear in addition to the regular fishing license. After further protest, the state took away the extra restriction and required only the regular license.

Elizabeth and I always enjoyed entertaining guests in our home. In later years when I became more involved in Indian work, we had a continual stream of these visitors at our house, staying for longer or shorter periods. Elizabeth took all this in her stride and was always very sociable.

George Nash, a Cayuga from Grand River, lived with me for sixteen years and never paid a penny. He really became a part of our family. He would help around the farm and was a good companion in every way. George was an older man and very old-fashioned. He wore his hair long, and could speak several Indian languages. He spoke the Tuscarora language perfectly and knew some of the very old expressions. In the summertime, he would build himself a bark house and live there. There is no one left on our reserve today who knows how to make these old bark houses.

Sometimes a visitor would give us a little trouble. We had a fellow staying at our place once who was quite bold. He was fond of drink, but we never kept any alcoholic beverages whatsoever in our house because neither Elizabeth nor I approved of drinking. Elizabeth did make cider vinegar every year, and as everyone knows, before the apple juice becomes vinegar, it turns to hard cider. Unknown to us, this fellow had discovered the crock of apple squeezings down in our cellar and, to Elizabeth's wonder, used to make frequent trips to the cellar.

One day, Elizabeth happened to take a look into the crock to see how the vinegar was coming along and was most distressed to discover that there was hardly any liquid left. Her whole winter's supply of vinegar was gone before winter had even started. She of course knew at once who the culprit was. She rushed upstairs into the kitchen, got the box of Epsom salts out of the cabinet, and hurried back downstairs. She dumped a generous portion of the salts into the remaining cider, replaced the box in the cabinet, and said nothing. Our visitor very soon received what we felt was just retribution for his deed.

Our family life was a happy one. I considered myself very fortunate to have such a good wife. Especially in the later years of our marriage, when I became involved in work for Indian rights, Elizabeth stood by me in everything, even though my work meant added work for her. I thanked the Great Spirit that he had brought us together.

4

Indian Leadership

ABOUT THE YEAR 1920, I began to be active in Indian affairs outside my own reservation. It was at this time that Edward A. Everett was chairman of the Indian Commission of the New York State Assembly. This committee had the responsibility of investigating the claims of the Six Nations Indians against the state of New York. Mr. Everett visited Indian reservations, met with Indian groups, and did much research on Indian treaties and other legal aspects relating to our claims. Indian interest in this project was very high. I myself very carefully followed the progress of this investigation.

On August 19, 1920, some friends and I were in Albany attending a special meeting on Indian matters relating to the Everett investigation. While there, we met Mrs. Lulu G. Stillman, who was secretary for Mr. Everett's committee. Through this work she was eventually to become interested in the problems and grievances of my Indian people and would prove to be a lifelong friend to us. At the time, she recognized the financial condition of those of us who had journeyed to Albany and so she prepared sandwiches for us to take along on our return trip. That thoughtfulness certainly was appreciated for we would have had to go without eating otherwise. This was just one example of the kindheartedness of this great lady. In later years she would stand by us in our troubles and give us much good advice, continue to do legal research for us, and also provide material assistance for our people.

When the Everett Report was finally presented to the assembly, February 25, 1922, I attended as a delegate from the Tuscarora Nation. This report was highly favorable to the Six Nations and demonstrated in detail how we had been cheated out of eighteen million acres of land at bargain prices for the buyers. The other members of the committee did not agree with Mr. Everett's carefully reasoned report and neither did the members of the New York State Assembly. The report was

49

therefore not accepted because it was too favorable to Indian claims; nothing was ever done about this great wrong.

It was also during this period that I became a chief. My father had come to see my point of view that the system in the council had to be changed, so I agreed to his urgings to accept a chieftainship. The sachem chief of my Beaver clan was Marcus Peters, but he was elderly and ailing. Since he had a very serious case of rheumatism, he did not attend council meetings, and he was willing to surrender his chieftainship to me. My mother was Beaver clan mother, or chief matron. Both Marcus Peters and my mother laid this matter before our Chiefs' Council, according to our custom. Marcus Peters went before the council and resigned his chieftainship. My mother thereupon presented me as the new chief. Then I was led into the silver circle,[1] and the crown of honor, or chief's headdress, was taken off the head of Marcus Peters and placed upon my head. Also, Marcus Peters' chiefly name of Rowadagahrade,[2] or Loud Voice, was bestowed upon me. The chief's wampum then passed to me. This string of white beads stands for peace and is the mark of a sachem, or peace chief.

Marcus Peters at that point told me: "You will remain a chief so long as you do what is right and just to all people."

In all my work, I have always tried to live up to my charge. A chief is supposed to be an upright man, always protecting the weak and the oppressed and seeking justice at all times. He is not to think of his own advantage and is not to use his chiefly office to enrich himself or to prey upon those who are less fortunate. He must never abuse his power. The opportunities for a chief to misuse the powers and privileges of his office and to forget the obligations are always present, and the temptations are very great, so a man must constantly seek the guidance of the Great Spirit in everything. When chiefs ignore the traditions, then both they and their office lose the respect of the people, and the government declines. I was always very attached to the old traditions. I learned the customs of my people and these customs I honored.

One of the great things we were able to accomplish during my early years as a chief was the building of the gymnasium. My father-in-law Titus Patterson and I worked together very closely on this. Titus was a member of our basketball team, the Tuscarora All Stars, which used the old council house for its games. The chiefs were sometimes reluctant to let the team have the building, and frequently there was tension between the two groups. Also the council house was actually very inadequate for purposes of athletics. It had two kerosene chandeliers, which gave inadequate light, and two wood stoves at either end, which were a danger to the players and a fire hazard if ever they should be tipped over. Titus saw the need of a separate building which the team could use whenever it needed and which would be of benefit to the community. I pushed this idea and was able to get it accepted. My mother, who always worked very hard for the welfare of our community, vigorously supported this project and aroused enthusiasm for it.

Since we wanted the building to last, we could not use green lumber but had to wait for it to season. We therefore took about two years to build the gym. The logs were cut from our own woods and hauled by my ox team up to our reservation sawmill, which was operated by Levi and Lyman Johnson. I worked severely hard doing all the heavy hauling of logs to the mill and boards to the storage and building site.

The building of the gym received the enthusiastic support of the whole nation. It united our people as nothing else had in many years. Many people donated their labor to make the project a success. We had a lot of fun working together on this, knowing that our work would benefit our nation far into the future. It was Titus and I, however, who put in the most work on the building, with Titus contributing by far the greatest effort of all of us. For my part in this undertaking, I was made a life trustee of the gym.

The realization of Titus Patterson's dream turned out to be the greatest tragedy for him. Titus played jump center on the team. During one game when jumping for the ball, Titus' opponent kneed him. Some thought that this was intentional, but Titus claimed it was an accident. He was in agony from the injury and was taken home and the doctor summoned. The doctor told the family: "Just give him coffee and I'll return in the morning." Titus got worse, and his son Wesley called the ambulance and had him taken to the hospital in Niagara Falls. There he died of a ruptured appendix. This was during Christmas week of 1921 and saddened our lives greatly. His wife Julia was helpless from a paralytic stroke at the time, and many thought she would not survive the second blow, but she did live on several years longer.

With my new role as chief came added responsibilities in the community. I was very active in the Chiefs' Council and was frequently chosen for special work. When the chieftainships are all filled, there are generally fifteen chiefs on the council. There are two chiefs for each of the seven clans: a sachem and a chief warrior, or sub-chief. The additional man is the pine tree chief, elected by the council and not by the clans. We consider this office to be very high and distinguished. Since 1914, my uncle Andrew Garlow had served as the pine tree chief. One office I held quite early was treasurer of the Chiefs' Council. Also, I was on a committee to investigate the claim the Tuscarora Nation had against North Carolina for its old lands within the boundary of that state. There were also other difficult cases to handle. I was chosen as one of a committee of three chiefs to assist in handling the affairs of an orphan girl who was not on our rolls. Her father, recently deceased, had been a Tuscarora, but her mother had not been. Since children take the lineage of their mother, this child could not inherit her father's property. But since we wished to see justice done and this child cared for, we worked out a means for her support, based on the rental of her father's estate. She, of course, was permitted to continue living on the reservation.

We also had a longstanding dispute with many of our lawless white neighbors who, from time immemorial, had come onto Indian lands to cut and steal our timber which we ourselves needed for fuel and building purposes. There was a New York State ordinance forbidding non-Indians from cutting wood on an Indian reservation, and we posted printed notices to this effect. Needless to say, those determined to take our belongings were not discouraged by knowledge of the existence of this law, and we had to be always vigilant to catch the culprits and deliver them up. I regret to say that this type of theft goes on to this day.

Another problem we fought to overcome and on which our nation was almost unanimous was the bill in Congress to force citizenship on the Indian people. I say "almost unanimous" because there may have been a few in our nation who were favorable to it, but I do not recall their names. Even the so-called progressive Indians in our midst were opposed. The Six Nations Confederacy spoke with one voice on this issue, and all protested the intent of the Congress to press us into becoming United States citizens. We were well aware of the unfortunate circumstances of the Western Indians who had had this dubious blessing imposed upon them in the nineteenth and early twentieth centuries and had had their lands taken away in the process, leaving them homeless paupers begging the government for support.

White people were always thinking up schemes to improve us poor Indians and to make the "Indian problem" disappear. The most favored of these continual grand programs was to make us into imitation whites. This plan was a lot more flattering to whites than it was to us. By the United States government forcing citizenship upon us, it could have greater control over us. We would lose most of our independence. By our ancient treaties, we expected the protection of the government. The white man had obtained most of our land and we felt he was obliged to provide something in return, which was protection of the land we had left, but we did not want to be integrated and assimilated into his society. United States citizenship was just another way of absorbing us and destroying our customs and our government. How could these Europeans come over here and tell us we were citizens in our own country? We had our own citizenship. We did not want or need the white man's type of citizenship. We feared citizenship would also put our treaty status in jeopardy and bring taxes upon our land. How can a citizen have a treaty with his own government? To us, it seemed that the United States government was just trying to get rid of its treaty obligations and make us into taxpaying citizens who could sell their homelands and finally end up in the city slums. We knew some white people were sincere in backing this Indian citizenship bill because they were trying to do what they felt was right by us. They just did not look far enough into the future and they did not understand our feelings in the matter.

The Citizenship Act did pass in 1924 despite our strong opposition. By its provisions all Indians were automatically made United States citizens whether they wanted to be so or not. This was a violation of our sovereignty. Our citizenship was in our own nations. We had a great attachment to our style of government. We wished to remain treaty Indians and preserve our ancient rights. There was no great rush among my people to go out and vote in white man's elections. Anyone who did so was denied the privilege of becoming a chief or a clan mother in our nation.[3]

Occasionally also we were completely frustrated in obtaining justice by the hard-hearted attitude of unbelievably stupid New York State politicians. I can remember particularly my sad experiences with the state government on a few occasions during the winter seasons of the

1920s. The state had a contract with a private individual in Niagara County to clear snow from the roads on the Tuscarora Reservation. This was not for Indian benefit only, because white travelers also used the roads on our lands. When we received no service after several heavy snowfalls, I recruited a number of men from the reservation and we worked many long hours in clearing the snow ourselves, without any modern equipment. I then submitted a bill for this labor to the proper state official. Since the man under contract had not lived up to his contract, I saw no reason why he should be paid for the work that we had to do because of his neglect. I received a curt letter back from Theron M. Ripley, Division Engineer of the Department of Public Works for the Fifth Division, telling me that the contractor's truck had broken down and since I had not submitted a requisition for this labor ahead of time, my statement could not be honored.[4] Now, everyone knows that snow removal is an emergency. Were we to have starved, immobilized in our houses, while waiting either for the spring thaws or the glacial speed of the state's approval for our industry? If our roads had not been public but for Indian use only, it would have been a different matter. As it was, our roads at that time were used far more by whites than by Indians. In the old days, we used to maintain our roads ourselves. Now that the reservation had become a public thoroughfare for white people, we felt that the white community, as represened by the state, should do its share in keeping the roads in order. Evidently Mr. Ripley's bureaucratic mind could not function except in the familiar channels marked out by governmental red tape.

I have related a few of the many problems our Chiefs' Council had to deal with, but my most serious controversy in my early years on the council came with Chief Grant Mt. Pleasant. The whole dispute concerned Grant's continual greed for more land. My mother-in-law, Julia Patterson, cared for her sister, Emeline Garlow, for two years or more before the latter's death. When Emeline Garlow died, August 7, 1920, Grant Mt. Pleasant, who was married to her other sister, Minerva, produced a will written by Emeline, stating that she willed all her property to him. Julia Patterson and her children contested this will, and the dispute was brought before our Chiefs' Council in May 1923.

Our Chiefs' Council disallowed this will of Emeline Garlow's on the grounds that it was obtained under undue influence and also that Grant had accumulated property far in excess of what he needed since he owned about six hundred acres or nearly one tenth of the entire reservation. The council granted to Julia Patterson a portion of money equal to the value of the estate promised her by Emeline. This was to be paid to Julia Patterson by Grant Mt. Pleasant. Grant refused to honor this judgment, so the Chiefs' Council granted that portion of Emeline's estate to her sister Julia. My father, Chief George Rickard, my brother Chester, Julia's son Harry Patterson, and I went in and took possession of the property, cut wood and picked apples for the benefit of the woman to whom the property had been awarded.

When Grant lost in council, he took the case to the white man's court, which we as a sovereign nation claimed had no jurisdiction over our affairs. He charged five of us with larceny. Grant came to my place with a mob of his followers and the United States marshal. In my yard, Grant struck me. I told the marshal to put this mob off, and he did. I then had Grant arrested for assault.

The case against us came up in the United States District Court. There I gave my testimony and related the whole history of this man's method of accumulating property from people in distress, taking a mortgage, and then foreclosing the mortgage immediately when they could not pay. I told the court:

"For many years Mt. Pleasant has made a business of gathering up all the old people who are ready to die and taking them to his house to live during their remaining days. He feeds and clothes them, but before they die, he has them make a will bequeathing their property to him.

"Then when the old folks die, he buries them and collects profit from from the lands, houses, and other property which they have willed him. Their survivors are left, in many cases, nearly destitute. Neither is this the limit of his activities.

"Mt. Pleasant buys farms and property at an extremely low figure from worthless Indians who anticipate skipping out. The day after they have gone, Mt. Pleasant appears on the scene with a deed to the property and evicts the faithless man's family. Recently he foreclosed a mortgage on property one day after it was due."

Under examination by Assistant United States Attorney Samuel J. Dickey, Mt. Pleasant admitted owning an extensive amount of land and several expensive automobiles, but he denied my charges.[5] Grant had also misrepresented this case to Warren K. Moorehead, a member of the Board of Indian Commissioners, when he came to visit our reservation in 1923. Grant got Mr. Moorehead's ear and told him, in referring to the chiefs who had decided against him in council: "These other Indians claim that the property should be divided up among themselves according to old custom on the grounds that I already have enough, that no law can stop them cutting [timber]." This misrepresentation was printed in Mr. Moorehead's official report. We did not want this property for ourselves but for the rightful owner. Grant also bragged to Moorehead that he owned a Cadillac, had numerous fruit orchards and extensive lands all built up by his own hard labor, and was worth $200,000. That also got into Moorehead's report since he wished to hold Grant's great success story up as an example to other Indians.

Grant even called those chiefs who opposed his greedy ways "Longhouse chiefs," and this government man, without question, printed this false statement in his report. He did not even bother to find out that we had no chiefs of the Longhouse religion on our reservation.

Now Grant was always quick to brag to white folks that he was a self-made man who started out in a small way and through his hard work alone became very rich. He contrasted himself with other Indians who were still at the bottom of the ladder, so to speak. And he accused those who were opposed to him of blocking progress. There were some details that never got into print, however, such as his grasping methods of accumulating land and his methods of trampling on the rights of others. For instance, years ago, one of our worthless men gave Grant a mortgage on his place for $400 and then disappeared from the reservation, leaving his wife and children destitute. The wife worked and scraped to save $400 to pay back the mortgage. The day it fell due, Grant came to put her out. She presented him with the money but he refused to accept it, saying: "I didn't make this agreement with you!" He put her and her family out that very day and seized her house and land for himself.

As soon as I saw a copy of Moorehead's report, I wrote him and protested its prejudiced and uninformed nature and asked him to print the truth. He had never bothered to investigate all sides of the story.

Moorehead wrote back to me saying he could not consider the points I had brought up in my letter and could not print them because if he did, he would become involved in a "small argument." This was a joke. He had already involved himself in a small argument the moment he printed his biased report. I truly believe he was not man enough to admit he had made a mistake and really knew nothing about what was going on on our reservation.

The case that Grant had against us resulted in both justice and injustice. It was thrown out of the district court, but I was later charged in county court, and the sheriff came onto my place and levied on one hundred bushels of my wheat to be sold at public auction in order to pay the judgment and court costs. This meant that the state superseded our authority to govern ourselves and set aside the decision of the Chiefs' Council. On many counts this was a great wrong. But I did win my assault case against Grant. The judge accused me first of inconsistency and asked: "How can you have him arrested? You assume the state has no jurisdiction."

I replied: "This man assumes state jurisdiction. Why not use that law on him?"

The judged answered: "That's his right," and proceeded with the case.

The United States marshal who was witness to the affair testified on my behalf, even though I had not had him subpoenaed. The result was that Grant was found guilty and fined $25 or imprisonment until the fine was paid. Grant had to borrow this money from his lawyer there in the court in order to escape jail.

The publicity from this case did result in Grant Mt. Pleasant's downfall as president of our council. Warren Brayley was later elected as president of the Chiefs' Council and Grant's influence declined.

It was told all over the reservation in later years that, while on his deathbed, Grant became extremely emotional, cried out continually that his bed was on fire, that flames were coming from under the mattress, and that the room was full of smoke. People said that he could see where he was headed after death. Grant then pleaded with his family to give back all the land he had secured by hook or crook. After his confession, it was said that he rested peacefully and never cried out again about fire. Shortly thereafter, he died. His family never carried out his deathbed wish, but kept all the land which they inherited from him. Folks on the reservation said that because these instructions were not complied with, all that land would come to nothing. That is exactly what has happened. Today Grant's fine farmlands have declined, gone to bush, and are unproductive.

In the early 1920s, I became acquainted with Deskaheh, or Levi General, the Cayuga sachem from Six Nations Reserve on the Grand River, near Brantford, Ontario. He was their leading chief, speaker of the council, and a man of the utmost integrity. He was an advocate of the traditional Iroquois ways and was always very much attached to the teachings of our ancestors. I admired him greatly and was honored to assist in his work on behalf of our people.

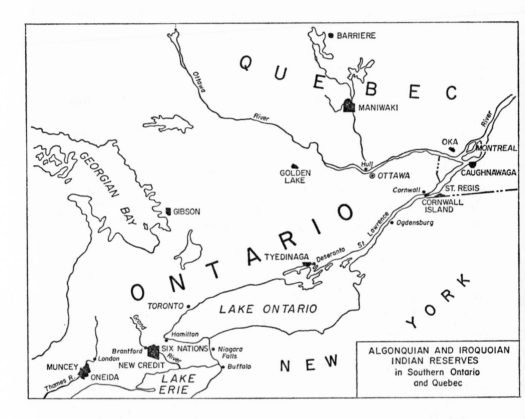

Deskaheh and others of the Six Nations Reserve were very disturbed because the government of Canada had been dominating the Indians and forcing foreign laws on them, refusing to let them run their own affairs. The Six Nations had many grievances on this account. A group of so-called Loyalist Iroquois, representing only a minority, was supporting the Canadian government's attempt to change the government and customs of the Six Nations. I tell Deskaheh's story as he told it to me personally and as he told it many times both in speeches and in newspaper interviews and in his letters.

The government of Canada changed its outlook toward Indians after the First World War. Three hundred young men from the Six Nations fought for Canada in that war, and forty of their number were left dead in Europe. After the soldiers returned home from the war, the Indian Office decided to force Canadian citizenship on the Indians. It was called "enfranchisement."

Six Nations Indians always had their own rights in their own nation and tribes, their own government and rulers, and freedom of movement within their own community. This citizenship proposal was a move to integrate Indians into the white man's life and community and to destroy the Indian community. The Iroquois do not wish to be subjects of any foreign nation. They served as faithful allies to the white man in many wars but never wished this alliance to be turned into bondage. The Six Nations Confederacy held fast the covenant chain of friendship with the Europeans who came to our shores. Now these white men had found a way of turning the covenant chain into a fetter for Indians.

The Dominion of Canada enticed Indians into enfranchisement by an attractive offer of money to anyone who took up Canadian citizenship. This money was taken out of Indian funds.[6] Then these Indians were taken off their tribal rolls forever and had no more rights to own Indian land. Scores of these Indians who chose to become British subjects squandered their enfranchisement money and then returned to their former Indian brethren as British paupers, asking to be cared for.

The Indian Office also had the power to buy and sell Indian lands without the consent of the Indian councils. Self-government was denied to Indians, except insofar as the Indian Office gave its approval. There was great fear that the Six Nations would be scattered to the winds and would disappear forever.

The Chiefs' Council of the Six Nations resisted the encroachments of the Indian Office and the dominion government, not wishing to live under a totalitarian white man's government but as Indians and as a free people. The Six Nations had a perfectly good government before the coming of the white men to this continent. Our people had their own way and did not wish to be made over as white men. That is no insult to whites. We feel that the Great Spirit has led us in our way and that our way is good. If white men have another way, then we do not quarrel with them, and we do not try to change them. We ask only to be left to our way and our traditions. We want the same freedom for ourselves that the whites wanted when they fled European tyranny and sought liberty in a new land.

Those Indians who were loyal to the Six Nations hereditary government and who were opposed to an elective council as approved by the Indian Department and a minority of the Iroquois were marked out as troublemakers by the Canadian government. The Royal Canadian Mounted Police raided the homes of patriot leaders and sent those they could find to Canadian jails to be tried in courts in which Indian tradition and custom were held of no importance, before juries that contained no Indians.

I myself received word from friends in northern Quebec that the Mounted Police were arresting a number of Indians from reserves there because these people had neglected to ask leave of the Indian Department to cut wood for fuel on Indian land, as they and their ancestors had always done. No Canadian farmer ever had to ask permission of his government to cut wood on his own property. This was the way in which Indians were discriminated against and treated as children and strangers in their own land. Indians were forced to conform to white men's laws which they had no part in making and which hindered their way of life.

The Mounted Police would have arrested Deskaheh, too, had he been available, but his people had sent him south of the Great Lakes for safety. The Mounties did raid his home on the pretense that they were looking for liquor, though Deskaheh was never a drinker. This was simply harassment and was meant as intimidation.

Deskaheh traveled on a Six Nations passport. He had first had a Five Nations passport but was told at the border by the authorities that they never heard of the Five Nations but they had heard of the Six Nations. Then he returned to his council and received a Six Nations passport.

He waited in safety among friends south of the border while his people at home raised money to send him to England. I also assisted in raising funds for his travel abroad. While staying in New York State, he became acquainted with attorney George P. Decker of Rochester, who later accompanied him to Europe to help in presenting his cause before the British government and the League of Nations.

In 1921 Deskaheh traveled to London as the representative of the Six Nations Council. In England he found many official doors closed to him, but he did make many friends among the people. The colonial secretary, however, told Deskaheh that the old covenant chain was no longer good, that the king had let go of it, and had let his faithful allies, the Six Nations, drift away. The British crown, the secretary said, was no longer responsible for the Six Nations. The Six Nations denied that the Dominion of Canada could take up this responsibility without the consent of the Indian people, which consent it had never sought. The Six Nations Indians wanted to be a free people subject to no one. They wanted to keep their old alliances and their old agreements.

The British government, through General Frederick Haldimand, October 25, 1784, granted to the Six Nations Indians who supported Great Britain in the war against the American colonies a tract of land on the Grand River, purchased from the Missisauga Indians and guaranteed to the Six Nations and their posterity forever. The king promised in this Haldimand Grant to protect this land belonging to "His Majesty's faithful allies." By withdrawing his protection from his old allies and by turning them and their affairs over to the Canadian government without first consulting the Six Nations, and by the Canadian government's not allowing the Six Nations to have control over their own lands and their own government thereafter, the white man had gone back on his word to the Indians and had attempted to subject them and destroy their freedom. It was this treatment that Deskaheh as spokesman of the Six Nations Council was protesting.

Deskaheh went again to Europe in 1923 in company with Attorney Decker. He visited many places in England and Scotland and made numerous friends. Also, he traveled to Geneva, Switzerland, to lay the grievances of the Six Nations before the League of Nations.

The situation had gone from bad to worse on the Six Nations Reserve on the Grand River. A small group of loyalists, so-called, were in favor of an elective council rather than a hereditary council of chiefs, chosen in the old way by the women of each clan and confirmed by the clan members and council. The government of Canada acceded to the request of these loyalists and required a vote on the issue from the Indian people on the Six Nations rolls. Voting in this fashion was a white man's custom, not an Indian tradition. The patriots also resented being forced in this way by the Canadian government. Deskaheh's people therefore boycotted the election. The result was that 10 percent of the reserve voted for an elective council. The overwhelming majority, in favor of the traditional government, did not vote. The government of Canada then proceeded to dissolve the traditional Iroquois government by an Order in Council of September 17, 1923. Royal Canadian Mounted Police were sent in to back up this action. The white man's government then attempted to prevent the Six Nations from governing themselves in their preferred way, but the traditional council continued to exist despite this setback, and most of the people on the reserve supported it. The Canadian government forcibly supported the elected council. Thus many quarrels and much hard feeling grew up among these people with two rival governments on the same reserve.

On November 4, 1924, Deskaheh presented an official proclamation from the Six Nations to the League of Nations. This proclamation explained the independence and sovereignty of the Six Nations, as recognized in many treaties heretofore concluded between them and representatives of the Dutch, British, and American governments. The said proclamation concluded by stating:

> And whereas the said Six Nations as a peace-loving and law-abiding, autonomous and independent state are desirous of availing themselves of the Hague Convention of 1899 (1) and 1907 (2) for the pacific settlement of international disputes,
> Now therefore I do by these presents proclaim and it is witnessed by my signature and seal hereunto duly fixed that the people of the Six Nations hereby adhere and by this Act will hereafter adhere to all the rules and regulations now made or to be made under the auspices of, and by virtue of, the said conventions and will do all things necessary in order to further the undertakings of such conventions for the purpose of the pacific settlement of international disputes, and the due execution of any award made thereunder.

The League of Nations refused to hear the petition of the Six Nations. The Iroquois had organized the original League of Nations, formed by Deganawideh and Hiawatha long before the coming of the white men to our shores, and had helped to make possible the modern-day League of Nations by fighting on the side of the Allies in the Great War from 1914 to 1918. Despite these contributions, the Six Nations were now turned aside and ignored.

Deskaheh returned from Europe in 1925 and went to stay in Rochester, New York, for a short while before returning to Ohsweken on his reserve. While he was so close by—Rochester being only a short distance from the Tuscarora Reserve—I renewed my acquaintance with him and offered to assist in carrying on his work. It had been my honor previously to help in raising money for his endeavors. Now I wished to do all I could for this noble man to aid him in securing justice for our people.

He was living in Rochester without any means to support himself except what he had saved or what friends had donated. He felt it necessary to stay there for a while in order to consult with Attorney Decker and to speak before various groups to make the cause of our people known. While he was living there in modest circumstances, the rumor began to be circulated among some of the more jealous of our Indians that he had built himself a fine house in Rochester with money collected from our poor people and that he would bring his family there to live in splendor. I have seen and experienced this sad fact more than once in my life that jealousy is the great weakness of many of our people and the reason for so much disunity among us.

I secured two speaking engagements for Deskaheh on March 5 and 7, 1925. On March 5, he appeared before the Red Jacket Lodge of Masons in Lockport, New York, dressed in full Indian regalia, and spoke of the grievances of the Six Nations and his work to solve the difficulties. He had with him the original copy of the Haldimand Grant, written on parchment. This was read to the gathering by Howard C. Townsend. Deskaheh made a very favorable impression on the nearly 150 Masons assembled at that meeting. They felt that it had been a real treat to hear this great man speak to them.

On Tuesday evening, March 10, he spoke over the local radio station in Rochester, again explaining his work and the troubles the Six Nations had been experiencing. We did not know it at the time, but this was to be Deskaheh's last public appearance. I had secured an engagement for him to speak on a Philadelphia radio station but was saddened to receive a letter from him written just two days after his Rochester broadcast telling me that he was too sick to make the Philadelphia appointment. His doctor had forbidden him to leave the house.

Deskaheh's sudden illness grew worse. He was taken to the Homeopathic Hospital on Alexander Street in Rochester. There he was confined for eight weeks. Nine doctors who worked on him were unable to cure him. He then made a request through Attorney Decker to come and stay at my home, where he believed he would improve. Decker informed me that Deskaheh was so weak that he would need nursing care for a while and would have to be waited on until he regained his strength. My wife and I never hesitated to consent to having him come to live with us. He was accordingly brought to our house from Rochester in an ambulance and we gave him a bed in our parlor.

Our new guest now asked me if I could secure a medicine man to treat him. I therefore went to his reserve to comply with his request. There were two medicine men who came to see him and who stayed in the same room with him for a week treating him. They gave me instructions not to let anyone in to see Deskaheh who was an immoral person, who indulged in liquor, or who had a bad character in any way. Any evil person would interfere with the medicine and counteract the treatment.

At the end of the week, when the medicine men came out of Deskaheh's room, he came out with them. They had brought him to the point of recovery. He could walk about normally and could do his work again. The medicine men then left and returned to their own reserve.

I later went to Grand River to secure another medicine man named David Otter to continue giving Deskaheh treatments. Altogether I made three trips to Grand River on Deskaheh's behalf.

During the time Deskaheh was with me, he had a number of visitors from his own reserve. Friends from Grand River came over to see him regularly. Now I do believe that the Canadian rulers were convinced that some plot was being hatched in my house for they did a very strange thing. The government of Canada sent Royal Canadian Mounted Police over into the United States and into the Tuscarora Reservation. These mounties rode up and down in front of my house intimidating us. It was a threatening act against a peaceful people who never did anything to harm anyone and who never wished to endanger the Canadian government in any way.

Our people at this time faced a very great threat to our rights as a result of legislation passed by the United States Congress and signed by the president. I am referring to the Immigration Act of 1924, sponsored by Senator Hiram Johnson of California. One portion of that Act was aimed at exclusion of Orientals, in keeping with American race prejudice of that day. Section 13(c) of the Act stated: "No alien ineligible to citizenship shall be admitted to the United States." This provision not only hit at Chinese and Japanese, but also at American Indians. Only people of the white and black races were therefore permitted into the United States. Orientals and North American Indians coming into the United States from Canada were excluded. This Immigration Act therefore made the original inhabitants of this continent the victims of American racial prejudice.[7]

In the middle of June 1925, the Immigration Service began to apply this act to our North American Indian people who were coming into the United States from Canada. Indian visitors coming over to see Deskaheh were thereupon barred, even though they might have been temporarily admitted under Section 3 of the act, which states that temporary tourists or those conducting business might come to the United States on a nonimmigrant status for a brief time. I received many complaints by mail from my friends at the Six Nations Reserve saying they were stopped at the border, in violation of our old treaty rights. Members of Deskaheh's own family, who had not seen him in two years, were prohibited from coming over to visit him.

One day I delivered a letter to Deskaheh as he sat at the table eating. He opened it and read; then he dropped the letter on his plate. He said: "My medicine man can't come over any more. What will I do? I'm done!"

Up to this point, he had been with me for six weeks, had been in good spirits, and was recovering his strength after his cure by the medicine men. Now he got up from the table without finishing his meal, went in and lay down on his bed. He never got up again. Several days later, he took chills and we piled all our blankets and quilts on him to keep him warm. Nothing, not even the white doctor, could save him. He died at 6:30 P.M., June 27, 1925.[8] He was only fifty-two years old and one of the finest men I have ever met. Deskaheh was one of the true natural-born North American Indian Freemasons, though he was not a member of the Craft.[9]

We sent his body back to Ohsweken the next day. His family, who had not been permitted to see him alive, could see him now only as a corpse. I was overcome with grief and anger at this great wrong.

The white doctor told us to burn all the bedding he had used and to disinfect the house. This we did, at great expense to ourselves.

Deskaheh's funeral was held at his home on June 30, and I attended. There were between fifteen hundred and two thousand mourners come to pay their last respects to this great man who had worn himself out in the service of his people. Visitors from various tribes as far away as Maniwaki in Quebec came to attend this funeral. It was the most impressive ceremony I have ever witnessed. In all that throng, there was not a dry eye. We all were grateful for his life and sorrowful that he had been taken from us so soon.

I made the acquaintance of a number of people at this funeral, among whom was Chief John Chabot of the Algonquin Indians of Maniwaki, Quebec. This would be the beginning of a long and important association with the people of that tribe.

Deskaheh's Ten Day Feast was held on July 7.[10] I took a number of his friends from Lockport and Rochester up to Grand River to participate in this ancient ritual to console the family of our departed friend. Arthur C. Parker from the Rochester Museum was present and gave a very encouraging speech. This event marked the end of the mourning period. I was quite convinced, however, that we could never find another man like Deskaheh to carry on our work.

I had a double sorrow at this time. On July 6, just the day before Deskaheh's Ten Day Feast, my mother, Lucy Rickard, passed away as a result of an attack of acute nephritis. She was just a few days short of being sixty-four. Her funeral was held July 8, 1925. It was a great loss to me for she was a good woman and greatly beloved by many. Alexander J. General, brother of Deskaheh, knew her well and wrote me a letter of consolation which very fittingly described by mother's character.

Ohsweken, Ontario, July 10/25

Dear Friend:

If anything could have caused me especial pain, it was of your said bereavement. How I remember your dear mother! Lovely, intelligent, and affectionate, ever displaying a thoughtfulness beyond her years, and to lose such a promising mother truly brings a deep and a shadow; but remember that light sometime will break through, and there will be glad and happy reunion in the great beyond. It is, indeed, been a heavy blow, and I scarcely know how to expressed of consolation under so bitter an affliction. But think of one who careth for us all and who loves all. I can say no more;

human consolation is weak. May Great Spirit bless you in the hour of sorrow, is the wish of Your Friend

Alex J. General

Despite these setbacks and discouragements, I was now more determined than ever to carry on the border fight to obtain justice for our Indian people. The Jay Treaty of 1794 between the United States and Great Britain had, in Article 3, given Indians the right to cross the border with their own goods at any time. Article 9 of the Treaty of Ghent of 1814, which closed the War of 1812, restored these rights to us. The Immigration Act of 1924 had thus deprived us of our treaty rights and even more, for long before the white man came over to our country, we passed freely over this land. Now since the coming of the Europeans, a border has been set up separating Canadians and Americans, but we never believed that it was meant to separate Indians. This was our country, our continent, long before the first European set foot on it. Our Six Nations people live on both sides of this border. We are intermarried and have relatives and friends on both sides. We go back and forth to each other's ceremonies and festivals. Our people are one. It is an injustice to separate families and impose restrictions upon us, the original North Americans, who were once a free people and wish to remain free.

In addition to my new activities to obtain justice from the government for our people, I carried on my duties as chief in my own Tuscarora Nation. I was elected treasurer of the Chiefs' Council in 1925 and was also given other responsibilities. One of these was to make arrangements for our National Picnic, which was always held in August. I was in charge of securing speakers and invited New York Indian Agent W. K. Harrison of Salamanca and Attorney George P. Decker of Rochester. Also, I called for a large representation of Indians from the Six Nations Reserve on the Grand River. Through my efforts, and through writing to various officials in Washington, the Immigration Service was beginning to let Indians come from Canada into the United States as temporary tourists if I would go to the bridge and vouch for them.

George Decker was the featured speaker at our picnic that year. He read Deskaheh's last address over the Rochester radio station and also gave the departed chief much praise. We were to find out in later years, however, that Decker was a man we could not depend on. He frequently gave bad advice and tried to charge us huge sums for doing a minimum of work on our cases. My people, in their long struggle for justice, were often victimized by lawyers of this type.

Two hundred-fifty people came from the Six Nations Reserve to attend our Tuscarora picnic, for an important announcement was to be made at the festivities. I had made arrangements with the immigration officials for this group to cross but had to be there at the border at the time they came on August 15. The visitors were thus able to get over to our side without any trouble.

The Six Nations Council had chosen successors to Deskaheh to continue his work, and the names were to be announced at our picnic. Three of them were from Grand River: Chief Chauncey Garlow, Mohawk; Warrior Alexander J. General, Cayuga, brother of Deskaheh; and Chief Robert Henhawk, Onondaga. The fourth person chosen was myself. I was honored that my Six Nations brethren had placed this confidence in me. Also I felt that it was noteworthy that it would take four of us to carry on the work that Deskaheh had been doing himself.

For my part, I determined not to rest until the victory was won. The last words Chief Deskaheh had said to me before he died were: "Fight for the line," meaning the border. And I intended to do just that.

I knew the road ahead of us would be rough, but I also knew there could be no turning back. I asked the Great Spirit, who is the One True Living God, to give me strength that I might carry on this work and never let my people down. With His help, I was confident that we would overcome all obstacles and that justice would prevail.

5

The Border Crossing

THE YEAR 1925 began a long struggle to secure the border crossing rights for our Indian people as guaranteed by the old treaties, which were still in existence. These were specifically Article 3 of the Jay Treaty of 1794 and Article 9 of the Treaty of Ghent of 1814. The United States government had ignored these treaties in passing the new immigration legislation, and it was now up to us and our sympathizers to carry on the fight to gain justice.

I now had to take a great amount of time away from my farm to travel and to write letters to Indian and white friends and to government officials, for I was receiving mail all the time from Indians, and I was also obliged to protest to the government this prohibition of our free movement across the border. In all my work, my wife Elizabeth provided constant encouragement and assistance. She served as my secretary for many years. I would write out my letters and she would copy them over in her fine hand. She was a very intelligent woman, with more formal education than I, having completed eighth grade, which was the most education the average Indian could get in those days. In addition to all the other duties a farm wife has, she took on this extra duty readily and cheerfully. Many a time in the years ahead my wife and I would sit at my desk from morning to morning writing letters. Oftentimes I would be called away from my farming to aid some Indian brother or sister in difficulty. Our house was always open to visitors and strangers, and they came frequently, often staying long periods. Sometimes we would not even know the person in distress who called at our door, but we took him in. As I became better known in this work, the visitors became more numerous. The financial drain was often great, and the farm frequently suffered. Despite all the difficulties, I can gratefully say that in all this work my wife stood beside me and bore the burden with me. Whatever success I had, the credit should be shared with her.

On September 11, 1925, Henry Hull, commissioner general of the

Bureau of Immigration, United States Department of Labor, replied to a previous letter of mine by saying that North American Indians might be admitted over the border if they were coming temporarily for business or pleasure, since this was permitted by the 1924 Immigration Act. The letter went on to state that the subject of their permanent admission was under consideration by the Department of Interior, but: "It is the practice of the Immigration Service at the present time to deny such admission to members of the red race under the section of law mentioned above."[1]

We therefore had only a partial victory. The fight was a long way from being completely won. In fact, on September 7, Chief Hoheoneane had been turned back at the border with no explanation given. Also, the American immigration officers stopped Indian Baptists from Grand River from coming over to revival services at the Tuscarora Baptist Church.

I had previously written to Senator James W. Wadsworth, Jr., and Indian Commissioner Charles H. Burke on this border crossing problem. I told Attorney Decker about the replies from Wadsworth and Burke and requested him to correspond about this problem with Senator Wadsworth, who had been of great assistance to us. I wanted the senator to ask the Secretary of Labor to notify the immigration stations along the border, especially at Buffalo, Niagara Falls, Lewiston, and Rochester, of the fact that there was no ruling excluding North American Indians from crossing the border for temporary purposes. We could see, however, that there was much more work ahead of us.

In appreciation for my work in opening the border, in the fall of 1925 the Algonquin Indians of Maniwaki presented me with a beautiful Indian costume made out of moose hide and expertly beaded. I had told these Indians about Sir William Johnson's second speech to the Six Nations. This speech was represented in beadwork on the front of the jacket. A red hand and a white hand held fast the covenant chain of friendship, signifying the alliance between the two peoples. Six stars represented the Six Nations Confederacy. There were also an eagle and thirteen stars indicating that our people had established a friendship with the thirteen original United States. The eagle is an Indian emblem adopted by the United States government. This costume was made by Mrs. Frank Meness of the Algonquin tribe and was sent to me by head chief John Chabot.[2] All I needed now was to secure a headdress to make my regalia complete.

For many years it had not been the custom to dress in Indian fashion on our reserve. I remember some of the older folks like Susan Thompson who had some beaded clothing to wear on special occasions, and old Alvis Hewitt, who had a beaded leather costume. In my youth I also remember a few of the older men who wore long hair. Other than those, the rest of the people all dressed white man's style at all times. I began wearing my costume on all special and ceremonial occasions and also encouraged other Indians to wear Indian clothing. I received much opposition from some of my Tuscarora people on this account and was even accused of "going back to the blanket." This opposition has gradually been overcome. Today when you attend our Tuscarora National Picnic, you will see many of our people dressed in Indian regalia, even some of those who originally opposed me for doing so. I have a good laugh at this sometimes, but I am proud to have revived the custom.

In December 1925 we faced a new setback at the border. On December 17, I went to Grand River to attend the condolence for departed Cayuga chiefs at the Sour Springs Longhouse. It was at this time that Alexander J. General was condoled to succeed his brother Levi General and to assume his title and chiefly name of Deskaheh. I took with me Job Henry, a Tuscarora from Grand River who had married one of our women and had lived and worked on our reserve for thirty years, with the exception of occasional visits back to Grand River. On the way back to the United States December 18, we tried to cross at Lewiston Bridge but were turned back by the immigration official whose name, as nearly as I could make out, was John McClay, and told to go to the Lower Arch Bridge in Niagara Falls, which was eight miles away. He certainly was no gentleman but talked to us as though we were dogs. I had been subjected to much embarrassment and delay by this same man on several past occasions when I tried to cross the border alone but was released when I showed him letters from Senator Wadsworth and Indian Commissioner Burke.

We followed McClay's instructions and proceeded to Niagara Falls. In the meanwhile, McClay telephoned on ahead and told the immigration office at that bridge to hold us. At the Lower Arch Bridge, we were asked why we tried to pass there when we were rejected at Lewiston. Then I was allowed to pass but Job Henry was refused on the grounds that he was illiterate, which he was. In fact, he spoke only the Indian language and little or no English. A 1917 immigration law barred illiterates from the United States and now for the first time this law was being used against my people. Job Henry, aged fifty-five, had a wife and two sons on our reservation. He had lived ten years straight on our reservation, from 1895 to 1905, and after that time he and his family returned occasionally to the Grand River Reserve. He worked for Titus Patterson first and then for Willard Gansworth and always had been known as a reputable person and a good worker. The 1917 law acted to separate him from his family and to leave these poor people in much emotional and financial distress. This was a great wrong perpetrated against the descendants of the original inhabitants of this continent by the descendants of European immigrants. Some of these border officers were themselves recent immigrants from Europe and could not even speak good English.

Nor was this all. Our people were continually stopped when trying to cross the border, despite the fact that no order had come from Washington to bar Indians. Just the contrary, in fact, for the letter I had from Immigration Commissioner Hull indicated that Indians might be admitted on a temporary basis. This discrimination against our people was directly the result of race prejudice on the part of some immigration officers. They held the power, and they were using it to humiliate and distress us.

I took up the case of Job Henry immediately. I wrote letters to Senator Wadsworth and to the Immigration Bureau in Washington. Senator Wadsworth gave us much assistance in supporting our right to cross the border at will. I myself went to the main office of the district director of immigration in Buffalo to protest this unjust exclusion and to plead the case of our Indian people who wished to cross the border. I had told the immigration officials that Job Henry was a native American whose ancestors had been here for centuries and who had been unjustly stopped at the border and separated from his wife and children. I did not consider that there was any such thing as "Canadian Indian" or "United States Indian." All Indians are one people. We were here long before there was any border to make an artificial division of our people.

While I was in the Immigration Office in Buffalo, January 22, 1926, I was advised by Arthur Karnuth of that office that he had received word from Washington to allow Job Henry to enter this country for a temporary period of six months. This was a great victory for us, but still a limited one.

Job came over the border February 4, 1926, and was allowed to stay until September 6, 1926. We made an appeal for him again in July to extend his temporary stay, because his wife and one of his children were born on our reservation and his employer was also on our reservation.

I had to interpret for Job while the immigration people questioned him. They kept asking him: "Are you a Canadian Indian?" And the poor man would reply: "Yes, yes."

I stood that as long as I could and then I interrupted and said: "No, he is not a Canadian Indian in any way whatsoever. He is a true North American Indian, even as I am. Our ancestors were here long before you people and your ancestors were. We should therefore not be restricted from moving about on this continent, which is our homeland."

Congressman S. Wallace Dempsey helped us to get Job's stay extended for one year. But our struggle had to go on to open up the border to our people in accordance with the Jay Treaty and the Treaty of Ghent. Also, it was our belief that the white man's border should never be used to separate our people. We once had complete freedom to go and come at will before the white man took the country away from us. But this continent was still our country, too. We could not bear to have our lives restricted as though we were aliens in our own land. This was why Job's fight and the fight for all my people had to continue until righteousness prevailed.

In 1926, the Algonquins made me their wampum keeper so that the Indian agent or the Royal Canadian Mounted Police would not seize the belts, as has been done on the Six Nations Reserve at Grand River. Also, the Algonquins wished me to use these belts in my continued work to open the border, to educate white people in Indian history. Frank Meness and his wife Teresa were the ones who brought these two belts across the border to me.

These wampum belts had an interesting history. The ancestors of these Algonquins came originally from Lake of Two Mountains, Oka. They left that place because the French priest there was bothering them, and went to the neighborhood of Maniwaki. But once there, they discovered that they had forgotten the wampum belts, so Frank Meness' great grandmother, Mrs. Amikonini,[3] went back after them by canoe.

About 1895, the Canadian Indian Act was extended to Maniwaki. Mrs. Meness' father, John Tenasco,[4] had been elected a chief and had served in that capacity for twelve years. His brother, Peter Tenasco, said that the Indians no longer needed the wampum belts because they were going to use the Indian Act. The wampum was then put away and nearly forgotten.

In the 1920s, a man named Philip Nattoway had the wampum belts in his possession. He lived with his son Alex at the Algonquin settlement of Barriere, about ninety miles north of Maniwaki. The younger generation had forgotten the meaning of the wampum, and Alex thought it had no great importance. Alex had a hunting cabin, and he used the wampum belts to stuff in the chinks of the cabin to keep the wind out.

When Frank Meness went up to visit Philip Nattoway one day, the old man told Frank that he better take the wampum belts down to Maniwaki where they would be cared for properly. Frank did so and finally brought them over to me for safekeeping in 1926.

Both of these belts are very old and have the hand-made shell wampum beads strung together on rawhide strips, in the traditional manner. The larger belt is about seven felt long, of purple beads with seven white diamonds across its length. The middle diamond is double. This is known as the Grand Council Wampum Belt, and the diamonds represent the tribes.[5] The other is known as the Hudson Bay Wampum Belt. The background is of purple beads, and there are the figures of three men in white beads holding hands in friendship. These three signify Indian, white man, and Hudson Bay Company. The belt tells how the Indians accepted the white man as a friend and allowed a trading post in their territory. Off to the side is a cross in white beads, signifying the white man's religion. It is standing apart from the figures to indicate that the Indians did not immediately accept this new religion because they did not know if it would do good to their people. They said they would just watch this religion for a while and see what it was like.

I was also given five strands of white wampum tied together. This was used in tribal meetings. The people touched the strings to signify that they agreed to a proposal under consideration.

A couple of years later, in appreciation for my work on behalf of Indians, I was given a small belt called the Peace Belt. This has a purple background with a white line running the whole length of the belt. At each end, there are four short white lines. The belt signifies that there is a peace, that Indians may go from one place to another, and that there is no border for Indians to cross. Ever since I received it, I have used this belt to inform people, both Indian and white, about Indian history. I have also used it in adoption ceremonies, pledging the adoptees to spread peace wherever they go.

I have now kept the wampum safely all these years. Several times people have tried to get the belts away from me. I would, for instance, receive a letter from some one at Maniwaki or Rapid Lake settlement north of Maniwaki telling me that the tribe had decided to call these belts back so that the young people could learn the traditions and that a delegation would visit me to receive the belts. Always Frank Meness would tell me: "No, don't give them up! Those fellows are the kind who would sell our wampum for drink!" There have even been attempts to steal the belts, but I guard them with my life. During these many years, I have often displayed these ancient and sacred wampum belts to instruct the people in their meaning, but always I have protected them carefully, as I have been charged.

In early 1926, I became acquainted with David Hill, a Mohawk from Six Nations Reserve who was living in Niagara Falls, New York. Huron Claus, the Indian evangelist, appealed to Dave for help on the border question, telling him that many of the Indians crossing the border were forced to lie as to their origins, saying they were from the Cattaraugus or Allegany Reservation or our Tuscarora Reservation so that they would be permitted entry into the United States. Claus thought this was a very bad situation.

Dave agreed and asked: "What can we do about it?"

Huron told him: "I was over at Chief Clinton Rickard's last week and I saw copies of the two treaties he has that say our people have the right to cross the border."

"I'd like to go over to see this Chief Rickard," Dave said.

Huron then made arrangements to take Dave out to my place at 1:00 P.M. that day. When they arrived, my wife directed them back to the sugar bush where I was boiling sap. This was early spring and I was hard at work tapping the trees and making syrup and sugar.

Dave received quite a shock when he first laid eyes on me. I was dressed in old, worn-out work clothes. I had on two sets of trousers, with the underneath pair poking through the holes in the top pair. I had not had my hair trimmed in quite a while, and there I stood, bushy-headed, with an old hat and tattered clothes, looking for all the world like a tramp.

Dave took one look at me and later told me that he had thought to himself: "What good can *he* possibly do us?"

When Huron hailed me and introduced Dave, I stepped forward, shook my visitor's hand, and greeted him heartily. Sometime after we had become good friends, Dave laughingly told me that at this point, when he felt my handshake and heard my large voice, he completely reversed his first opinion and told himself: "This is the man we're looking for!"

From that point on, Dave and I worked very closely together. He is a most upright, honest man, generous and kindly, and a devoted worker for justice. The Great Spirit has always been his guide.

One March day in 1926, Dave met a Mohawk friend, Leslie Martin, on the street in Niagara Falls. Leslie was the son of Sophie Martin, a most upright, honest lady who has always defended the rights of our people. Dave told Leslie about the border trouble and said they ought to have an organization, if only they had a place to meet and organize.

Leslie said: "You can have my house any time." He lived right in Niagara Falls, New York, and thought this would be a good central place.

They agreed on a meeting time. It was to be held the same time as Leslie's second wedding anniversary celebration. There would be a number of people there then. Leslie's wife refused to postpone the celebration, so they had both together.

Mrs. Henhawk, the mother of Leslie's wife, was on her way over the border to attend the celebration at her daughter's house. There were some other friends in the car with her. A white man was driving. When they got to the bridge at Niagara Falls, they were stopped by the immigration officials, who would not let them into the United States. They called Leslie and he got in touch with me. I dropped everything to go and speak on their behalf to the immigration officials. I was successful, and we all went on to Leslie's house. There we talked about the necessity of having an organization to work for our rights.

During the summer and fall, we worked on getting an organization together. On December 1, 1926, we finally formed the Six Nations Defense League. We later broadened our organization by changing the title to the Indian Defense League of America. We encouraged our friends in other areas to form branches of the league to unify themselves for our fight and to make our cause better known. Our first goal was to obtain our border-crossing rights. After victory, we would decide whether to continue. This was an all-Indian organization. We later began adopting some of our faithful white friends who had given us much assistance, and they were thereupon made honorary, but not voting, members of our league. We also made a place as honorary members for those persons who had less than 50 percent Indian blood.

I wrote up the following brief set of regulations for our organization:

(1) Quorum shall not be fewer than eight present, with the President or Vice-president.

(2) Any member who is not in good standing will not have a voice or a vote at any meeting.

(3) Anyone who is under the influence of liquor will not have a voice or vote at a meeting.

(4) Anyone who is in arrears of dues two months will lose all benefits and voice.

(5) This organization was formed by Chief Clinton Rickard, and its main object is to redeem our border crossing rights as they were before the border became restricted; it will continue until some relief is obtained. Thereafter the Defense League and the President and Vice-President will call a general meeting, and if two thirds of the members wish to continue, the organization can do so.

(6) Election of officers shall be called once a year. At that time all the members will be notified.

(7) Membership fees will be two dollars; dues will be one dollar per month until the border problem is over.

After our league was organized, I continued with my travels and speaking engagements to publicize our problem both to Indians and to whites. My Masonic brothers and my comrades in various veterans' organizations were most helpful in inviting me to speak before their groups and also in passing resolutions which were sent to Congress on our behalf. I knew when I first began this work that there were many good white people who favored our cause, but they were not active. It was my job, and that of other Indians, to tell these people the truth and to encourage them to become active on our behalf in fighting for justice.

Another tactic I used during the summertime to publicize our cause was to dress in my Indian costume and visit the tourist camps around Niagara Falls to speak to the many visitors who came to that city from all over the nation. I told these people of our problem and asked them to write to their congressmen when they returned home. In this way we were able to gain new friends and also put more pressure on the government to secure our rights.

We did have a number of friends in government who sympathized with our cause. Among those most active in our defense were Congressmen S. Wallace Dempsey and Clarence MacGregor of New York and Senators James W. Wadsworth, Jr., of New York and William King of Utah. Senator—later Vice-President—Charles Curtis also gave much encouragement. I am sure that Charles Curtis' sympathy for us came from the fact that he himself was part Indian.

The border problem was very complicated, for it involved not only the simple rights of crossing but also the head tax of $8.00 on immigrants. In late January 1927, I received a very distressing letter from Lizzie John in Middleport, Ontario, asking me to help her two daughters, Adeline and Vera, to get out of the Erie County jail. These two young ladies had been in this jail since January 7, 1927, for not paying this head tax and were awaiting deportation. Attorney Robert M. Codd, Jr., assisted us in this case. I asked him to get a writ of habeas corpus, and this he did. So the girls were out of jail in about two weeks' time. They could then be free while awaiting their court case.

Early in 1927, I took two trips to Washington to testify on Congressman Dempsey's border-crossing bill, H.R.16864, but we were not able to get it out of committee. Attorney Codd accompanied me in February.

On March 1, 1927, I had a conference with Second Assistant Secretary of Labor W. W. Husband. This man was a true friend to my people. He told me he would do what he could for our cause, and he meant it.

We began having trouble with Attorney Codd about this time. He submitted to us a bill for $731.00 for his work on deportation cases on behalf of seven people we were interested in helping. The Indian Defense League paid him $371.00 on account, but not one of these cases was ever called. I wrote to Secretary Husband for advice in this matter, and he asked me to talk with Mr. Flynn at the district immigration office in Buffalo. I complied with this advice and had a conference with Director Flynn, showing him Codd's bill. Mr. Flynn told me this bill was

not worth a cent and advised me to tell my people not to go to this attorney any more. He added: "You and I can settle all the difficulties."
We accordingly dismissed Codd.

This man Codd was not to be outdone, however. He began working
with a factional group in the Indian Defense League at Grand River,
convincing them that he was just the one to solve the border problem.
My Indian people sometimes find it hard to work together, and this fact
often leads to unwise decisions. Jealousy is one of the most serious
factors in causing Indians to defeat themselves.

To add to our difficulties, hostility to our cause developed among my
own Tuscarora people. Most unfortunate of all, the man who was the
most active against the free border crossing was our head chief, J. Warren Brayley. For many months, he had been writing here and there to
officials in Canada and the United States saying that the Tuscarora
Nation was opposed to the entry of Indians from Canada into the United
States. He wrote to Congressman S. Wallace Dempsey opposing a bill
that he had introduced on our behalf. Congressman Dempsey showed
me this letter on one of my trips to Washington and told me how dam-
aging it had been to our cause. The letter stated that these "Canadian
Indians" wanted to cross the border in order to take employment away
from United States Indians. "Not only that but they come over to our
reservation and squat on our lands and use our firewood, and Sundays
when our Tuscaroras go to church we see these Canadian Indians drunk
and disorderly." He said, furthermore, that the "Tuscarora Nation of
New York Indians are opposed to letting down the bars of the Immigration Act. We are favorable to more strict enforcement of said laws."
Congressman Dempsey told me that we would have to overcome the
effects of this letter.

Even though Brayley was president of our Chiefs' Council, he lived
in town and hardly ever came out to the reservation. He considered
that no Indian who was worth anything would live on the reservation.
No doubt he got these notions from his father, who was a white man.

I immediately called a council of our Tuscarora chiefs, for Brayley
had for some time been inactive and I was now vice-president of the
council. We met at the Council House on February 26, 1927, and had a
very heated debate. I could see Brayley's sentiments were held by others.
The border crossing and the recent case of Job Henry came under discussion. Chief Lucius Williams of the Snipe clan vigorously opposed me

on my defense of Job and said I was not telling the truth when I said he had lived here for thirty years. Lucius was thinking about Job's travels back and forth to Grand River during the past twenty years.

At this point, when tension was very high, Chief Philip T. Johnson spoke up. He was a very distinguished person, son of the late Chief Elias Johnson, and was of the same clan as my father. He had studied medicine at a Canadian university and was a physician in Erie, Pennsylvania, but came back to the reservation periodically so that he could hold his chieftainship. I had called him back particularly for this important council.

Chief Johnson explained to the council and especially to Chief Williams that the Jay Treaty rights belonged to all our people and not just to Indians from Canada. If we asked that this right be annulled, then we would be depriving ourselves and setting a dangerous precedent. He spoke very feelingly and very intelligently and showed himself a true Indian in every way. Even though he lived apart from the Indian community, his heart was still with us. Lucius Williams also became convinced by Chief Johnson's words.

This noble speech by Philip Johnson saved the day for us. The council thereupon passed the following resolution without a dissenting vote:

> Legally constituted council of the Tuscarora Indians was held at the Council House February 26, 1927.
>
> Whereas there is what is known as Dempsey Bill No. H.R. 16864 also a Wadsworth Bill S. 4304 both regarding Immigration Act of 1924, and whereas that there is a letter written by Warren Brayley purporting that this letter was the spirit of the Tuscarora Nation as against the passing of the above said bills,
>
> Resolved herewith the Tuscarora chiefs in council moved and seconded carried unanimously: That the said chiefs are sincerely and humbly requesting the great U.S. Congress to pass either of the said bills pending.
>
> Vice-President, Chief Clinton Rickard
>
> Secretary for the Council,
Chief Edgar H. Rickard

I went to Washington and placed this resolution before the Committee on Immigration and Naturalization. I also testified against a bill that had been introduced that would have allowed only Iroquois Indians to cross the border. When committee members expressed surprise at my attitude, I explained that this bill, if passed, would cause great confusion. It would prompt other Indians who wanted to cross the border to represent themselves falsely as Iroquois. The congressmen then asked me what the Jay Treaty said, and I told them that it referred to Indians in general but not specifically to any tribe or tribes. I added that I was working to restore the Jay Treaty as read. The congressmen saw my point and told me that they would take up the matter when Congress reconvened that fall.

Despite the resolution passed by our Chiefs' Council, sentiment against Indians coming over to our reservation from Canada was growing, and feeling was beginning to be high against me among my own Tuscarora people. I was accused of bringing "Canucks" over. Children pick up what their parents say and learn their thoughts and habits. So it was that some of the schoolchildren came to taunt my son William because of my work on securing our border-crossing rights. One day after school, four boys grabbed William and beat him unmercifully in order to get even with me. Then they threw him to the ground and jumped up and down on his chest.

When William did not come home from school for hours, I went out looking for him and finally found him at 10:00 o'clock at night, half dead, lying in a ditch. I took him to the doctor and learned that his chest had been crushed.

William only partially recovered from that beating. Although his chest healed, it was constricted, and every winter regularly we could expect him to have pneumonia. He eventually developed emphysema and bronchiectasis and was unable to finish school or ever enjoy completely good health when he became a man. He used to remark in his later years that those four boys, then grown, never amounted to anything in their lives. This statement was true. All four of them turned out to be ne'er-do-wells. My son's health, and eventually his life, was the price my family had to pay to secure justice for our people.

I received further discouragement from a man who was one of the best-known members of our tribe. This was the Smithsonian ethnologist John Hewitt—or J. N. B. Hewitt, as he was known professionally. He came to my house in his car one day especially to talk me out of my work in securing our treaty rights.

He said: "Chief, when the government takes anything away from you, you'll never get it back."

I was very annoyed at this and told him: "We are going to continue on and on and eventually obtain justice for our people."

I was not going to be turned aside by anyone, no matter how educated he was. But it is interesting to note that John Hewitt's elder brother, Alvis Hewitt, was a member and faithful supporter of our Indian Defense League.

The reason I was so certain of the rightness of my work was because I had always appealed to the Great Spirit to bestow upon me the knowledge and wisdom to defend the rights of my people. I did not let a night go by without seeking this guidance before I lay down to sleep. I do feel that the Great Spirit answered my prayers.

On August 7, 1927, there was to be a dedication of the new Peace Bridge which linked Buffalo, New York, with Fort Erie, Ontario. This ceremony was to be attended by many outstanding dignitaries, including Prime Minister Stanley Baldwin of Great Britain and the Prince of Wales and the Duke of York.

Attorney Robert Codd sent for a delegation of Indians from Quebec to come to this celebration, promising them $5.00 each and expenses. A delegation of eight Algonquins from Barriere and Maniwaki therefore made this long trip. Some of them had to travel a great distance by foot and canoe until they reached good roads. They were bringing with them $300 to help us with our work on the border question, and $200 for their own expenses. They hid this money by carefully sewing a patch on a pair of trousers and hiding the money under the patch. When they came to the place where they were to leave their canoe, they got out and left some of their clothing behind. When they got to Maniwaki, they discovered that the clothing with the money in it was missing. Some of them went back to find the clothing and the money but discovered that it was gone. They then borrowed money to continue their trip.

At the border, they were absolutely refused entry. I received a message to come and help them. I dropped everything and went to the border, where I met a stone wall of refusal from the officials. After an argument of about half an hour, I did finally succeed in securing their entry.

Once these people who had come so far at Codd's urging were over here, Codd never came near them and never kept his promise to have them included in the Peace Bridge celebration.

Our Defense League did have its own Peace Bridge celebration on August 6, 1927. This was a big affair, held at The Front, the large park near the Peace Bridge in Buffalo, and featured Indian dances and a speech by City Judge Patrick J. Keeler. It was our tribute to the dedication of the Peace Bridge. Our Six Nations Confederacy was the first League of Nations and was known as the Great Peace. This was why we wanted to perpetuate the symbol of peace in our own day.

I kept the eight Algonquin visitors at my house until they could get money from their reserve to go home. Their friends sold horses to raise the money for them. My brother Chester took the last two chiefs home in his car.

All during the 1920s, the world was looking for ways to bring about international understanding so there would be no more wars. It was on November 30, 1927, that I therefore wrote these words: "I believe that justice should prevail regardless of creed or color. While the people are seeking for everlasting peace in the world, let us help to solve the great problem by giving to all races their rights and by honorably preserving the agreements made by all nations."

In 1927, a famous case on the border fight was tried in Philadelphia. A Caughnawaga Mohawk ironworker named Paul K. Diabo had been arrested in Philadelphia in 1925 for illegal entry into the United States and ordered deported on the grounds that he might become a public charge. This despite the fact that he was earning $70 a week working on the Delaware River Bridge! Diabo had traveled continually across the border from 1912 to 1925 while pursuing his profession but was finally caught up in the tangle of the Immigration Act of 1924. Diabo retained a Philadelphia law firm to defend him and determined to fight this case to the finish.

On February 20, 1926, I began corresponding with James H. Ross, a Caughnawaga Mohawk friend of Diabo's living in Philadelphia, and told him about my work on the border problem. In a later letter in March, I offered to send him or the lawyer copies of all the documents I had gathered which pertained to Indian rights in crossing the border. I learned that the law firm of William N. Nitzberg in Philadelphia was handling Diabo's case. Ross let me know that the members of this law firm and Diabo were going to Washington, D.C., in April to plead the case before the Labor Board of Review. I went to Grand River to try to raise a delegation there to go to Washington in support of the appeal, but just as I returned home, I took sick for a month and was not able to follow through. Ross wrote and told me that the Labor Board had rendered a decision against Indians, claiming that the Jay Treaty was no longer in effect. The lawyers were now going to take the case to court. Ross also told me that he had already contributed $300 of his own money for this fight and was going to try to raise more from friends at Caughnawaga.

Early in 1927, William N. Nitzberg argued the case before Judge Oliver B. Dickinson in the District Court of the United States for the Eastern District of Pennsylvania. I wrote to the judge before he rendered his decision and sent him copies of treaties and other documents relating to Indian border-crossing rights.

On March 19, 1927, Judge Dickinson rendered his decision in favor of our people as follows:

> The boundary line to establish the respective territory of the United States and of Great Britain was clearly not intended to, and just as clearly did not, affect the Indians. It made no division of their country. The Jay Treaty of 1794 recognized this fact in the provision that the Indians residing on either side of the line, which was between the United States and Great Britain and established as a boundary line, should be unaffected in their right to pass the line at will. It has been argued to us pro and con that this treaty was abrogated by the War of 1812. We do not see that the rights of the Indians are in any way affected by the treaty, whether now existing or not. The reference to them was merely the recognition of their right, which was wholly unaffected by the treaty, except that the contracting parties agreed with each other that each would recognize it. The right of the Indian remained, whether the agreement continued or was ended. The question of the right of a relator to enter the territory of the United States does not turn upon any treaty with Great Britain, although, of course, if we have an agreement to permit him to enter, we will make good our promise, unless it has been duly revoked.
>
> The turning point of the question of whether the Indians are included among the members of alien nations whose admission to our country is controlled and regulated by the existing immigration

laws. The answer, it seems to us, is a negative one. From the Indian view-point, he crossed no boundary line. For him this does not exist. This fact the United States has always recognized, and there is nothing in this legislation to work a change in our attitude.[6]

I quote this historic decision at length because it represented an important turning point in our fight. For the first time, our viewpoint was reinforced by a high United States judge. This decision could therefore not be ignored.

The United States government took this case, *McCandless, Commissioner of Immigration,* v. *United States ex rel. Diabo,* on appeal to the United States Court of Appeals, Third Circuit. Attorney Adrian Bonnelly represented Diabo at this hearing before Circuit Judges Buffington, Woolley, and Davis. On March 9, 1928, the Third Circuit Court upheld Judge Dickinson's decision, and the Solicitor General of the United States decided not to carry the appeal further.[7]

Meanwhile, in the fall of 1927 there were eleven bills introduced in Congress favoring our right to cross the border. I looked them over and picked out the bill written by Senator William King of Utah. It was known as S. 716. Congressman Clarence MacGregor's bill, which was similar, was H.R. 11351. King's bill read as follows:

> That the Immigration Act of 1924 shall not be construed to apply to the right of American Indians born in Canada to pass the borders of the United States: Provided, that this right shall not extend to persons whose membership in Indian tribes or families is created by adoption.

I knew that we had a lot of support behind us and were close to winning our case. For that reason, I wanted to spread the news around among our people to keep them from hiring lawyers uselessly when the issue was near to being settled. I was especially anxious that our brethren at Six Nations Reserve should not lose their money, for a small group of them had hired Attorney R. M. Codd, Jr., to work for the border crossing. Codd had been supporting a bill which would permit only Six Nations Indians across the border, and this I considered most unjust. Other than that, he was getting nowhere on this issue.

On January 21, 1928, I was invited to a meeting at the Six Nations Reserve at Grand River. The Indian Defense League delegated four of us, including David Hill and myself, to attend. We drove the ninety miles in an open car in zero weather, with gale winds at sixty-five miles an hour. When we arrived at the reservation, we had to walk the last four miles because the roads were not cleared of snow and my automobile could not get through. We had started our trip at 4:00 P.M. and arrived at 8:00 P.M.

The meeting was held in 69 Corners Hall, which was packed with people. The hall was like a basket with the wind blowing through. All sat there with hats and coats on trying to keep warm. Attorney Codd had visited the reserve sometime previously and had asked a large sum of money for getting the border crossing rights restored. Some of the ladies were there cooking cabbage and turnips and tea and charging a small sum for this lunch in order to raise money to pay the lawyer.

I had letters with me from Washington, from senators and congressmen and others, and from various people across the country. These letters showed that the border fight was well on the way to being won and that bills were already introduced in Congress to give us our rights. We therefore did not need any lawyers to take our money. I had come to warn my people of this fact.

Chauncey Garlow, who was in thick with Codd by this time, spoke to the people in Mohawk, which he knew I did not understand, but which Dave Hill translated for me, and warned the people that I was leading them to the great pit. I think he would have been more of a gentleman if he had spoken in English.

Chauncey Garlow was my second cousin—the grandson of my grandfather Garlow's brother. But even if it is a member of my own family who does wrong, I will oppose him.

I spoke to the people for an hour warning them about the attorneys and told them that all the hard work was nearly completed. The Defense League had watched all movements and had thrown its voice continually for justice. They would soon see the results of our efforts without payment to any idle lawyers.

It was plain to me at the time that the greatest trouble with us Indians was in looking too much to some of the white people and in being afraid of them. We were afraid of offending them. For that reason, we could often be very easily led by outsiders. I could see that Indians were often hesitant to trust themselves to learn the true facts. This is what we in our organization, the Indian Defense League, have tried to overcome. We have provided a way for Indians to work together and to speak out on their own.

During the early months of 1928, Senator King's bill was progressing very well in Congress. It passed the Senate on March 21 and went to the House. There, Congressman Clarence MacGregor substituted this bill for his, and it passed on March 29. President Coolidge then signed the bill into law on April 2, 1928.[8]

My wife heard this news over our radio and relayed it to me. I was so elated that I took the whole day off. After three long years of struggle, we had finally won!

Elizabeth and I had written letters steadily for five months before the passage of this bill. Altogether in all the time of our working on the border question we had sent out five hundred letters. We now saw this great burden transformed into victory and hoped that we could at last relax and attend more fully to our own affairs once again.

Many letters of appreciation came to me after the border fight was won. One of those letters that I cherished the most was from W. W. Husband, Second Assistant Secretary of Labor, who had given support to our cause all along. It is dated April 26, 1928, and says:

> My dear Chief Rickard:
> Mr. Horner acknowledged receipt of your letter and the picture which you so kindly sent me, but I want to tell you personally that I appreciate your kindness in remembering me in this way. It is certainly an excellent picture of you, and you may be sure that we were all interested in seeing you in the splendid regalia which you had with you on one of your trips to Washington.
> As I have said in another letter, you certainly are to be congratulated on the successful outcome of your work in behalf of your people in connection with the modification of the Immigration Law.

I made a trip to Grand River after our bill had passed to warn my people not to pay Codd for supposedly getting this bill through Congress. There was a council on this matter at the Sour Springs Longhouse, and the building was packed. Chief Chauncey Garlow, who was part of the faction that had hired Codd, did his best to keep me from speaking, but he could not cut me off, because the people wanted to hear me.

When I took off my coat and stepped to the middle of the floor, they applauded for about five minutes before I was able to speak. Then I told them the whole history of our struggle. They were more than surprised to hear of all the work that had been done in achieving our victory. This was a great moment for all of us.

During our border fight, we had difficulties with various lawyers who had represented us briefly on different occasions. When I first began working on the border case, I consulted Attorney George P. Decker of Rochester. He told me to forget about writing letters because it would only waste postage. He would take the case himself, he said, but it would cost between $800 and $1,000. I did not see what he could do for us for that amount that we could not do for ourselves, so I dismissed him. He later charged $300 for writing one letter to Washington. R. M. Codd, Jr., was hired by a faction at Grand River, headed by Chauncey Garlow, after I had warned them not to hire him. He submitted a bill to them for $500 for the victory that we had won in Congress, though he had done nothing toward securing passage of this legislation. Dave Hill later heard that Codd rendered a bill of $2,600 to the people at Grand River. Codd also had another money-making project to present. He was going to sell identification cards to Indians for a dollar apiece. These cards were to have the person's photograph attached. In other words, this was to be a sort of passport to get Indians across the border. I went to the district director of immigration in Buffalo and asked about this proposal. He told me it was entirely unnecessary and that Indians should save their money. Passports were only for foreigners.

After our bill had passed Congress and had been signed by the President, I told Dave Hill: "This calls for a celebration!" I wanted to preserve this moment in history and have a thanksgiving observance after our many years of effort. Dave agreed and we began to work on the program.

The planning took three months. There was, first of all, to be a parade which would come across the bridge from Niagara Falls, Ontario, to Niagara Falls, New York, and end in the athletic field, where we were to have our program. I wrote many letters to get the entertainment and also to invite our many white friends who had helped us. We wanted to stress Indian culture particularly and also the Indian as he was two hundred years ago. Two chiefs from Maniwaki, Quebec, came in mid-June to help me. I also had the cooperation of the chamber of commerce and the mayors of the two cities.

The celebration was held on July 14, 1928, and was a great success. People said that Niagara Falls had never seen anything like it before. Indians came from all over to participate. Sixteen persons traveled the eight hundred miles from Maniwaki, bringing many attractions such as sleigh dogs, a birch-bark canoe, moose and wolf hides, and several very old and fine wampum belts which had remained hidden with these Indians for over a hundred years. We had a band, Indian dancers, and a lacrosse game at the park grounds. I had also invited representatives of the American Legion and other veterans' groups that had been so helpful in sending petitions to Washington on our behalf. There were both Indian and white speakers at the festivities. The entire program was very satisfactory to everybody concerned and accomplished just what we wanted it to do. It celebrated our victory and publicized our culture to white people.

Many people at the time thought that this celebration would mark the end of our struggle. We had won. Why continue our organization or our publicity? It was true that I was relieved to be out from under the burden of this long campaign to win the border-crossing right but I felt that we could not rest on our victories. My work over the past three years had shown me too much about the needs of my people. Some other faithful members of our Defense League could see the importance of keeping our organization going. Since we were sure that we would have much to do in the future, we determined to continue the Defense League.

6

Tragedy and Turmoil

THE PENDULUM OF LIFE always seemed to swing back and forth between victory and defeat for me. My life was full of extremes. The disappointments of my early days led to my enlistment in the army. There the Great Spirit protected me through all the terrors of the battlefield and preserved me when malaria struck me down. The high point of my life, my marriage to Ivy, was soon followed by her death and the death of my little boy. Not long after, the sun scattered the dark clouds when I was admitted into the Masonic Order, and later when I married again. Our family grew, the farm prospered, I was made a chief. Save for the continual remembrance of Ivy, my happiness had been restored. Then tragedy struck repeatedly and, without the help of the Great Spirit, would have overwhelmed us. In succession, our third son died, my people were deprived of their border-crossing rights, Deskaheh died in our house, many of my own tribesmen began to hate me and dispute my leadership because of my fight for justice, and my son William was cruelly beaten. Our great border-crossing victory only intensified the hostility against me from my Tuscarora people because so many of them resented other Indians coming into our country. No matter how much my people might turn against me, I would never turn against them. I would continue to fight for justice for them and for all others. There was always much discouragement, but my wife Elizabeth stood loyally by my side, and my good white and Indian friends constantly strengthened me.

So it would go. Happiness and despair, victory and defeat, good fortune and tragedy would follow me in succession all the days of my life.

Elizabeth was expecting another child not long after our border-crossing victory but had a premonition that this birth would mean her death. She would occasionally awaken me at night expressing this fear. I remember one time in her sleep she threw her arms around me and cried out that she was going to die. I shook and shook her, but could not awaken her. My wife's unsettled condition disturbed me greatly.

On April 18, 1929, Elizabeth gave birth to a boy at our home. Two hours after delivery, she suffered a stroke and went into a coma. The doctor was not able to revive her. She died of an embolism the next day, April 19, aged thirty-two. Once again I was plunged into the lowest depths of despair.

I was lost in the darkest clouds with the passing of my dear wife. She had shared with me in everything over the years, and had taken up the burden of the border struggle with me. She had faithfully looked after all my correspondence of many hundreds of letters and had foretold two years before our victory that we would win our rights. My one consolation was to realize that even one hundred years is short, and we, too, can be called at any hour. This sudden loss taught me the shortness and frailty of human life. It seemed this world was just a testing place to prepare us for that life everlasting where there is no parting or heartache. We do not know why these things happen and will not understand until we reach that stage in the beyond.

Before her death, Elizabeth had expressed a desire that her sister Nellie Gansworth should raise our child, for she knew that our home would be without a mother. I complied with her request and gave the baby into the keeping of Nellie and Willard.

We had not chosen a name for the child, and I therefore turned to a very dear friend of ours in Chicago to do the honors. William F. E. Gurley, professor of paleontology at the University of Chicago, was a fellow Mason and had been very close to us over the past three years. He had given us continued encouragement and occasional financial help. His thoughtfulness in our periods of distress, when I had to neglect my farm in order to carry on my work for our people, proved him a true friend. I therefore wanted him to have the privilege of naming our boy. He chose the two names, Eli Zabeth, from my wife's name. When Eli grew a little older, his school chums used to call him "E" for short.

Despite the very great sorrow of the loss of my wife, I knew that my work for my family and my people must go on. The question arose whether there should be another border-crossing celebration again in 1929, as we had had the previous year. I therefore went to see my good friend Dave Hill, who had always given our organization splendid support. When my family was in financial need because of my Indian rights work, he came to our assistance many times. I knew I could depend upon Dave in every way.

I said to him: "Are we going to have a celebration this year? You know I have a farm. I have given a lot of time to the Defense League, but I have to take care of my farm, too. Others should help us. When the farmer plants seed, he has to work the ground to keep the weeds out. That's what we should all do—work the ground so our organization will be strong."

Dave told me: "There's a lacrosse practice in Buffalo every Friday night. A lot of Indians go there. I'll go and see what I can do."

He then went to Buffalo to Front Park where the practice was held. One Indian spotted Dave and called out: "There's Dave Hill. He wants me to work on the celebration again. I can't do it."

Since Dave is a wise man, he saw that an opening had not yet presented itself, and he waited. He kept his feelings to himself until the practice was over and people were leaving. Suddenly a shower came up and many of the players and spectators ran to the bandshell for protection. Dave worked his way to the center of this crowd and then spoke up.

"Fellows, I have something to say. If you want to hear it, all right. If not, we'll forget about it."

"Sure, let's hear what you have on your mind," some of them said.

Then Dave began to tell them how the government had taken away their border-crossing rights and how I had worked to restore them. He told how I had sacrificed and neglected my farm for nearly three years to work on this problem. He repeated my words to them.

"When you have a farm and plant seed, you have to work over the ground to keep the weeds out. We all have to help to make these rights work. The educated Indians haven't backed us up," he continued, thinking of how John Hewitt had tried to discourage me, "and we have to depend on ourselves. Should we forget about this celebration?"

"No, let's continue it," they said.

"What do you want us to do, Dave?" asked several of the men.

Dave told them he wanted them to support our celebration by coming out and being part of it. And when a collection was taken up at the park grounds on celebration day, he asked them to give what they could; otherwise, we could not continue with our work.

"If we don't make our expenses, we'll need extra help," he reminded them.

There were many promises of support from the men, some pledging three or five dollars or various other amounts.

"All right," said Dave. "I'll hold you to it. If we don't make expenses, then I'll come around to see you. I'll put down your names and the amounts you said you'll give. Does anybody have paper and pencil?"

Some one gave him paper and pencil and he took down the names and the amounts. Thereby he got these men interested in our Defense League.

This was the answer we had been looking for. I do truly believe that the Great Spirit had sent that rain.

We had the celebration as usual that July and experienced the same success with it as we had the previous year. This celebration has now become permanent and has been held every year since 1928. Through this means we not only commemorate our great victory but also educate our own and the white people as to our history, customs, and rights. Every year we attract new recruits to our cause. In this way, our work goes on.

For many years during the 1920s, a number of us had been working on what we called the Cayuga claim. This effort was an attempt to get payment for the Cayugas of Grand River for their old lands around Cayuga Lake, which they had lost many years ago through the treaties of 1788, 1790, and 1795. A lump sum was to be paid at the time these treaties were negotiated, and New York State was to pay a perpetual annuity of $2,300. This perpetual annuity had been paid to the Cayugas who remained south of the Canadian–United States border but not, after 1811, to those who lived on the Six Nations Reserve at Grand River. What the Cayugas wanted was either the right to their land or a settlement of the claim and their annuities from 1811, with interest.

A consideration of this claim was agreed to by the American-British Arbitration Tribunal in 1925.[1] The members of the tribunal were Sir Charles Fitzgerald, former chief justice of Canada, serving for Great Britain; Dean Roscoe Pound of Harvard Law School for the United States; and Alfred Nerinez of Belgium as the neutral member and president. Great Britain was insisting that the United States owed the Cayugas one million dollars, and the United States, of course, was contending that this claim was so old that it never should have come up. Fred K.

Nielsen, agent for the United States, said that the Treaty of 1853 had arranged for the United States and Canada to bar all claims prior to that date.

For a number of years thereafter, we did not hear anything of a settlement being made. As a result, my brothers from the Cayuga Nation at Grand River appealed to me to help them, for we had heard that the responsibility for settlement lay with New York State. I accordingly wrote to the attorney general of the State of New York, who was an old army acquaintance of mine, and asked for an interview with Governor Franklin D. Roosevelt. The attorney general and the governor both honored my request and arranged a meeting for a date in November 1929.

A delegation of four went to Albany to call on the governor. There were three from Grand River to represent the Cayugas: George Nash, Chauncy Isaac, and Robert Davey. I was spokesman for the group.

I had with me a photostatic copy of the Treaty of Cayuga Ferry of July 27, 1795. This treaty specifically stated that New York State would protect and preserve this land for the Cayugas and their posterity and would prevent outsiders from residing on that land. We wanted the state to live up to its agreement.

Both the attorney general and Eleanor Roosevelt greeted us when we arrived for our meeting with the governor. The attorney general told us not to be disappointed if the governor did not stand up when we entered his office, for he had suffered an attack of infantile paralysis many years ago and had been left a cripple.

After we had greeted the governor, we proceeded to bring up the question of the Cayuga claim and asked for a settlement based on the treaty and the land once owned by the Cayugas. The governor said to us: "I will immediately investigate that part."

Sometime later we learned that Attorney General Hamilton Ward announced that the state of New York had awarded the Cayugas a settlement of $100,000. Governor Roosevelt also wrote me a letter saying that the Indians had requested the Canadian government to seek this money from the United States government; therefore, the state would be compelled to turn the sum over to the government of Canada for payment to the Cayugas. These Cayuga Indians of Grand River now receive a small annuity on this claim to this day.

In 1930 a serious threat faced our Six Nations people in the form of the Snell Bill in Congress, which would give control of our Six Nations to New York State. We Indians have always feared being under the thumb of the state rather than continuing our relationship with the federal government because it is a well-known fact that those white people who live closest to Indians are always the most prejudiced against them and the most desirous of obtaining their lands. We have always had a better chance of obtaining justice from Washington than from the state or local government. Also, in turning us over to the state, the federal government would be downgrading our significance as a people and ignoring the fact that our treaties are with the United States. For these reasons, we strongly opposed this bill which had been introduced by Congressman Snell from Potsdam, but actually written by Henry S. Manley, the assistant attorney general of New York State. Manley had lobbied for this bill in Congress, telling in glowing terms how much New York State had done for the Indians in the past.

In order to organize ourselves for more effective opposition to the Snell Bill, many of us Tuscaroras felt that there should be a change of administration on our reservation. We always have our general election for officers in the Chiefs' Council on the second Tuesday in April. We had our council meeting at this time for our 1930 election, and I as vice-president tried to get Chief William J. Johnson to take the chair as president. He was a fine upstanding person and would have made a good leading chief. At the last moment, he declined. The result was that I was elected president. Those voting for me were Chiefs P. T. Johnson, William J. Johnson, George Rickard, and Pine Tree Chief Andrew Garlow. Those favoring William Chew as President were Lucius Williams, Jonathan Printup, and my brother Edgar Rickard. I did not seek this office, but I humbly accepted it. The other officers elected at this time were my father, Chief George Rickard, as vice-president, Harry Patterson as secretary, and Chief William Johnson as treasurer.

This election caused a split in the council. I had served as vice-president for six years and upon several occasions had filled the president's chair when he was absent from council. My work had always been for the betterment of my nation and also for all North American Indians. Unfortunately, some of my people had a grievance against me because of my work on behalf of all Indians, no matter where they came from.

Many people in our tribe were particularly opposed to what they called "Canadian Indians," and therefore they would let our government and community be torn apart by a needless feud, since they blamed me for befriending these Indians.

There were those who let themselves be carried away by jealousy and resentment. My brother Edgar was bitter at having lost the election as secretary, for he had held that office ever since 1912. William Chew, who was an unobjectionable man personally, allowed himself to become a tool of the insurgents. He was illiterate, and whereas that might not have been of great importance in years past, it was a serious drawback in the modern day when the president of the council had to conduct much business with the white man's government and be able to read the newspapers, treaties, legislation and to correspond widely. A man who could not read and write was at a disadvantage in this office. One of the warriors who was the most hostile to me was Robert Anderson. He had been furious with me for a long time because of my work to open the border for our people. What he called "Canadian Indians" were obnoxious to him, as they were, unfortunately, to a number of my Tuscarora people. Anderson therefore made it his project to block my work on the council.[2]

These three were the leaders of the insurgent faction. The chiefs who opposed me held their own meeting and elected Chief William Chew as president and Edgar as secretary. Then they came to our council meetings and created a great disturbance, to the extent that we could not proceed with business. Edgar and Robert Anderson were particularly loud in shouting me down and in not permitting me to give a report on my trip to Washington to testify against the Snell Bill. Jealousy and rivalries were once again getting in the way of the welfare of our tribe. I was forced to call in the United States marshal so that we could carry on our meetings.

The situation was further complicated by the fact that, since my mother's death in 1925, there was no one in our Beaver clan who was as yet eligible to be clan mother. The only qualified person was too young. A woman who had absolutely no qualifications whatsoever for this office put herself forward and was recognized by the insurgents. She was a member of the adopted Shawnee Beaver clan and therefore ineligible, since this office should be held by a Tuscarora Beaver woman.[3] It is also our longstanding tradition that no immoral woman should ever be a clan mother, and this woman lived a scandalous life. This is the way our customs are destroyed.

In all this controversy, my father gave me his complete support. Edgar had written a letter to the *Niagara Falls Gazette* which was published on April 24, 1930, condemning me and my work, the Jay Treaty, and the wearing of feathers. My father wrote a strong letter backing me and this was published on April 26, 1930. He said in part: "Edgar Rickard has been a trouble maker in the Council and also in the churches. I, George D. Rickard, father of four sons, declare that Edgar Rickard has always been the worst trouble maker in the family. This is nothing new. Cain slew Abel through jealousy, and Joseph was sold by his brothers through jealousy. This should not occur among our people."

Edgar had always been unpredictable. Some years before this controversy, I had come home from church one Sunday and was still in my Sunday clothes putting the horse away in the barn. Edgar was down the hill below my house with a gun and shot up at me. I went down and took the gun away from him.

The year 1930 was one of great turmoil in our Tuscarora Nation. We scheduled our National Picnic as usual, but the insurgents met and set the date for their picnic one week before ours. Their picnic went off without incident. These insurgents then did all they could to destroy our regular National Picnic the next week, such as tearing down our signs and disrupting our ceremonies.

Many things were said against me personally by the Chew faction. Willy Chew himself claimed that I could not be a chief because I was a member of a white man's organization, meaning the Masons. This was not logical, because Chief Philip T. Johnson, whom no one disputed, was also a Mason, and so was Warren Brayley, who by now had become active again and had joined the Chew faction. Also it was said that my name, Rowadagahrade, or Loud Voice, was not a legitimate chiefly name, though it was the name Chief Marcus Peters had borne, and no one questioned his chieftainship. Many years later, my son William found confirmation of my name among Indians in Virginia who told him that Loud Voice was the name of the chief who had led his Tuscarora people northward through their area after the wars with the white settlers in North Carolina.

Also, a number of the Tonawanda and Onondaga chiefs, especially Jesse Lyons of Onondaga, began to take up the cry against me, saying

I was working too much for "Canadian Indians" and was also not fit to be a chief because I was a Christian and a Mason. This was not honest on the part of the Seneca chiefs because they had at least one chief who was both a church member and a Mason, Nicodemus Billy by name. One of their most famous chiefs, Ely S. Parker, had also been a Mason. Years later, some of the newer Seneca chiefs admitted to my son William that the old feeling against me had been all jealousy.

The next year, 1931, we had an even worse crisis on our reservation. I, as president of the council, called our regularly scheduled meeting for April 14 at 2:00 P.M. The insurgents met one hour ahead of time at 1:00 P.M. and proceeded to hold an election, even though only five were present, which was two short of the required quorum. They elected Willy Chew as president, Thomas Isaac as vice-president, and Edgar, my brother, as secretary. J. Warren Brayley was elected trustee of Mt. Hope School and Lucius Williams as janitor and wood inspector. Then they adjourned and refused to attend the regular meeting at 2:00 P.M.

The situation in our council became intolerable. Our whole reservation was split. Neighbor was against neighbor. Jealousy has always been the downfall of our people. For several years, we had two sets of Chiefs' Councils and two National Picnics. It was indeed a sad situation for all our people, when resentment and hatred ruled our nation. As my father said, these things should not be.

At the same time that we were in the midst of this tragic chaos on our reservation, the famous Marchand murder trial, involving two Indian women, was in process in Buffalo. Lila Jimerson and Nancy Bowen were both from the Cattaraugus Seneca Reservation and were charged with the murder of Clothilde Marchand, wife of the artist Henri Marchand. The murder took place on March 6, 1930, and the investigation and trial lasted well over a year. It was quite a sensation in our parts. The newspapers were full of accounts of the trial for months.

One Sunday, my father read in the newspaper that the United States government had refused an appeal from the Cattaraugus Indian leaders to provide legal assistance for Lila Jimerson, who was to go on trial the next day. Nancy Bowen was to be the star witness against her. The Senecas claimed that Indians were the wards of the United States government and therefore entitled to the government's protection. The response was that the Senecas at Cattaraugus had signed their treaties with the state of New York and therefore were not in the same category

Sophie Martin, Mohawk of the Six Nations Reserve on the Grand River, and one of the original founders of the Indian Defense League of America. She is wearing the traditional Iroquois women's dress, made of figured cloth rather than the more usual plain cloth. The picture was taken in 1971 when she was ninety.

David Hill at the time he first became acquainted with Clinton Rickard. *Courtesy of Clinton Rickard family*

Frank Meness, Algonquin of Maniwaki Indian Reserve. It was he who entrusted the Algonquin wampum belts to Chief Clinton Rickard. He is wearing a headdress of owl feathers made by his wife, Teresa Meness. *Courtesy of Teresa Meness, Maniwaki Indian Reserve*

The Algonquins display their wampum belts. Left to right, Nonan Papate of Barriere, Frank Wabey of Baskatong, Moses Odjick of Maniwaki, Frank Meness of Maniwaki, and Louis Machewan of Barriere. Only the long grand council belt, the short peace belt on the far left, and the Hudson Bay belt in the center were given to Chief Rickard for safekeeping. The long belt hanging on the string of corn at far right always remained with the Algonquins. The picture was taken at the Rickard farm after one of the early Border Crossing Celebrations, either 1929 or 1930. *Courtesy of Clinton Rickard family*

John N. B. Hewitt (1859–1937), Tuscarora tribal member and noted Smithsonian ethnologist, who attempted to discourage Clinton Rickard in his Indian rights work. Photo 1923. *Courtesy of Smithsonian Institution, National Anthropological Archives, Bureau of American Ethnology Collection, Washington, D.C.*

Civil War veteran Alvis Hewitt, elder brother of Smithsonian ethnologist J. N. B. Hewitt, and his son and World War I veteran Silas Hewitt. Alvis Hewitt gave early encouragement to the Indian Defense League of America. *Photograph by Hare, Buffalo, New York. Courtesy of Clinton Rickard family*

Clinton Rickard and Second
Assistant Secretary of
Labor W. W. Husband
holding the peace belt.
The picture was taken at
Rickard's farm right after
the 1933 Border Crossing
Celebration. Husband had
given great encouragement
to Rickard in his
Indian rights work.
*Courtesy of
Clinton Rickard family*

William and Clark Rickard holding the Hudson Bay wampum belt at an early
Border Crossing Celebration, either 1929 or 1930. *Courtesy of Clinton Rickard
family*

A few of the dignitaries at one Border Crossing Celebration pose for the photographer. Left to right, Chief Alexander J. General (who inherited the title of Deskaheh from his brother, Levi General), Mayor Ernest M. Hawkins of Niagara Falls, Ontario, Chief Clinton Rickard, honorary member Joseph Fornero, and David Hill. *Photograph by Ron Roels*. Niagara Falls Evening Review, *Niagara Falls, Ontario*

Presenting the Cayuga Claim to Governor Franklin D. Roosevelt in Albany, New York, in 1929. Left to right are Clinton Rickard, George Nash, Robert Davey, and Chauncey Isaac. Rickard and Isaac wear Plains headdresses, and Davey wears a traditional Iroquois headdress. Both Davey and Isaac are wearing Plains-style trousers. *Courtesy of Clinton Rickard family*

Mayor E. Dent Lackey of Niagara Falls, New York, Mayor Robert F. Keighan of Niagara Falls, Ontario, and Chief Clinton Rickard join hands in a gesture representing the unity of the American, Canadian, and Indian peoples at the 1965 Border Crossing Celebration. *Photograph by Ron Roels.* Niagara Falls Evening Review, *Niagara Falls, Ontario*

Lila Jimerson during the sensational Marchand murder trial of 1930. The relationship between the noted sculptor Henri Marchand and his attractive Indian model brought on the murder of Marchand's unsuspecting wife. Because of Henri Marchand's international renown as an artist, the trial received worldwide publicity. Enterprising American reporters had a heyday with the case, and two of them even invented a fraudulent "Lila Jimerson's Diary," which was nationally syndicated. This "diary" contained such typical White stereotypes of the Indian as: "Me take canoe, me paddle up river, me see great man." *Courtesy of* Buffalo Evening News

Nancy Bowen, the accused murderess of Mrs. Marchand, in custody at the time of the Marchand murder trial of 1930. She confessed to the murder and testified that Lila Jimerson had persuaded her that Mrs. Marchand was a witch who had brought about the death of her husband, "Sassafras Charlie" Bowen. Mrs. Bowen's clothing, long out of fashion by 1930, bears eloquent testimony to her basically humble life style, conservative nature, and lack of touch with modern ways and thinking.
Courtesy of
Buffalo Evening News

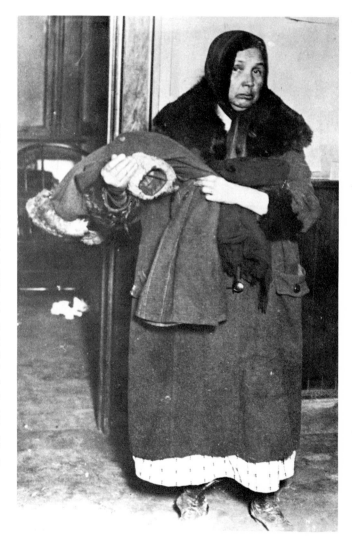

Tuscarora visitors pose with Algonquins at Maniwaki during the Second Grand Council of the Algonquin Indians in September of 1931. Chief Rickard stands in the center. To the right of him in light jacket, holding camera, is his bride, Beulah Rickard. Directly to the right of her are Teresa and Frank Meness (holding hat). The group is standing in front of a birch bark tipi. Shortly after this picture was taken, Chief Rickard was arrested by the Royal Canadian Mounted Police and thrown into jail on a false charge. *Courtesy of Clinton Rickard family*

Chief George D. Rickard around 1932 after he had gone to live with his son Clinton. *Courtesy of Clinton Rickard family*

Charles Curtis Rickard, eldest child of Clinton and Beulah Rickard, in 1932. *Courtesy of Clinton Rickard family*

Clinton Rickard was the last farmer in Niagara County to use oxen. Here son Clark handles the ox team.
Courtesy of Clinton Rickard family

An IDLA picnic in 1940. Clinton Rickard is at the far left in the third row. Third and fourth from the left in the third row are his sons Clark and William. Beulah Rickard sits directly in front of William. George Nash is at far left seated with the children in the front row. In the fourth row, David Hill is second from left, Angus Horne is sixth from left, and Sophie Martin is third from right. *Photograph by Muriel Kelley. Courtesy of Clinton Rickard family*

Fred Shipston and Clinton Rickard at a veterans' banquet in honor of Memorial Day in 1961. Ten years later, they were the last two surviving members of M. B. Butler Camp No. 7, United Spanish War Veterans. *Courtesy of Niagara Falls Gazette, Niagara Falls, New York*

Working with young people was one of Chief Rickard's favorite pastimes. Here he explains the wampum belts to a group of Cub Scouts.

Six Nations Indians with their UN representative, Emery Kocsis, participating in the cornerstone-laying ceremonies at the United Nations building on October 24, 1949. Left to right, David Hill, Emery J. Kocsis, Clinton Rickard, Harry Patterson, Angus Horne, Thomas Beauvais, and Lone Wolf. *Picture from* New York Daily Mirror. *Courtesy of Chicago Tribune–New York News Syndicate, Inc., New York City*

Chief Rickard meets Soviet Foreign Minister Andrei Y. Vishinsky (left) in the delegates' lounge of the United Nations at Lake Success, New York, October 23, 1950. The next day, the Indian delegation which Chief Rickard headed laid their grievances over treaty violations before United Nations Secretary General Trygve Lie. *Photograph by Alfonso Preindl. Courtesy of Clinton Rickard family*

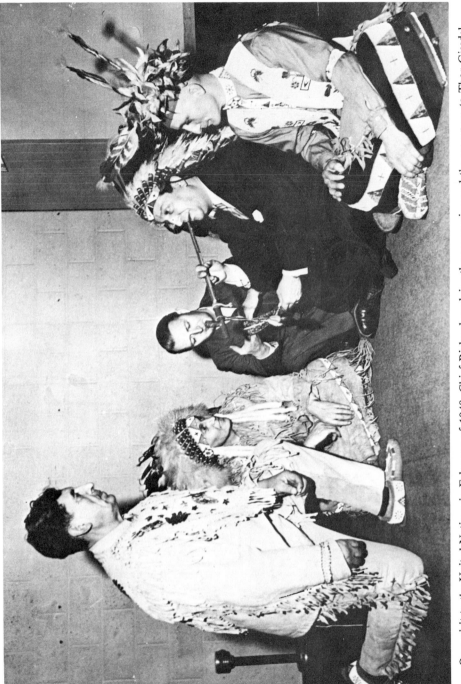

On a visit to the United Nations in February of 1948, Chief Rickard explains the peace pipe and the wampum to Thor Gjesdel of Norway and Dr. Benjamin Cohen of Chile (holding pipe). Flanking them are David Hill (left), wearing Plains headdress, and William Smith (right), wearing Iroquois headdress, both Mohawks of the Six Nations Reserve, Grand River. *Associated Press–Wide World Photos, Inc., New York City*

as other Indians and not wards of the United States. The court had appointed attorneys to defend Lila Jimerson, who was to go on trial first. My father showed me the article and asked me if I could help. I determined to try.

The next day I went to Buffalo to visit United States Attorney Richard H. Templeton and asked him to represent Lila Jimerson, as he was required to do by law. He became very angry at this and claimed that there was no such law. He said it was not the business of his office to help murderers. He and I argued quite heatedly for a time, and then I produced a law book that contained my proof. It was the 1926 edition of the *Code of the Laws of the United States* and had been given to me by Congressman Clarence MacGregor. Title 25, Chapter 5, Section 175 said: "In all States and Territories where there are reservations or allotted Indians the United States district attorney shall represent them in all suits at law and in equity."

Upon reading this, Mr. Templeton put in a call to Washington, D.C. While he was in his office making the call, his assistant told me: "He's going to beat you with a bigger book!" The response from Washington, however, reaffirmed my claim. Thereupon, Templeton called the court, where the trial was in process, and requested a recess until he could enter the case.

The story behind this Marchand murder trial was a strange one. Marchand was a sculptor and had become attached to his model, Lila Jimerson. Lila was persuaded to tell Nancy Bowen that Mrs. Marchand was a witch and had killed Nancy's husband by her witchcraft. This was the beginning of a plot to get Mrs. Marchand out of the way. Mrs. Bowen, through a Seneca interpreter, Clifford Shongo, testified in court that she and Lila went to visit Mrs. Marchand in Buffalo to ask whether she was a witch. Mrs. Marchand was somewhat amused by this question and replied that she was. Mrs. Bowen then claimed that she took a hammer and killed her.

It was during these courtroom sessions that I met the Episcopal minister Glenn B. Coykendall, who was a good friend of the Indians and was doing all he could to help these women get a fair trial. The lawyers had asked him and Clifford Shongo to bring Arthur C. Parker, the noted anthropologist, from Rochester for the trial. Dr. Parker, who was part Seneca, was an authority on Six Nations Indians. When this distinguished man did appear at the trial, Erie County District Attorney

Guy B. Moore was very insulting to him. Moore also asked the Reverend Coykendall when he was on the witness stand if he knew the Ten Commandments. The Reverend Coykendall replied that he did know something about them. Moore then told the jury that all Indian women were immoral—not only Senecas, but those on other reservations as well. If they doubted this charge, they could come to his office and look at his files.

I later received an anonymous letter stating that Marchand and a friend had killed Mrs. Marchand and then took the two Indian women to Canada and gave them money and clothes to say that they had done the killing. This sounded like a reasonable explanation of the events, but there was no definite proof available to confirm the statements in the letter.

The outcome of the trial was that both women were set free.[4] A further result of the trial was the happy defeat of Guy B. Moore as district attorney at the next election.

The publicity given to this case revealed the very inferior educational system on our reserves.[5] Those of us who knew the state Indian schools at first hand had always known how inadequate they were. It was for that reason that parents who could afford to do so sent their children to the Quaker school near the Allegany Reservation or to Hampton Institute in Virginia or to Carlisle in Pennsylvania. Our schools were far below the standard of the white country schools, and they went only as far as eighth grade. Parents who wanted their children to have more education had to send them off the reservation to white schools and pay the tuition and cost of books and supplies. By 1930, New York State appropriated only $60,000 a year for all Indian schools, not counting the Thomas Indian School for orphans. Only $2,000 a year was spent by the state on textbooks for Indian children. There were never enough textbooks to go around, and none of them were very new. Also, the state classed our schools with prison schools. Facilities were very poor, sometimes hazardous, and the teachers usually not well trained. Our people were therefore very much at a disadvantage educationally.

These facts were now made public for the first time through my speaking before various groups, pleading equality of education for my people, through newspaper interviews with me, and through independent investigation of Indian education on our Six Nations reservations by various newspaper reporters. Concerned white people were thereby aroused to right this wrong. Several bills were introduced into the state legislature to increase the annual appropriation for Indian schools and to permit Indians to attend high schools at state expense. We owe especial thanks to State Senator Nelson W. Cheney of Eden, New York, for his work in the legislature in 1930 toward making high school education available for Indians. Since that time, my people have been attending high schools regularly to the extent that today we have a well-educated population among our younger generation.

Throughout these trying years since the loss of my wife, I carried on the best I could with caring for my family and upholding the rights of my people. Sometimes the fight was very lonely, but I had to continue it. Many years ago I had asked the Great Spirit for strength to help those in distress and he responded to my request; therefore, I knew he had a purpose for me. Through my work, I also met very many great and good people. It was the highest privilege to have their friendship and to work with them. Even as I helped others, so these friends helped me. This is the way the Great Spirit wants the world to be, with everyone working together to help one another and to overcome all evil.

7

Legalized Treachery

ABOUT TWO YEARS after my wife Elizabeth had died, my old friend Nelson Mt. Pleasant and his wife Margaret came to my house to discuss with me the possibility of marriage to their daughter Beulah. Nelson Mt. Pleasant had been one of my closest school chums and had always liked me. Now he and his wife expressed their desire to have me for a son-in-law. I accordingly began courting Beulah and we were soon married.

My new wife was a member of the White Bear family line in the Bear clan, but her father, like my previous father-in-law, was an Onondaga Eel, born and raised on the Tuscarora Reservation. This White Bear family had originated during the time my Tuscarora people lived in North Carolina. The white settlers were always kidnapping our children and selling them into slavery. This crime, and the Europeans' greed for our land, caused a series of wars between us and them. At one time, a child was kidnapped from the Bear clan. In order to keep peace, the settlers returned to us a substitute child—a little white girl who was one of twins. She was adopted into the Bear clan to replace the stolen child and became the mother of the White Bear family. Before this time, twins had not been known among the Tuscaroras. Now the birth of twins became common among the White Bear people. This White Bear line is often called in our own day the "Twin clan." People also often refer to "White Bear clan" and "Black Bear clan," the latter being the descendants of the original Tuscarora Bear people and the former being the descendants of the white child whom the Bear people adopted. This tendency to think of the Bear clan as two separate clans has sometimes caused intermarriage between White Bear and Black Bear people, but this is not proper. They are both of the same family.

My wife and I, along with my brother Chester as our driver, left shortly after our marriage to go to Maniwaki in Quebec to attend the Second Grand Council of the Algonquin Indians. This was to be not only a business trip, but also a short honeymoon for my wife and myself.

The first time I had ever been on the Maniwaki reserve was in 1926 when I was invited up there to explain the border problem. Some of the Algonquin chiefs came to visit me a couple of years later after we had won our border fight. I showed them around our Tuscarora Reservation and even took them to our little one-room schoolhouse. As inadequate as our school was, these Algonquins thought it was wonderful. They were disturbed because at their reservation school so much religion was taught during the school hours that there was little time left for learning anything else. They asked me to come up to their reserve the next year for their First Grand Council, to be held in August of 1930, and explain our ways to their people. This I did.

It was a large affair with about five hundred people present. Several white officials were also invited to this council, among whom was C. C. Parker [no relation to the Seneca anthropologist, Arthur C. Parker] from Ottawa, a special Canadian government investigator of Indian agencies. Mr. Parker was called away from the gathering early and asked me to preside in his absence and also to bring the resolutions of that council to his office on my return. I did comply with his request in this regard. Also while I was at the reserve at that time, I was asked by the commissioner of education to speak at the school. I did so and told them the type of education that we had on our reservations and mentioned particularly that we had no more than one half-hour of religious services or instruction in any one day. The commissioner then informed me that he was issuing orders for a limitation of one half-hour per day on religious services in the schools and congratulated me for calling this matter to his attention. The Indians were also well pleased with my visit and invited me back for the Second Grand Council, to be held in September of 1931. It was this second council that my wife and I were now headed for.

We arrived late at night on September 15 and got a few hours' sleep before the beginning of the council the next day. The morning after our arrival, we went about visiting and taking pictures while waiting for the opening of the first session, at which I was scheduled to speak. There were about a thousand people there for the meeting. Two mounted policemen, dressed in plainclothes like civilians, were also present. They walked about like tourists, taking pictures of the birch bark tepee and other interesting things, and never introduced themselves. People thought they were the invited government representatives.

In the afternoon, when people were resting, the mounted police came up to me and asked me if I would like to go on a sightseeing tour. I agreed, and my wife and I got into the car.

The mounties took me right over to the Indian agent's office. I was asked by the agent: "Can you read English?"

"Well, I can try it," I said.

He shoved a paper in front of me and I saw that it was a warrant for my arrest. It read as follows:

WARRANT IN THE FIRST INSTANCE

CANADA
Province of Quebec
County of Hull

TO THE PEACE OFFICERS IN THE SAID COUNTY
WHEREAS   CLINTON RICKARD
has this day been charged upon oath before the undersigned, for that he, on divers dates between the 16th day of April, A.D., 1931, and the 15th day of September, A.D., 1931, at Barriere in the said County of Hull did unlawfully, without consent of the Superintendent General expressed in writing, receive, obtain, solicit or request from certain Indians a payment or contribution for the purpose of raising a fund or providing money for the prosecution of a claim which the tribe or band or Indians has or is represented to have for the recovery of a claim of money for the benefit of said tribe or band, contrary to Section 141 of the Indian Act.

THESE ARE, THEREFORE, to command you, in His Majesty's Name forthwith to apprehend the said CLINTON RICKARD and to bring him before me or some other Justice in and for the said County, to answer unto the said charge and to be further dealt with according to law.

Given under my hand this 15th day of September, in the year of our Lord one thousand nine hundred and thirty one at Maniwaki, in the said county of Hull.

E. S. Gauthier, J. P.
Indian Agent
County of Hull

This warrant was false from beginning to end. I had never been to Barriere and had corresponded with only one person there, Chief Alex Nattoway, on the border problem.[1] Nor did I ever solicit money at Barriere or elsewhere to sue the Canadian government. I had been paid for my travel expenses to Maniwaki in 1926 by the Algonquins. People from there had also collected money to help us with our border fight, but this did not concern any grievance against the Canadian government. Now at this time, in September of 1931, the people were taking donations to pay me for the money I had spent in boarding five of their number at my house for a considerable period and in lending to these five men to get home. The money I had spent to help these men came to $140, and the people were trying to reimburse me for this expense. Of the charges laid against me, however, I was completely innocent.

Despite my protestations of innocence before the Indian agent and my explanation that, so far from taking money from these people, I had in fact lent some of them a sizeable sum, I was roughly thrown into jail. The next day, I was taken by the mounted police to the city of Hull, eighty-five miles away. They secured a taxi to take me to jail.

One of the mounties looked at the pin in my lapel and asked me: "Is that an Indian sign?"

"No sir," I replied, "that is a Masonic emblem."

This mountie seemed very displeased at my reply.

When we arrived at the Hull jail, one of the mounted police stopped to pay the taxi driver, and the other took me inside the building behind the door, quickly pulled out his wallet, and slipped me a five dollar bill in American currency. He told me: "Get in touch with your Master. I see what you are up against." Then nodding in the direction of his partner, he added: "We can't do a thing with him; he's K of C," meaning Knights of Columbus.[2]

I was taken into the jail and constantly interrogated. They tried to pressure me into admitting that I had solicited the money as charged and had taken $500 from the Barriere Indians to sue the government of Canada. They would not allow me to see my wife or brother, to write, or to call anyone. The only outsider I had contact with was an attorney named Jean Daoust who hung out around the jail seeking cases and who came to see me and offered to help me get free. I did not send for this man, and I really did not formally hire him, but I did agree to sign over to him from time to time sums of my money which the police were holding so that he could try to get me freed of the charges against me. I needed help, the police kept everyone but this man from me, so what could I do?

Meanwhile the police were continuously trying to get me to plead guilty, and I just as continuously refused because I had done no wrong. Nor was I ever faced with my accuser or even told who he was. The Indian Department and the police had no witnesses on hand to accuse me and absolutely no proof of any wrongdoing.

I was thrown into the dirtiest cell in this world, I do believe. The cell was about 25 feet by 10 feet and housed twenty other prisoners. Usually our food was just cold oatmeal, or porridge, as they called it, and salt that was half dirt, a piece of dry bread, and water. For supper we usually got mush. At night when I tried to sleep, I found that the cell was full of bedbugs into the thousands. I had been remanded here for a week and bail refused. Later bail was set at $500 and then $250— none of which I could meet.

After a week's stay in jail, I was remanded again for another week. The reason they later gave for keeping me in jail and refusing to release me on bail was that they had to send a man to Barriere, ninety miles north of Maniwaki, to get witnesses and that the trip must be made by canoe from Maniwaki, as there were no roads most of the way. I later learned that a mounted policeman named Charron on his way to Barriere met Chief Alex Nattoway and questioned him sharply, trying to get him to confess that I had solicited money from his band. Chief Nattoway denied this charge and could not be shaken. Later, Charron again accosted Nattoway and grilled him, threatening him with jail and hanging if he did not confess. He asked the chief if he were going to Hull to the trial. Alex said yes, he would, if he were wanted. Charron thereupon ordered him to return to Barriere.

During all the time I was in jail, Daoust kept coming to my cell and getting me to sign over more money to him so that he could withdraw it from the keeping of the police. He told me he needed this money to get me free. I could not see what he was doing for me, since I was still in jail, but Daoust kept holding out hope and I kept signing until he had taken all the money that I had in the world.

My story was beginning to be printed in the Canadian newspapers. While I was still in jail, Dr. James Cotton of Toronto, an honorary member of the Indian Defense League of America, had a letter printed in the Toronto *Telegram* giving the whole account of my arrest and treatment. The newspapers in both Niagara Falls, Ontario, and Niagara Falls, New York, also carried the report of my false arrest. More than two hundred letters were sent by my friends from Niagara Falls, Ontario, alone to authorities in Ottawa calling for my release.

After I had been in jail six days, I was given a special treat for supper. In addition to being fed the regular garbage, I was given soup that evening. I was the only prisoner to receive such food. I finished it up unsuspectingly. In the next half hour after I ate, the guards took me into the doctor. This doctor grilled me and grilled me, though I did not see what business it was of a doctor to act as a police interrogator.

Suddenly the doctor noticed that I had started to quiver and shake and perspire. He became excited and said to the policemen standing by: "Take him back! Take him back!"

I felt as though my insides were on fire. My eyesight was growing dim, pains were shooting through my body, and I was having convulsions. When the police dragged me up the stairs, I found that I could not use my legs. I made one flight of stairs and then I dropped, unable to go any farther. Right then, I threw up. After getting rid of whatever poison they had given me, I felt much better.

The police then put me in a cell that contained sentenced prisoners. They took off my shoes, and as they did so, a letter that I had hidden in one shoe dropped out. They pounced on it like cats after a mouse. It was from a special friend in New York telling me he hoped I would be able to help my Indian people and overcome the problems that they had. The police opened it and read it and then commented: "Oh! another Gandhi!"

For four days I lay ill in the jail with no medical care whatsoever. I suffered in the extreme during all that time. The prison doctor later told me that I had had a paralytic stroke. I would never have believed, if I had not experienced it, that I would have received this most inhuman treatment from a supposedly civilized nation. And they call *us* savages!

My brother Chester meanwhile had gone to the Indian Department in Ottawa with a companion and asked for C. C. Parker. He was told by the official in charge that Parker was out. Chester then told his story and asked if this office could help. The answer was: "There are no

Americans who can come over here and tell us how to take care of Indians. We take care of them right!"

Chester turned to his friend and said: "We can get no help here," and left.

In addition to the pressures upon me by the police to confess, even lawyer Daoust tried to get me to plead guilty. On September 25, the tenth day of my imprisonment, he came to me and said: "Well, Chief, I have it all fixed up so you may go home today. All you need to do now is plead guilty and they will give you eight days, which you have already served, and they will pay your fine of $27."

I told him: "No, I cannot tell a lie against myself or against my people."

On the same day, Mr. Miller of the Indian Bureau came and asked me if I wanted to go to the hospital.

"Yes," I told him, "it's a better place than here."

I was taken before the judge at this time and still pressured to plead guilty. Whenever my witnesses had shown up, the police and judge had postponed the trial. Now they decided to release me on my own recognizance, despite the fact that I was so sick I could hardly walk.

After my release, Chester and I called on a number of high officials in Ottawa to gain redress for my false arrest. One was the American consul. We also went to see Prime Minister Bennett and spoke with his secretary.

We made a special trip to see the commander in chief of the Ottawa Consistory, Masonic Lodge. He called the Indian Office on my behalf. I could not hear what they were saying; but when he hung up, he told me: "You'll hear the news when you get back."

We then returned and met my wife at Hull. She told me that the government had withdrawn the charge and that we were free to go.

I said: "No, we can't go home until I have something on me to prove that the charges have been dropped."

I went to see lawyer Daoust and told him: "You have all my money and there has been no hearing and no trial. I have to have something to prove that charges have been withdrawn. I see what they are up to. They have released me on my own recognizance. Now they want me to leave the country so that they can charge me with being a fugitive. You draft a statement to the effect that the government did withdraw the charge."

The lawyer had no papers from the court or the Indian Department or the police, but he did give me this statement on his personal stationery:

September 30, 1931

This is to certify that in a case of the King against Clinton Rickard, the charge was withdrawn by the plaintiff who, in the matter, was the Department of Indian Affairs.

I may say personally that the Chief would have never been convicted of the offence laid against him because he was absolutely innocent.

Jean Dauost
his attorney

We were now almost penniless. The $100 which my fine friends had collected to reimburse me had been turned over to Chief Michel Cote of Maniwaki to give to me. Chief Cote, who had been, as I thought, my close friend, now kept this $100. I never did see it. In fact, Cote told me curtly that my presence was no longer needed at Maniwaki. My brother Chester had also been arrested by the police for trespassing on the Maniwaki reserve and fined $11.35—all the money he had with him. We then turned homeward, completely destitute.

In Toronto, I stopped off to see Dr. James Cotton and thank him for the assistance he had given my case while I was in jail. He gave us $10 and something to eat. Then in Niagara Falls, Ontario, we stopped to see our very dear friends, Mr. and Mrs. A. J. Holman. They also gave us $10 and something to eat. Many, many of my good white Canadian friends had stood by me in my darkest hour. They had all brought pressure on their government to release me and undo this great injustice, and they had supported me in my greatest financial distress. I thanked the Great Spirit for their friendship.

When we returned, we went to Nellie and Willard Gansworth's to pick up my two boys, Clark and William, who had been left in their care. Nellie was most surprised to see my condition when I got out of the car, for I was bent over and had to walk with a cane. I had gone away a young man and had come back an old man, she said. We took the boys back to our house and tried to pick up our life again. It would not be easy, for my earning power was impaired for many long months.

I went to our doctor for treatment and he confirmed what the prison doctor had told me in saying that the symptoms I described sounded like a stroke. I do firmly believe that the poison given me in jail brought on the convulsions which in turn caused a stroke. My father, who knew herbs, also nursed me back to health.

We experienced a great financial loss because of this trip. Altogether the trip cost me $500. We had intended to stay only a couple of days and then return immediately so that I could harvest my fruit. My jail sentence ruined my opportunity to get in my crop. I lost all told two hundred bushels of peaches and all my prune crop. The fruit just fell from the trees and rotted—a whole year's labor gone to nothing.

I now began a long campaign to gain redress from the Canadian government. Friends helped me in my efforts to secure a public investigation of this scandal. The Algonquin Indians sent an appeal to both the Indian Department and Prime Minister Bennett, saying:

> We, members of the Maniwaki, Que. reservation, appeal to you for mercy and for justice. We feel very badly about the act of our Indian agent E. S. Gauthier. They arrested our best friend, Chief Clinton Rickard, for no reason whatsoever, arrested him when he had never asked one penny of any of our people. He had come to our second annual grand council at his own expense. We just invited him as we did last year.[3]

Senator Lynn J. Frazier, Senator Royal S. Copeland, Vice-President Curtis, and Seth T. Cole, who was deputy commissioner of the Bureau of Law of the New York State Department of Taxation and Finance, all gave me great assistance in pressing for an investigation by the United States government. Senator Copeland and Mr. Cole particularly did much work in my behalf to help me secure justice. Had it not been for these two, the investigation would not have proceeded so far or uncovered so much.

My attempt to obtain redress was blocked at every step by both the American and Canadian governments, with the latter telling falsehoods and the former, for the sake of friendship, accepting them. Secretary of State Stimson was forced to investigate my case because of the pressure brought on him by Mr. Cole and Senator Copeland, but his report was a complete whitewash of the Canadian government's actions.

The government of Canada sent Stimson a report that was a tissue of lies the whole way through. The American consul general in Canada accepted this false report and backed it up all the way. The acting secretary of the Canadian Department of Indian Affairs said that I was "prosecuted under the Indian Act by reason of a complaint in writing received by the Indian Department from the chief of the Barriere Band of Indians and . . . the complaint was withdrawn by the Indian Department owing to the fact that it later appeared that the collecting of money complained of had been made more han six months previously and was therefore barred as evidence."

No one would reveal the name of this supposed chief who complained against me. Finally, through Mr. Cole's efforts, the name was revealed as Chief David Macacouse. My brother Chester then went up to Barriere in July of 1932 to find this Chief Macacouse. Chester located him and found that the man could neither read nor write and could not speak English. How could he have written the complaint? Lie number one.

The charge that I was collecting money to sue the Canadian government and had secured $500 at Barriere, as the government claimed, was lie number two. We never had that much money contributed to us by these poor Indians; I had never been to Barriere; and I was interested only in fighting the border case, which did not concern the Canadian government. Maniwaki Indians occasionally sent a small amount to us to aid in our border fight prior to 1928. We collected nothing in order to sue the Canadian government, however.

I had attempted to help the Maniwaki Indians in some others ways. Exavier Odjuck of that reserve had lost his only son in World War I and received no compensation. Through my efforts an appeal was sent to the Indian Department. I succeeded in securing him a small pension of $15. This certainly had nothing to do with suing the government. I had also supported the right of the Algonquins to unrestricted hunting, fishing, and trapping, since this was their complete and only means of livelihood. The Canadian government was making these Indians comply with the laws passed to regulate white sportsmen and so was pressing them into poverty. White people were also going into Indian territory, competing with these Indians for game, and deliberately destroying their traps and stealing their kills, I helped them in making an appeal to the Indian Department for protection. All my activities in this regard were open and honest. We kept no secrets from the Indian Department.

Both the acting secretary and the deputy superintendent of the Indian Department of Canada further stated that an officer of the Royal Canadian Mounted Police visited me in jail at Hull and asked if I wished to go to the hospital and I refused. No policeman ever visited me and made this offer at any time I was in jail. Lie number three.

I was asked only on the *tenth* day of my imprisonment and *only* by Mr. Miller of the Indian Department if I would like to go to a hospital. I said: "Yes, it's a better place than this." Shortly after I made this reply to Mr. Miller, on the same day, I was released from jail but *not* sent to any hospital. The Indian Department said in its report that when this mysteriously unnamed RCMP asked me if I wanted to go to the hospital I said "No," but later changed my story about my answer when I made complaints to the authorities about my treatment in jail. In their long list of lies, this was lie number four.

The warrant against me had stated that my supposed collection of money at Barriere, where I had never even been, had taken place between April 16, 1931, and September 15, 1931. Then the deputy superintendent of the Indian Department stated that I was finally released because they found that I had collected the money more than six months previously and was accordingly not tried because this supposed collection was "barred as evidence, as Section 141 above quoted provides for summary conviction, the department although convinced that the offences were committed, had withdrawn the charge."

They arrested me on a lie, refused to let me bring witnesses, refused to confront me with my accuser, and then released me on a lie. From April 1931 to September 1931 is five months, not six months. When did the supposed collection of money take place? The truth is, the government could not stand before the facts and so did not want an open investigation.

My treatment made me realize that the Canadian government thought no more of an Indian than they did of an insect. It is obvious that the agents of the Indian Department thought they could do to me the same as they had always done to Indians. The government would throw my people into jail when they complained too much in order to shut their mouths. In my case, they were surprised at the great publicity given their unjust act. They knew they had a case that could not stand up in court, so they released me on a flimsy excuse in order to cover up their illegal behavior. As Seth T. Cole wrote to me in a letter of

December 16, 1931: "The peculiar point from the standpoint of the Canadian Government seems to me to be that they did not discover that the alleged offenses had taken place more than six months previously to your arrest until after you had been arrested and thrown into prison. To say the least, it would seem to me that in making the arrest they acted upon inadequate information."[4]

The truth was, this charge was merely a subterfuge. I was arrested not for collecting money but for my work in getting better schools for the Indians at Maniwaki and for my known sympathies for the traditionalists and hereditary chiefs rather than for the elected councils. Proof that I was arrested more for my beliefs than for my actions is contained in the report the Indian Department issued on me. It accused me of sympathizing with those who had "imaginary grievances" against the Canadian government. It would seem that no Indian was permitted to have a point of view differing from that of the Indian Department. Canadian white people had several political parties but the government would not permit the same freedom of thought to Indians.[5]

What hurt most in all this controversy was the way in which Secretary of State Stimson and the United States government dismissed my appeal and considered me a liar while accepting the lies of a foreign government against me. What was one Indian more or less? Even my army service on the field of battle for the United States was not taken into consideration. I had defended the American government and now that government refused to defend me.

The Canadian government was so embarrassed by the publicity given my case that on March 8, 1933, it refused the entry of my wife and myself into Canada on the false grounds that I could not prove that I was not entering the country as an immigrant. We were attempting at the time to go across the river to visit friends in Niagara Falls, Ontario, and in no conceivable way could be said to be immigrants. It was well known to all that my home was on the Tuscarora Reservation. I made an appeal in April to the Department of Immigration and Colonization at Ottawa, but my appeal was dismissed and I was barred from further entry to Canada.

When Border Crossing Celebration time came around in July, I walked to the middle of the bridge and waited for the parade from the Canadian side to come over and meet me. The photographers were all there to record this interesting event. For about three years, I was denied entry to Canada, and at each celebration time, the reporters and photographers made a big thing out of my waiting in the middle of the bridge. The publicity which the Canadian government received as a result of denying me entry was not favorable. I believe that it was to avoid further embarrassment that the government finally lifted the ban and allowed me entry as usual.

Although I was once more permitted into Canada, I was never given any redress for my false arrest in 1931. I kept appealing as late as 1938 to the United States government to protest this most barbarous act, but all my efforts were futile. Also I continued to press my claim against the government of Canada for $10,000 damages for personal injury, false arrest, and financial loss. Needless to say, I never received a penny.

Nothing made more plain to me the contempt with which Indians are treated by both governments than this incident. Justice is given out only when it is to the benefit of the government to do so or only when the people are strong enough to force it to do so. Only a very few statesmen live up to the high ideals that are written on paper. But we will never give up in the struggle for our rights. We have been shown the way and we know what to do. I have always known within myself that our lives are not our own; they are only lent to us by the Great Spirit. When we realize that, then no one or no government, however powerful, can ever turn us aside.

8

Depression and Oppression

As a result of my treatment in the Hull jail, my health was broken for many months and my family suffered from my inability to work steadily. My chronic attacks of malaria, dating from my army years, added to my distress. My wife and my friends all gave me great encouragement through this period of trial. Nor were those days easy times in general, for the United States was going through its greatest depression in history in 1931 and after. It was during this period, when work was scarcest, times were hardest, and our needs were the greatest, that I was the least able to provide for my family. Also, my army pension, which was my only income during my illness, was reduced to $8.00 per month because of the government's economy program, putting me back to the 1906 standard. Gradually, however, I began to recover my health and was once more able to do a man's work.

Now that I was married again, my boys were once more eating good meals and were well cared for. I was proud of both of them. They were good scholars in school and seemed to be promising in every way. Clark was husky, but William was still sickly. He never fully recovered from the beating he had received as a little boy. The result of this assault was a permanent constriction in his chest which caused him constant difficulty and pain the rest of his life. Every winter we could depend on his having pneumonia. He was, though, a very sensitive and kind-hearted boy. I looked forward to the day when he could begin to help our people. I knew that he would carry on my work.

William's sickness soon caused his dismissal from school. He had just started tenth grade when he was sent home permanently with the word that he had tuberculosis. The diagnosis was mistaken, but his formal education came to an abrupt end. This setback did not discourage his love for learning. He used to say that he would be his own teacher and so continued to read all that he could and informed himself on many topics.

115

One day, not long after I had remarried, William came running into the house and said: "Pa! there are surveyors down there surveying! They're moving the boundary over and taking our land away from us!" I therefore hurried down the hill toward our north boundary to see what the trouble was.

We live on the northeast side of the reservation, not far from white man's land. The boundary is the woodland that is the border between the white farmers and our reservation, and we have always known how much of that woodland belonged to our reservation. There were still the marks on the trees where there had once been a fence. This land down the hill to the north of my property consists of a large field and a wooded stretch and was owned by Marcus Peters and later by his grandson, Truman Johnson. Some years later, after this incident, I bought this tract to add to my farm. On the other side, north of the wooded strip, was white man's land.

Once down the hill, I saw that the United States government surveyors were at work and were running the reservation boundary a good distance south of where it actually belonged. They were completely ignoring the woods, leaving it all on the white man's side, and were also cutting about twenty yards off the open field to the south of the woods and giving that to the white man also.

I informed the surveyors that they were surveying too far south, on Indian land, that the boundary was several yards north. They became very impudent and told me they knew what they were doing.

With that I lost my temper and began yelling. I told them that we and our ancestors *and* the white man *always* had known where the boundary was and there was never any question about it. The white man had always stolen Indian land, but we were not going to stand for having it stolen right under our noses. If they put those markers down, I said I would pull them up. I told them they were trespassing and I would run them off. My wife later said she could hear me yelling all the way up to the house.

In the midst of all this, my brother Chester came over for a visit, and my wife gave him the news about our troubles. He came rushing down the hill also and began yelling at the surveyors along with me.

The end result was that the surveyors did move the markers over. But we were not able to follow them all around the reservation boundary to see what they later did in other places. We suspected that they were just picking out the spots where it was easiest for them to make their surveys, without any regard for accuracy.

My father, who was now a widower and ailing, came to live with us and remained until his death in April of 1934. He had a bad heart condition and as a result suffered greatly from swollen legs and dropsy. It was painful for him to lie down, and he usually slept sitting up in a chair. One morning, my wife found that he had slit the skin on his legs with a razor blade in order to drain out the water. The newspapers which he had spread around his chair were soaked and the water was still oozing out from the slits in his skin. It was not long after this incident that I came home from a Chiefs' Council meeting one time to be met by my wife with the news that my father had had a heart attack. We got him ready and I took him to the hospital. There the nurses made him lie down, even though it was impossible for him to do so and still breathe properly. He lived in misery a few days and then died.

After my father's death, I stopped attending Chiefs' Council meetings. The disruption in our nation had become too disturbing to me, and therefore I devoted myself entirely to working through the Indian Defense League of America.

The first child born to our marriage was a boy. I again asked my good friend, Professor W. F. E. Gurley from the University of Chicago, to name our new child. The Gurleys had always been so good to us that I wished to show my appreciation in this manner. The professor chose the name, Charles Curtis, after the then vice-president of the United States, who was part Indian.

Charles was not yet two years old when my father died, and before father's death often used to play around the old man. One day as he watched Charles, my father said to my wife: "I hate to tell you this, but you won't raise this boy. His spirit is not here."[1]

Her grandmother, Sophronia Thompson, had made a similar prediction. She said to my wife: "You must be good to this boy because you won't raise him."

We thought little of these words at the time, but they turned out to be true. Charles was accidentally killed when he was thirteen years old. He was a big, strapping fellow at the time and would have been a powerful man had he lived. We lost him one day in 1945. My son Clark had just come home from the army and all four brothers—William, Clark, Eli, and Charles—were going out hunting. They were in a cut-down jalopy, such as the men and boys on our reserve use for hunting. William and Clark were sitting in the front with a loaded rifle propped up against the seat, and Eli and Charles were standing in the rear. Just as they drove down the driveway to the road, the car went over a bump and the rifle was jolted and discharged. Charles was hit in the head and was killed instantly. My wife and I were in town doing the shopping at the time. When we came home, the body of our son still lay by the side of the road covered by a blanket, waiting for the coroner. We were not permitted to see him since he was too badly shattered for viewing. Once again tragedy had struck my family. I had had many hard blows in my life, but this one hit me the hardest.

The Lord gave us six more children besides Charles. A large family meant more work for myself and my wife. We had no electricity and no indoor running water. Our water supply came from Black Nose Spring just across from our house, and had to be carried up in buckets. The larger our family became, the more water needed to be hauled, the more washing to be done, the more food to be grown. We took the work in our stride, for it was all a part of making a home.

William and Clark were becoming old enough to help with the chores and were learning to be good farmers. They could drive the ox team which I used for plowing. We used horses for cultivating. I had bought a second-hand tractor once, but it did not work properly and I returned it. It was hard for Indians to accumulate the money to buy the latest farm equipment that the white man used. We made out the best we could with our modest-sized farms but knew that it was difficult to keep up with the white farmers about us, who owned more land than we and who could produce more with their mechanized equipment. A crop failure was always a greater financial blow to us than it was to the big white farmers. My boys were both in our Tuscarora 4-H Club, however, and they did therefore learn many of the techniques of modern scientific farming.

In later years, my son William became interested in breeding an early-maturing variety of Indian corn. Many of our farmers raised the original Indian corn in addition to the hybrid varieties of sweet corn that had been developed by the white man. We still use Indian corn in making old Indian recipes such as corn bread and corn soup. The Longhouse people on the Onondaga and Seneca Reservations and at Grand River use it in all their ceremonials. The Indian variety takes much longer to mature than does hybrid corn used by the white man. Some years when there is an early frost, the Indian corn is killed before it is ready. William was experimenting to produce a variety of white Indian corn that would have larger kernels and mature earlier than usual. Clark worked very closely with him on this. They bred in with the white corn both the red and the purple Indian corn to get the extra qualities they wanted. The final result was a white corn that was superior to the old variety. A professor of agronomy at Cornell University, Dr. Frank P. Bussell, took an interest in William's project and pronounced it a success. The professor had one complaint, however, that the neck of the ear was too stout to permit the use of a cornpicker. William kept on selectively breeding until he developed a strain that could be used with a cornpicker. One year, when an early frost killed the Indian corn at the Grand River reserve, William had already harvested his crop and so sent several bushels up for our friends to use. He gave instructions that poor people were to have it free.

One time, William, my wife, and I were on our way up to Grand River with a sack of shelled Indian corn. William was doing the driving. We meant to take the corn to our friend Bill Smith on the Six Nations Reserve so that he could pass it out to those who wanted it—a quart to a family. As is usual in going over the border, we were stopped for questioning by a customs inspector at Niagara Falls, Ontario. He asked if we had anything in the car that we were bringing into Canada. William truthfully told him about the sack of Indian corn. That started the argument. The officials wanted us to pay customs duty on it, and we refused. We said that according to the Jay Treaty of 1794 between Great Britain and the United States, Indians had the right to pass the border unmolested with Indian goods. Indian corn was certainly Indian goods. The government of Canada, against all rules of international law, refuses to recognize this treaty, which it in all honesty should do. The customs men refused to give in and so did we.

William informed these customs inspectors that the corn we had was not commercial. "You can't buy this anywhere on the market," he said. "It is raised only by Indians, for Indians. You can't place any price on it."

We told them we had raised this corn ourselves. After we had harvested it and dried it for several months, we spent a whole month shelling and sorting it by hand to get that sack full that they saw. So far from making a profit on it, it had cost us to produce it. This was not white man's corn that sold on the open market. We wanted to know how or what the customs would charge us since no white man knew the value of it.

By this time, there were several customs officials gathered around arguing with us and refusing to let us into Canada with that sack of corn. We had quite a heated discussion with them, but we held our ground. One of them asked us if we intended to sell the corn when we got up to Grand River. William told him no; that corn was a gift to the Indian people. Since we had not bought it and since we intended to give it away, how could the customs charge us for it?

Finally one of the chief customs officials at the bridge put in a call to his boss in Ottawa and requested further instructions. The answer came back to let us proceed without paying customs.

We had been there at the border for about three hours arguing our point, and it was a point of honor with us. We were greatly relieved not only to have won, but to be on our way at last; however, we considered that encounter at the bridge as time well spent, for we had the satisfaction of seeing justice prevail.

The Great Depression that was sweeping the United States in the 1930s hit our Indian people everywhere particularly hard. In 1930 there were seventy-six farms on our Tuscarora Reservation.[2] During the distressing times of the depression, we had the utmost difficulty in securing enough money to buy seeds, horses, mules, or other necessities required for agriculture. When we were unable to farm, we were unable to be self-reliant. Our hunting was no longer sufficient to support all of us during the year, but could be used only as a supplement. We looked for wage work off the reservation but were discriminated against because of our race. The white people were taken care of first, and those of our men who were fortunate enough to find work were usually soon discharged to give the job to a white man. Even a recent European immigrant was always given preference over an original American. When we sought relief, we were turned away with the comment that our reservation was not in any relief district. White men less destitute than we were readily given work.

Here we can plainly see in this treatment we received from our white neighbors and local and state officials a major reason why we had never wanted to be under state control, even though the State of New York was constantly trying to assert control over us. The white people who live closest to Indians are always the most prejudiced against them and with few exceptions, the least likely to treat them equally with other races. If New York State ever assumed jurisdiction over us, we feared we would suffer continued discrimination and that even our lands would not be safe from the desires of our white neighbors. We knew that our treaties with the federal government were our best protection, if only Washington would honor its commitments to us.

The white people always had a notion that we Indians receive all our support from the government. They have the misconception that, since we have been getting "handouts" for years, we have become lazy and degenerate and do not rely on ourselves. Nothing could be more false. The only thing our Iroquois people have received on a regular basis from the United States government over the years is a small annual token gift of cloth amounting to forty cents per person. This "treaty cloth" as we call it is merely an acknowledgment that our treaty with the United States is still in effect, since the government promised to pay us a certain amount in perpetuity in exchange for our lands that we gave up and as a reward for our continued friendship to the people and government of the United States.

Article 6 of the Treaty of Canadaigua of 1794 actually states that the government shall set aside the sum of $4,500 yearly for the Six Nations "which shall be expended yearly, forever, in purchasing clothing, domestic animals, implements of husbandry, and other utensils suited to their circumstances, and in compensating useful artificers, who shall reside with or near them, and be employed for their benefit." These promises have never been met in full. The government covers all these obligations by merely giving us this payment of cloth. In past years, when a dollar was worth something, we received as much as fifteen yards of this unbleached muslin apiece. In later years, this amount went down and down until in 1929 it was four yards apiece. Later it became 2½ yards, sometimes paid every other year rather than annually. In the 1960s it was only 1½ yards, but since it symbolizes the faith of the government in abiding by the treaty, it is still important to us. So much for our "handouts."

In 1932 the state welfare department did issue an order for some of our more destitute families to receive groceries. It was in this same year, however, that we were told that no relief work could be provided for us because we were not in any relief district. Seven of our men who had received jobs three days a week in Niagara Falls were thereupon fired and white men put in their places. It was not until two years later, after much suffering, that my people were finally provided with a minimum amount of relief work. After all the lobbying in Congress the New York State officials had done in the past years to obtain complete jurisdiction over the Indians, with many tales of the great things the state had done for our people, the Albany government now showed itself none too eager to provide assistance to Indians in time of crisis. This attitude just demonstrated what we suspected all along, that the state wanted political control over us without assuming the federal government's treaty obligations to us and without treating us as equal human beings with other races. We had not made the Great Depression. That was the white man's doing. The white people had moved in and filled up the whole territory around our reservation so that it was no longer possible for us to live in the old Indian way. All we asked, therefore, was equality of opportunity with whites and other races in getting useful jobs so that we could support ourselves.

I was a member of a committee appointed by our Tuscarora people to plan relief projects for our reservation and submit these proposals to the Indian Bureau. Harry Patterson, Silas Chew, and Calvin Hewitt were the other committee members. The first project that was obvious to us was the improvement of the roads on our reservation. These were dirt roads and were adequate in bygone days when the horse and buggy was the means of travel. In the 1930s, many white people and a few Indians owned automobiles, and these were very hard on our dirt roads. We calculated that 95 percent of the traffic on our reservation was white-owned cars. Our roads had become badly rutted as a result of this constant through traffic. The money received in car registration fees and gasoline taxes could well have been used to pay for a project to repair our roads which the white people were wearing out. White and Indian would thus both be benefited by such a project. We accordingly petitioned both Indian Agent W. K. Harrison and Indian Commissioner John Collier to help us in securing this project. I also wrote to Mr. Collier requesting that the Bureau of Indian Affairs help us in establishing a practical trades or training shop so that our people might be trained for useful occupations. The United States government had two important treaties with our people: the Treaty of Canandaigua of November 11, 1794, and the Treaty with the Oneidas, Tuscaroras, and Stockbridges of December 2, 1794. These old treaties promised that sawmills and gristmills would be set up for us, young men trained as millers and sawyers, and husbandry established. By organizing a training school, or building these establishments in accordance with the treaties, the government would just be living up to its old unfulfilled promises. We were asking for a modern application of this guarantee of economic assistance in order to help us over our present difficulties.

When the white men first came to this continent, they were few, weak, and feeble. Our people could have easily wiped them out, but we took them to be our friends. We gave them land to plant corn on for their women and children; we gave them many plant foods unknown to them, such as corn, squash, beans, and many more. We showed them how to get sap from the maple tree, told them how to make snowshoes, canoes, and moccasins. We taught them how to hunt and take care of themselves in our country. When famine walked among them and their little ones cried for bread, it was the Indians who gave them meat, corn, and fish. The hand that fought for the white man in all his wars—the Revolutionary War, the War of 1812, the Civil War, the Spanish-American War, and the World War—was now open to him for relief.

We did not get our road project or our training shops. The Indian Bureau dallied for many years, and then, when my people, in despair, began to argue among themselves, Agent Harrison wrote me in early 1936 and told me that because of the attitude and sentiment of our people, there would be no opportunity for any projects on our reservation. The bureaucrats were using our most recent disagreements as an excuse not to give us projects, though when we made the request, the sentiment was unanimous for them. I wrote to Agent Harrison complaining of his unfortunate attitude toward my people. "Do the Democrats, Republicans, Socialists, and Communists all agree?" I asked. "They do not, but they get the projects just the same."[3]

Some of us were able to get work on federal projects like WPA, though this work was never steady. When the weather was below 10° above zero, there was never any WPA work carried on. My Indian people would have worked in any weather, and that is why we craved work on our own reservation. Whenever we experienced a cold winter, many days we traveled into Niagara Falls only to be told that work was suspended for the day. A twenty-mile round trip for nothing and more money for transportation gone out of our pockets!

There was much incredible bungling in dispensing the relief assistance that did come our way. White men who worked on WPA received issues of national food surplus. When we Indians obtained work on the WPA, our surplus food issue was immediately discontinued. What we had been receiving was not given us in the initial issuing along with white people, but was just what was left over from nearby towns and districts. Issues of surplus food were frequently late in reaching us or did not reach us at all. When I inquired in the Buffalo office one time why we had not received our issue, the lady who spoke with me told me she did not know we had not received our portion and it was too bad because she had already sent it back. On a number of occasions I had appealed for food for our Tuscarora people to George Elson, who was in charge of this relief office and was told by him that we had nowhere to store it on our reservation. This was a stupid answer for we always issued the food as soon as we received it and had no need of a storage depot. On another occasion, I learned that there had been some Red Cross clothing meant for our use stored at our schoolhouse for many months over the winter and never given out. The nurse and Miss Helen Wayne from the relief office were in charge of this clothing. During the winter, some of our men suffered frozen feet and hands while working out in the cold, but this clothing sat unused in boxes in the schoolhouse when it could have been used to keep our people warm.

Miss Wayne once remarked to me: "There is no use to give Indians a job because they won't save money." Now here was a strange notion indeed! A woman who has a steady job and not a care in the world thinks that Indians who can get work only two days a week—if that— can support their families, pay high food prices, and still have enough money left to put away in the bank. It was attitudes like this that made the depression even harder for Indians than for whites.

Were it not for our good white friends who voluntarily came to our assistance, we would have been in even more desperate circumstances than we already were. We were especially grateful to the Boy Scouts who, without regard to race and without thought of gain, collected shoes and other clothing for needy Indians. We were also thankful to the

Sisters of Christian Charity in New York City, who so mercifully sent clothing to be used by our needy.

Even though the depression had forced me out of farming for the time being, I was still able to continue with a smaller garden to provide food for my family. Also, I donated as much of this food as I could to my Indian neighbors who were in need. It was the old tradition that we should share what we have and help each other in time of trouble.

The depression also ruined the forest on our reservation. We used to have a fine stand of virgin timber, so thick that a person who was unfamiliar with the forest could get lost after going only a few yards into it. The old folks had always cherished our forest and said it would save us some day. During the depression, some of our people began cutting the wood in our national forest and selling it to the white people by the cord. We Tuscaroras all owned this woods equally, and to have a few cut and sell month after month meant the final destruction of our woodland and the robbing of the rest of the people of their future share. While the rest of us were compelled to work on WPA or support ourselves as best we could, these few made their living by the complete ruination of our timberland.

In the midst of the depression years, another threat arose to endanger our way of life. This was the proposal put forward by Indian Commissioner John Collier and by congress in the Wheeler-Howard Act, or Indian Reorganization Act. I had a copy of this act and had read it carefully, as had many of our Tuscarora people. There were many in the community who did not understand just what it was John Collier wanted us to do. It was plain that, among other things, the act required Indian nations to draw up written constitutions and incorporate, which were practices totally foreign to us. We had our own form of government and felt that our way was just as good for us as the white man's way was for him. We saw no reason to incorporate and reorganize our government just to please the politicians in Washington. If we wanted to change any of our ways, we would do so according to our needs, but we did not want outsiders telling us how to run our affairs. We did not tell the white man how to run his government. We would thank him to let us make our own decisions.

The Wheeler-Howard Act permitted incorporated tribal governments to handle federal money which would come to Indian nations and individuals as loan funds. Some of our people felt that there was a likelihood that the chiefs in power would just pass this money out to friends and relatives and the rest of the nation would not benefit.

My brother Edgar was one of the few members of our nation strongly in favor of the Wheeler-Howard Act. His attitude toward this legislation brought about a decline in his influence in the community and and on the Chiefs' Council, for our people were strongly opposed to Washington's attempt to reorganize our traditional government and customs.

All the nations of the Iroquois Confederacy overwhelmingly turned down the Wheeler-Howard Act. Within our own Tuscarora Nation, the vote was taken on June 12, 1935, and was 132 to 6 in favor of rejection.

While we were still attempting to pull ourselves out of the depression, World War II came upon us. I had been able to make out quite well in reestablishing my farm, especially since my two eldest sons were now able to help me and even undertake projects on their own. Others had also begun to establish themselves and become self-reliant once more. Now the war came and took our young men away wholesale. This was the unfortunate result of the 1924 Indian Citizenship Act. Prior to that time, the government did not draft Indians, as they were not considered citizens, but many of my Indian people throughout the country had always volunteered for every war. Now, we had no choice. We did not request this citizenship, did not want it, and opposed it. We now saw how it could be used in violation of our treaties.

My son Clark was drafted, even though he was a farm worker. It was much easier for white farmers to get deferments than it was for Indian farmers. The drafting of Indians into the United States armed forces was a violation of our sovereignty as Indian nations. It also had the effect of forcing many Indian farmers out of work when their elder sons were taken and making support of the remaining family more difficult.

In his army career, Clark went through some of the worst horrors of the war, including the Battle of the Bulge, but came out unharmed. William, my eldest son, was not taken into the army because of his continued poor physical condition. All the physically able young men from our reserve were drafted regularly into the armed services throughout the war.

We had two special grievances against the United States government at this time. One was the draft of Indians and the other was the Alien Registration Act. By this latter act, our North American Indians who came from north of the Canadian–United States border were required to register as aliens. We who once owned this whole continent from sunrise to sunset and who never knew of any Canadian boundary line were now considered aliens in our own land.

Our Indian Defense League fought this Alien Registration Act. At the Border Crossing Celebration, we demonstrated against this most unjust law which considered Indians to be foreigners. Dave Hill had thought up a motto which we had painted on a large sign to be carried in our parade. It read: WE DID NOT FINGERPRINT THE PILGRIMS. In addition to this demonstration, a delegation including Angus Horne, Ivan Burnham, and myself went to Washington, D.C., to protest this law. Indians in Canada were never considered Canadian citizens unless they had been enfranchised. This was the only way in which they could give up their Indian citizenship and take on foreign, or Canadian, citizenship.

For a number of years, our Indian people fought this law. Chiefs from Caughnawaga and Six Nations Reserves were particularly active in protesting, as was our own Indian Defense League of America. But the United States government still persists in considering our native North American Indians to be aliens. Actually, it is just the other way around. It is the white people who are the aliens in our own land and perhaps we should require them to register.

We also opposed the military draft of Indians. The Tuscarora General Council, which was the People's Council as distinct from the Chiefs' Council, determined to oppose this draft on the basis that we rejected enforced citizenship, in violation of our old treaties which promised that the government would not molest us. We were not United States citizens, no matter what the government said. We were Six Nations citizens. Harry Patterson, Noah Henry, and I were authorized to make a financial appeal to take this case to the Supreme Court of the United States. We had absolutely no objection to our young men serving in the armed forces, but we did object to a violation of our national sovereignty and a brushing aside of our treaties as well as the government's legislating for us. We had a test case involving Eldreth Green, a young Onondaga who was resisting the draft on the grounds that he was not a United

States citizen. The case was decided against us in the Federal Circuit Court of Appeals in November 1941. We hired attorney Wilfred E. Hoffman to take this case on appeal to the United States Supreme Court. Unfortunately, the court refused to recognize our treaties or our sovereignty in this regard.

At one time in the 1940s, our Defense League had a very unfortunate experience with the Buffalo Branch of the IDLA. There were some people in this group who became overly impressed with their own importance to the extent that they forgot that the purpose of our organization is to bring all Indians together in unity to protect the rights of our people. They set out to gain for themselves power and influence by wrecking our Defense League.

This group applied for and received a charter from the State of New York, calling themselves "Indian Defense League of America, Inc." They then proceeded to have their own border crossing before ours. At seven o'clock in the morning on the day of our Border Crossing Celebration, Ivan Burnham came to my house and warned me that this bogus IDLA had a warrant out for Dave Hill's and my arrest for misrepresentation. They said their group was the true IDLA.

William and I went to see the U.S. marshal and explained the matter to him, giving him proof that we represented the original organization. As I was speaking, the sheriff came in and heard the story. He clapped me on the shoulder and said: "Rickard is right!"

Our attorney informed us that we could easily have caught them in their own trap and had them arrested for fraud and for swearing out a warrant falsely. They lyingly claimed to be the original Defense League that had held border crossings since 1928, but according to their charter they had been in existence less than a year.

The marshal asked me if I wanted to have them arrested for swearing out a warrant falsely. I could certainly have done so, for not only had they broken the white man's law, but they had violated Indian custom. But Dave Hill said: "Oh, let them go!" And I let the matter pass.

The whole bunch of them were down at the bridge that day to see Dave and me get arrested. They were more than surprised to find that their little scheme had backfired. After that, this group just fizzled out, and we heard no more from them.

This was not my only experience with betrayers. One of the young men of our reservation came to my house some years ago and expressed a great interest in the Indian Defense League and in Indian affairs in general. I was happy for this young man's interest. Also, I discovered that he knew how to type. I thought that we had found some one who could help us in the Defense League and who would do good for Indians. William and I therefore took him and trained him in Indian affairs. He also expressed an eagerness to be my secretary, so we allowed him free access to my desk. One day he stole much valuable research material, including a document on Indian rights that William and I had been working on for months, and published this document word for word under his own name as his "Findings." Then he presented a bill for the printing expenses to the IDLA, which we of course refused to pay. Later I saw his dishonesty in land dealings with different people on our reservation. Money was a great object with him. At various times, he borrowed many hundreds of dollars from different individuals with the promise that he would soon pay these sums back because he was earning good wages, but he never paid back a penny. When his creditors tried to collect, he would either ignore them or take off on a trip for a couple of months. Dave Hill was one of the people he cheated in this way. He was also always bragging to the white people about his great accomplishments—most of which were imaginary, but some of which were things that other people had done and that he took credit for. Whenever Indians anywhere were working on a project, he was always there at the last minute to get in front of the newspaper or television cameras and to take the reporters aside and give them the most outlandish accounts of how he was the leader of this project and many others besides—all of which nonsense was printed as exact truth by these simpleminded white men. It was clear that his major aim was self-publicity and that he would stop at nothing to get it. Greatly disappointed, I determined I did not want him around me or in my house ever again.

Shortly after the end of the Second World War, the Indian Defense League of America fought an immigration case of great significance. Dorothy Goodwin, a Cayuga from Six Nations Reservation on the Grand River, married a white man from Niagara Falls, Ontario. According to the Canadian Indian Act, any Indian woman who marries a white man immediately loses her status as an Indian. Dorothy kept crossing the border at will, as guaranteed by the Jay Treaty and the act of April

2, 1928. When the American immigration officials discovered that she was married to a white man, however, they arrested her on July 13, 1946, and put her in jail for eight or nine months awaiting deportation.

I was asked to intercede for this poor woman who was being treated like a criminal simply because of her marriage. In order to protest this injustice, I was sent to Philadelphia by the Indian Defense League to the commissioner of immigration to plead this woman's case. Dave Hill went along with me to support our plea.

When we appeared before the commissioner, I explained the case in detail to him and complained that the United States was abiding by a foreign law in violation of its own laws. The commissioner commented: "Well, you did say enough to let the girl go, but the government wants a test case." Then he continued: "I'll do this. I'll give you a statement to have her released in your custody."

After securing the papers, I went to the jail where Dorothy Goodwin was being held to obtain her release. The person in charge said to me: "This is the first time that this has ever happened in the twenty years that I've been here that an Indian has been released in the custody of an Indian."

We reported to the Immigration and Naturalization Service in Buffalo, and the official gave me the privilege of saying how often Mrs. Goodwin should report to me during her parole.

I said: "This poor girl has suffered all this time for nothing. Once a month is enough." The parole papers were thereupon made out and signed on August 6, 1946. She reported to me for over a year while the case was pending.

Later, I traveled to Washington to appear before the Board of Appeals and review the case. I remarked to the four men on the board: "I do resent it very much that this country has brought a foreign law to jeopardize my people and put them in jail for no reason whatsoever."

The board members told me: "You said enough to let her go, but the government still wants a test case."

The board members were most sympathetic. In fact, one of them had been an officer of mine in the Philippines and remembered my service under him. I did feel encouraged by his good words to me.

The Indian Defense League had retained Edward E. Franchot, a very distinguished trial lawyer, to try our case, which was called for September 15, 1947, in Buffalo. It was to be tried before Federal Judge

John Knight. Attorney Franchot and I took Dorothy Goodwin before Judge Knight on a writ of habeas corpus and she was released in my custody in August of 1947, pending trial. The poor woman was much relieved at this, for she had been crying continuously on the way to the court for fear that she would be sent to jail again.

On the day of the trial, an immigration commissioner from Ottawa came to press the charge against Dorothy Goodwin. After the trial was over, he said to me: "Chief, you are not going to win this case this time."

I told him: "Sir, we're going to win this case if there is justice. If there is no justice, we are going to proceed and fight on!"

In November of 1947, Judge Knight rendered his decision in Dorothy Goodwin's favor. In the opinion of the court, Indians born in Canada or on reserves north of the United States border remained Indians racially without regard to their political status. Attorney Franchot had rightly claimed that there are no rules in the United States Immigration Service which interfered with the right of North American Indians to cross the border, whether they are married to whites or any other race. Judge Knight gave a good decision and Attorney Franchot did a splendid job in arguing the case for us.[4]

There was another reason why we felt grateful to our attorney. He was a lawyer of outstanding ability and could command a high fee. His law firm had worked hard on this case and had given us their best. But when it was over and we had won, Mr. Franchot told us he was reducing the charge from $3,000 to $1,500, because, as he said: "You are an oppressed people."

Attorney Franchot was much interested in minority groups and represented a number of our Indian people in various cases. It was thus with great sorrow that we learned of his tragic death in an automobile accident some time later. He had devoted considerable time to protecting our rights in the law courts and was always active in other civic and community affairs. We Indians and the residents of Niagara Falls lost a true friend with his death.

Beginning in 1948 and for several years thereafter, representatives of the Six Nations Confederacy made an annual trip to the United Nations headquarters in New York City. We brought our message of peace to this world body and reminded the delegates we met that we were the first United Nations. In 1949, a group of us from the Six Nations attended the cornerstone laying of the UN building in Manhattan. In 1950, we presented a petition to the United Nations protesting the attempts of Canada, the United States, and the State of New York to assume jurisdiction over our Six Nations Confederacy and called attention to our opposition to the attempts of these foreign powers to assimilate our people. In 1952, we petitioned the United Nations to admit the Six Nations Confederacy to membership. This petition was pigeonholed.

These trips to the UN were arranged for us by Emery J. Kocsis, who had been pastor of our Tuscarora Baptist Church from 1939 to 1945 and at the time of our visits was pastor at a church in New Jersey. He served as UN observer for the Indian Defense League of America and was one of our most active honorary members. Pastor Kocsis, who was originally from Hungary, had done much for our Indian people over the years and was very highly thought of on our Tuscarora Reservation. He was an especially good friend to me and my family. Our IDLA had adopted him and given him the name of Peace Messenger.

One of the great things our Indian Defense League of America was able to do around this time to preserve our heritage, despite continued attempts to assimilate us, was to initiate the annual Six Nations Pageant at Grand River. This pageant is held in a very beautiful outdoor setting and each year several thousand people attend to see the presentation of Iroquois history. Emily General has been the leading inspiration behind this pagant, and for many years it was held on her grounds on the reserve. After the IDLA's early sponsorship of the pageant, the group at Grand River that had worked so hard on it took over responsibility for its continuance. The pageant is now independent of the IDLA, but several IDLA members like Emily General and William Smith continue their good work with it.[5]

For many years, I have been very active in Boy Scout, veterans, and Masonic Lodge work. The work with young people is one of the things I enjoy most. I have frequently lectured to Boy Scout groups on Indian history and customs. In addition, I urge the boys to take their Scout oath seriously, to live clean, upright lives, and to keep away from things that will be harmful to them. A number of these Scout troops have made me an honorary member and have presented me with their official neckerchiefs.

In the spring of 1951, a scoutmaster friend asked me if a group of three hundred scouts might camp for a weekend on my farm. I agreed immediately and allowed them the use of my east field. This field is completely surrounded by bush and so provided them with privacy. The boys were so well mannered during their whole stay that we hardly knew they were around.

The two veterans' organizations that I have been most active in are the Veterans of Foreign Wars and the United Spanish War Veterans. I took the lead in organizing Tuscarora Post No. 8442, Veterans of Foreign Wars, on our reservation on April 24, 1955. We had a membership of forty, and I was chosen as the first commander. When I was no longer able to be active regularly, the post declined and finally dissolved. I then had my membership transferred to Niagara Falls Post No. 54, where, as a Spanish War veteran, I was made a life member.

I have also served for a number of years as commander of M. B. Butler Camp No. 7, United Spanish War Veterans. As these old veterans gradually pass away, our camp has declined to three members, representing three races. People call us the "Red, White, and Black." Besides myself, these comrades are Fred Shipston and Frank Robinson.

One activity that has been of great interest to me has been my work with the Niagara Falls Memorial Day Association, on which I have served both as president and honorary president. This group consists of veterans, military, and civic organizations and exists to sponsor the annual Memorial Day parade and tribute to veterans on May 30.

A special honor that I shall always remember came to me as a veteran on November 11, 1961, when four veterans from our reservation participated in a wreath-laying ceremony at the Tomb of the Unknown Soldier in Arlington National Cemetery. The group consisted of Chester Bomberry and Edward Chew, both World War II veterans; Sanford Pembleton, a Korean War veteran; and myself, a Spanish War veteran. This special ceremony was arranged by Lillian Valleau, who was a member of both the League of North American Indians, of which my son William was president, and of the Daughters of the American Revolution. Indians fought in all American wars, but I believe this was the first time an Indian organization had ever paid this tribute to our honored dead. As I placed the wreath on the grave, my thoughts flashed back to my comrades who had been burned alive in the Philippines, and I wondered if their bones might not lay here in this cemetery.

On that same day, I took the opportunity to visit Fort Myer, which is close by, and see again the place where I had soldiered sixty years before. There were many changes in the camp since I had last seen it as a young trooper.

We then caught a plane back home and arrived in time for the annual banquet of the IDLA at the Sheraton-Brock Hotel in Niagara Falls, Ontario.[6]

My lodge work has also been close to my heart ever since I first joined the Masons in 1913. I have been a member of Ransomville Lodge No. 551 now for well over fifty years. I am also a Thirty-second degree Mason and a member of the Buffalo Consistory and of Ames Chapter No. 88 Royal Arch Masons, Bruce Council Cryptic Rite Royal Select Masters, Palmoni Lodge of Perfection 15°, Palmoni Council Princes of Jerusalem 16°, Buffalo Chapter of Rose Croix 18°, Ismalia Temple of Buffalo, and the Seneca Shrine Club. Many years ago, I was made an honorary member of Ely Parker Lodge of Buffalo, named after the famous Seneca chief, who was a faithful Mason. I have been color bearer of this lodge for over forty years and have attended every installation ceremony except one, when the snows kept me home.

The work of protecting the rights of my Indian people also has kept me constantly busy. We could never relax, for there always seemed to be some danger to our existence that would come from the government. We had to keep an eagle eye on the politicians to prevent them from destroying our way of life.

During the administrations of Presidents Truman and Eisenhower, the Indian people faced some of the most severe assaults against their sovereignty, their way of life, and their well-being. In the late 1940s and early 1950s, we were constantly assailed by a government that wanted to be rid of its responsibilities to us in violation of our old treaties. We had ceded most of our land—this whole continent—from which the European settlers were now making great profit. All we asked was to be guaranteed the small portion of the country yet remaining to us and to be assured that the government would abide by the agreements it had made in return for the cessions of our lands.

As New York State had been doing for many years previously, it again resumed its attempt to gain control over my Indian people. Several bills were pending in Congress in 1948 which would have turned the Indians of the Six Nations over to New York State. New York would then exercise both civil and criminal jurisdiction over our reservations. We could not see why the New York politicians were so anxious for this jurisdiction unless they coveted our lands. We knew that the federal government was always a better protector of Indian lands than were the state governments. After the American Revolution, New York State made a very successful effort to take away Indian lands so that today we are left with only a fraction of what we once owned at the close of the Revolution. We have never forgotten this. Unfortunately for us, the federal government at this time was in the mood to "get out of the Indian business."

I went to Washington in March of 1948 and testified before the Senate Interior Subcommittee on Indian Affairs against the move to give New York State complete civil and criminal jurisdiction over our Indian nations. This would be a further threat to the tribal law which governed our reserves and a step toward a breakdown within our communities. The white man is always talking about making the Indians self-reliant, but he refuses to let them govern themselves in peace. These outside threats kept my people in a continual state of anxiety. They impressed upon us the feeling that the white man felt the Indian way to be inferior. How can we succeed if we are constantly being told that to be successful we must imitate white men in all ways? The white people tolerate within their midst such nonconformist groups as the Hutterites and the Amish. Why can they not also tolerate Indians who want to be themselves? We also want to be free to practice the ways that we think are good.

Despite the great opposition of our Six Nations people to New York State jurisdiction, this act passed Congress. The politicians once more had contempt for what Indian people wanted. We were not asked, we were told what was good for us. It is humiliating to my people always to be treated like children.

In 1949, the federal Indian office in New York was ordered closed. An agent had been sent in to terminate the last business of this office, and then he also was withdrawn. Although we opposed this ending of our relationship with the United States government, in direct violation of our treaties, we were not overly sorry to see this agent go. The government had provided a loan fund for Indians who wished to improve their farms, and my son William went to Buffalo to apply to Agent Benge for a loan of $500. The agent agreed, and handed William papers already filled out, only awaiting his signature. William saw that the papers were made out in favor of the Crandall Horse Company. He protested that this was not what he wanted.

The agent said: "Why, I assumed you wanted this loan for power on your farm."

"Yes," said William, "but I want to buy a tractor. I can plow ten times as much with a tractor as I can with a team of horses."

"Sorry," said the agent, "I can't authorize the loan for that."

William tore the papers up, threw the pieces into the agent's face, and walked out of the office.

The Crandall Horse Company sold only half-broken horses to Indians, and these were too dangerous to use. They would kick the side out of a barn. One of our farmers had his leg broken plowing with these half-wild animals and had to get rid of them. We believed that the agent and the horse company must have had some sort of agreement to channel business with Indians to the Crandall people. What good was the loan fund to us under those circumstances?

The beginning of the federal government's policy of terminating its trusteeship over Indian affairs and breaking up Indian communities was found in the Hoover Commission Report of 1949, which the Indian Defense League strongly opposed. The commission wanted to convert all Indians in the United States into full taxpaying citizens, taxing every inch of reservation lands. The commission also proposed putting all reservations and Indian affairs under the jurisdiction of the various states. Not only did this new plan violate our ancient treaties, it also threatened the many poor Indians who could afford to live in a house they called their own because they paid no taxes on their lands. Making them taxpayers would force them to give up their small holdings, to struggle for existence, and eventually to lose their houses and end up on city or county welfare rolls. The Hoover report also wanted Indians to be allowed to sell their reservation lands to whites. We saw what happened with a similar proposal in the nineteenth century when the General Allotment Act was passed. Western Indians became poverty-stricken and lost millions of acres of land to whites. The Hoover Commission plan was an unscrupulous proposal. Even though Indians bitterly opposed this project, it became a reality in the Eisenhower administration, and the federal government began "terminating" its responsibility for Indian affairs, tribe by tribe. The great disaster this policy proved to be to the Klamaths, the Menominees, and other tribes is now history.

The Klamaths were browbeaten by the Bureau of Indian Affairs to approve of termination and to take individual payments as the tribal assets were liquidated. Off-reservation Klamaths were brought back in droves by the BIA to swing the vote in favor of termination. Now the Klamaths' money is spent, their homelands are gone, and their extensive and rich lumber-producing lands have been sold off to private lumber interests and this once-perpetual income lost to them forever.

The Menominees were also forced by the BIA, against their wishes, to accept termination. Their reservation then became a county in the state of Wisconsin and the Menominees were forced to set up a county administration. The state also forced them to tax their lands to raise money to support this new county administration, which was an alien type of government to them. As a result of this land taxation, many poor people lost their homes and were in most desperate circumstances with no place to live. The BIA had always operated the Menominee lumber lands but had never given these Indian people training in operating the lumber business on their own. The result of the BIA's sudden pullout was a disaster for the Menominees. The state of Wisconsin also shut down the old BIA-run Indian hospital on the former reservation because it did not meet state standards. So, in addition to losing everything else, these poor people also lost their health care.

Events of the recent past proved to us that we could never relax. We always had to be on the alert to protect our people against injustice. The Indian Defense League of America continued to oppose termination and also the land-grab going on in Alaska at the expense of Indians and Eskimos. Everywhere we looked throughout the country, our way of life and our lands were in danger. We tried to live in peace, but the government would give us no peace. In the old days, the Indian was always going on the warpath to protect his rights. Now in our own day, we still have to go on the warpath. The only thing that has changed is that today we Indians use peaceful weapons. We organize, we write letters, we make speeches, we go to court, we have demonstrations, and we rouse up friendly white people to support us. We are determined to fight to the end for those things that are most precious to us.

The State Power Authority

THE GREATEST THREAT to my Tuscarora people since the days of the North Carolina wars and the removal to Kansas came in the 1950s as a result of the New York State Power Authority's attempt to grab our lands. In the long battle we waged with the Power Authority, we were brought face to face with the danger we had long feared from state encroachment on our lands. The state had not wanted control over Indians for nothing. Now we saw at first hand what this control meant.

To the white man, who is accustomed to buying and selling land as a business, the earth is only a commodity. To the Indian, the land is a gift from the Great Spirit, to be held in trust for the ever-coming generations. In the old days, before we were thoroughly hemmed in by Europeans, the land was our complete source of support. Now, even though many of our people have been forced to earn their way in the white man's world, our land still supplies much of our support. When I worked in an outside occupation, I would do a day's labor on the farm besides. Oftentimes my boys have worked late at night by the light of the tractor plowing and cultivating their fields after their daily wage work for the white man was finished. So it is with many of my people who hold a job off the reservation during the day and till their fields early in the morning and late in the evening, putting in two full days' work in a single day.

We love our lands that the Great Spirit has blessed and has given to us. All our men and boys hunt and fish on our reserve and some are very good providers for their families. Our streams and our woods provide less fish and game than in the old days, but what they do give us we gratefully receive as a gift from our Creator. The white man sees our woods and bush and thinks they are waste. We know better, for here we get our fuel and our timber, and here the wild animals have their homes. The land holds us together; it makes our community. Without our land, we are nothing. The white man can make his community anywhere. Wherever he goes across this continent, he can buy a house and lot or rent an apartment and melt into the neighborhood. When the Indian moves from his reservation, he leaves his community behind and becomes an outsider in the white man's land—a land that was once his own. To us, the earth is sacred. Only through our closeness to the earth can our spirit survive. This is why we were determined to fight to protect our land.

In January of 1957, William Latham, State Power Authority engineer, and a Mr. Smith came to my home and asked my assistance in getting authority for them to survey on our reservation. They said they did not want to use any of our land for the SPA project that was planned for Niagara County, but just wanted to survey a part of our reserve. I told them I did not have authority to grant them such permission but would arrange a meeting of our nation where they could present their proposals to our people. I suggested they get in touch with Hamilton Mt. Pleasant, who at that time was chairman of the General Council, or People's Council.

A meeting of the People's Council was held early in March of 1957 to hear Latham and two of his associates explain their proposal to our people. Latham told us that the SPA wished to conduct a survey on our reserve solely for the purpose of determining the depth of soil down to bed rock and would in no way interfere with any of our people. He stated that he had not come to buy land and that was not the issue. He was asked if he would buy reservation land, and he replied: "Yes, when and if we needed it." He said the SPA had not bought any land in Niagara County yet and kept assuring us that all the SPA wanted was to make surveys in the area to determine the most economical way of building a water storage reservoir for power purposes.

It was quite plain to us that the SPA did not wish to survey our land for the pleasure of surveying it. We knew that if they had an eye on our land, they had a plan to build the reservoir there. These engineers had come to us like wolves in sheep's clothing.

My son William moved to deny permission to the SPA engineers to survey. The motion was seconded by Harriet Pembleton and carried unanimously. The Chiefs' Council then also unanimously turned down this proposal from the engineers. We had only a small quantity of land, and we wanted to preserve it for our own use forever. It was all that we had left to us after many years of migration northward and westward in order to find a place where we could live out our lives in peace.

From the time he was a young boy, I had known that one day William would be able to help our people. For several years, he had been serving as my secretary. He had worked closely with me in the Indian Defense League and had taken a keen interest in Indian problems. Now, when our people were in danger, he was ready with wise counsel and determination to resist injustice. During our many months of controversy with the State Power Authority, I was undergoing a long illness and was not able to enter fully into the resistance campaign. William took this work upon himself, writing letters and reports, organizing meetings, and taking trips to Washington. My people called him "Fighting Bear." We knew we could depend upon him to stand for what was right.

Despite the soothing words spoken to us by the SPA engineers assuring us that they did not want our lands but just the right to survey them, we were shocked to find that the state planned to confiscate a large section of our reserve for a reservoir. In September of 1957, the *Niagara Falls Gazette* carried a map showing that the SPA planned to take 950 acres in the western section of our reservation. Our Chiefs' Council sent strong letters of protest to Washington, addressed to President Eisenhower, Secretary of Interior Fred A. Seaton, and Federal Power Commission Chairman Jerome K. Kuykendall.

These protests did no good. We were informed that our Six Nations people were no longer under the protection of the United States government but had been turned over to New York State. We had been thrown to the wolves, so to speak. We knew we could expect no mercy from the state. What the state wanted from us, it would take; we could depend on that.

In November of 1957, another SPA map was published in the *Niagara Falls Gazette* showing that the state now wanted 1,220 acres of our reserve for the reservoir. The situation looked very bad for us and we scarcely knew which way to turn for help. We were determined to resist in order to keep our lands. Fighting to protect our homes has always been the history of the Indian people ever since the Europeans first set foot in our country.

Late in the afternoon of November 8, 1957, we received word from some of our good white friends that a hearing would be held the next day before the Federal Power Commission in Washington, D.C. William, with Elton Greene and Harry Patterson of the Chiefs' Council, immediately left for Washington and arrived in time for the hearing. Both the commission and the SPA lawyers attempted to prevent our representatives from testifying because they did not have an attorney with them. Our men persisted and were finally granted permission to give their testimony but were warned that this was the last time they would be allowed to speak.

The hearings were then adjourned to Buffalo. William and my wife's sister between them attended every hour of the four-day hearings. Here they listened to representatives from the Town of Lewiston, in which the reservoir was to be located, protesting against losing so much of the township's taxable land. Their solution was to recommend that the SPA take nontaxable Indian land instead. Here again we saw too plainly how our closest neighbors would give us the least justice.

Shortly after these hearings the Federal Power Commission granted a license to the SPA to continue with its plans. To our shock, the SPA now announced that it intended to take 1,383 acres, or over one-fifth of our reserve. We now knew that we were in deep trouble for the government had decided against us. We would have to continue the fight on our own.

Through the efforts of Elon Crouse, my wife's brother-in-law, we retained the law firm of Spiegelberg, Strasser, Fried and Frank in Washington, D.C. This firm had much experience with Indian cases. With only two days left to meet the deadline, attorneys Arthur Lazarus, Jr., and Richard Schifter filed our protest brief for us.

The SPA did not remain idle while our case was in progress. On March 19, 1958, we received a call from a white friend informing us that SPA attorneys were in Lockport in the Niagara County Clerk's office searching land titles and filing maps of our reserve. Our friend told us that the SPA representatives intended to come right into our reserve and begin surveying.

Some members of the Tuscarora resistance committee then prepared to meet this threat. These people met in our house and decided to make warning notices which would be put up at every entrance to our reserve. The signs were posted by one of our young warriors, John Hewitt, who was a great-grandson of Alvis Hewitt. They read as follows:

WARNING!

TO

OFFICIALS, SURVEYORS, CONTRACTORS
AND EMPLOYEES OF THE NIAGARA
POWER PROJECT OF THE S.P.A.

NO TRESPASSING!

BY ORDER OF THE TUSCARORA NATION

The *Niagara Falls Gazette* published a picture on March 10, 1958, showing some of our people standing beside these notices. This annoyed the SPA and its chairman, Robert Moses, who sent out an open letter accusing our people of obstructing progress. Moses thought we should be glad to get the $1,100 an acre he was offering us for our land. To us, the land was priceless and could never be sold.

In April of 1958, the SPA got an appropriation bill through the New York State Legislature to permit them to take Indian lands. Governor Averell Harriman gave his approval to SPA expropriation of our homeland. The SPA then sent in surveyors on April 16. We gathered at the survey site to block the attempts to take over our land, and the chiefs ordered the trespassers off. That evening, the SPA issued announcements on radio and television saying that they would be back the next day with police protection to continue their work. Our people were ready for them. We had sent out a call for assistance to our brothers in the Six Nations and volunteers poured in from all the other tribes. Our young people going by bus to high school in Niagara Falls decided they were more needed back home and directed the driver to return to the reservation. They, too, joined in the passive resistance to block the surveyors.

On the morning of April 17, our reservation was invaded by SPA legal staff, workmen, and a small army of paid gun slingers. There were about thirty-five Niagara County deputy sheriffs, fifty state troopers, and a large number of plainclothesmen. In addition to the regular sidearms, these police invaders had riot equipment, tear gas, and submachine guns in their cars. With this show of force, they attempted to intimidate our people, assembled for peaceful protest, into giving up. They did not succeed. Our people—men, women, and children—stood firm.

A certain James Williams from the New York State Indian Social Service began ordering the chiefs to send the protestors home. My son

William confronted him and asked him what his authority was. Williams replied that he was there to carry out Governor Harriman's appropriation bill. William denied the authority of the state to appropriate Indian lands, and James Williams thereupon cited the Criminal Jurisdiction Act of 1948 and the Civil Jurisdiction Act of 1950, giving New York State control of Indian affairs. William continued to deny the validity of those acts, which were passed over the unanimous opposition of the Six Nations. He told Williams that he had been present in Washington for both hearings and that the bills were both pushed through at the end of each congressional session. Williams then discontinued his conversation and returned to the police.

As our people were standing about peacefully, on our own reservation, the police suddenly, without any provocation whatsoever, seized three of our men, whom they had recognized from their pictures in the *Gazette* a few days previously. All men were nonresisting at the time. Four deputy sheriffs attacked William, beat him to the ground, and dragged him to their car. The other men were also shoved into the police cars. With these arrests and the roughing up of our men, some of the women and children began shoving and scratching the police. A surveyor kicked one of our women, and only after our repeated insistance was he placed under arrest for assault.

It was fortunate for us that we had a local attorney on hand when our men were arrested, for, as it turned out, this arrest and punishment were all planned ahead of time. Legally, according to white man's law, these protesters should have been taken to the justice of the peace in the district closest to where they were arrested, which would have been Lewiston. Instead, they were taken out of the district to Justice of the Peace Gamble in Sanborn—a man well-known for his especially hard feelings against Indians. The justice of the peace in Lewiston, on the other hand, was always known to be friendly to Indians. When our men were brought into court, it was learned that William had been arrested for disorderly conduct and the other two for unlawful assembly. This on our own reservation!

William, when he saw that they were being taken before Judge Gamble, told the sheriff that this looked like a rigged affair. The sheriff made a grab for William but was pulled back by two deputies. He shouted at William: "I'll tell you where to go!" He then barred the newsmen from the court.

Our attorney asked that the charges against the three be dropped because the justice of the peace had no jurisdiction over Indians. Gamble denied the motion. Then the lawyer moved dropping the charges on the grounds of insufficient evidence. Gamble again denied the motion. Finally the attorney entered a plea of innocent and had the three released in his custody pending hearing on April 23.

When these three men with the attorney returned to the reserve, they were surrounded by newsmen who told them that, two hours before the arrest, Justice Gamble had issued a news release that the three had been arrested and sentenced to two weeks in the Niagara County jail. The newsmen had come to the reserve to get further details on the story and were much surprised to see the arrest just taking place. It was also shocking that Justice Gamble had pronounced sentence before either the arrest or a trial had taken place. Justice was in the pay of the State Power Authority.

The SPA also protected its surveyor who had been arrested for assault. When the trial was called, no notice was sent to the injured woman. The case against the surveyor was thereupon dismissed.

The case against our three men was adjourned three times and finally dismissed because no one appeared to press charges. The attempt to intimidate our people therefore failed. The SPA had wrongfully thought that resistance would collapse if a few persons were arrested. They misjudged our temper.

Our Washington attorney, Arthur Lazarus, had secured a restraining order against the SPA. On April 23, this order expired, and the surveyors again came in force to our reservation. They had with them a federal marshal with a restraining order forbidding the Tuscaroras from interfering with the surveyors. Our people looked upon this as most unjust and proceeded to stand in front of the transits. The marshal then served hundreds of these restraining orders and our people let them fall to the ground and continued with the peaceable protest.

We learned later from an article in the June 12, 1958, *Niagara Falls Gazette* that the SPA paid a total of $1,026 to the Niagara County Sheriff's office for all the gun slingers it had hired to intimidate our people during the time we were peacefully protecting our land.

During the period we were conducting our resistance campaign, our telephones were constantly tapped. There were telephone linemen working on our reserve twenty-four hours a day recording all our conversations. One day, a member of our nation called me on the telephone to discuss a particular situation. In reply, I commented: "If you are going to depend on *that,* we might as well give up." We were sitting in our parlor that same evening, watching a news broadcast on the Buffalo television station. The commentator announced that I had made an appeal to our Tuscarora people to call off our resistance since we were beaten and it was useless to fight on. To prove this lie, my voice was broadcast over the station saying: ". . . we might as well give up." We were thunderstruck. My telephone conversation earlier in the day had been recorded and the first part of the sentence deleted. Then this false report was sent to the local television station with my half-sentence to confirm it. Our enemy had stooped to the lowest depths in trying to defeat us.

William immediately telephoned the television station to protest this false report. The station denied having made such a statement and then cut him off. We never did get a retraction.

After this incident, whenever possible, we spoke over the phone in our own language. That stopped the spying. When our white friends called us and offered help, however, we had to speak in English. In these instances, the SPA was always able to anticipate our actions.

During our troubles, the writer Edmund Wilson came to our reservation to gather information for some articles he was writing for *The New Yorker* magazine. These articles were later published in a book called *Apologies to the Iroquois.* We do not take his book at all seriously because he was not among us long enough to know our people or our situation. There are a number of errors and misinterpretations in this book, some of which are very laughable. Everywhere he went on the different reservations, he was unable to understand or represent the Indian situation properly. Also, at least one person deliberately gave him misleading information, which he innocently printed as truth. But he did very accurately reveal many of these low tricks that had been used against us by Robert Moses and the SPA. In reply to Wilson's book, Moses issued a pamphlet entitled, *Tuscarora: Fiction and Fact,* on June 20, 1960. In it he denied the charges of unfair treatment by law enforcement officials and said of Wilson's charges of phone tapping: "He passed on completely ridiculous and false canards that the Indians' telephone wires were tapped and that a substantial number of them could talk Indian." If this was a canard, then let Holy Moses explain how my voice came to be recorded and this fraudulent report given to the television station.

A second restraining order against the SPA obtained by Attorney Lazarus expired on June 24, 1958. We could not get a renewal, and the surveyors and their lawyers poured in. They did not confine themselves to the 1,383 acres but roamed all over the reserve, claiming that their license gave them permission to work wherever they needed to. William obtained copies of all the Federal Power Commission orders and saw that the SPA license included *park* areas also. We feared then that the rest of our reserve would be turned into a park.

Some of the high-ranking SPA employees tried to make a personal profit out of our distress. William Latham, the chief engineer, and another engineer friend of his, came to my son William and asked him which land was his. William pointed out the land he and Clark and Eli had inherited from their mother. Latham then said that he would pay William big money if he would let them put a trailer court on it. Latham would then be able to rent this area out to the SPA workmen and their families, many of whom lived in trailers, and to other whites who owned trailers, and make a good income off our land.

William turned this offer down flat. He said: "We put crops on that land! Putting leach beds under it for trailers will ruin it for anything else. We'd never be able to farm it again." William was very angry. He told Latham that he would not do anything to help the white man exploit our reservation.

In the summer of 1958, representatives of the SPA came to our nation and held a meeting in the presence of our attorney. They offered us a $1,250,000 community center, new roads, free electricity, and the honor of having the SPA name one of its generating plants "Tuscarora." The people laughed and cried out: "Some deal!" We rejected this offer outright. The SPA later announced to the press that they would go to court to secure our land. We were prepared to oppose them all the way.

Finally, through our attorney, the SPA offered us $1,500,000 for our lands. This, they said, was their final offer. They had just paid Niagara University $5,000,000 for two hundred acres of land. Although our attorney recommended settlement, we directed him to fight the case in court. The land was not for sale. Lazarus urged reconsideration, for he said he had a very small chance of winning. He argued with us for hours. We would not give in but told him to go out and protect our lands. That was what he was hired for. We would take this case right on up to the Supreme Court of the United States.

Even though our appeal was still pending in the Court, Federal District Judge Burke of Rochester, New York, permitted the SPA to work on eighty-six acres of our land to erect power lines. Burke disregarded the fact that our case had not been finally decided in the courts when he issued this order. When the SPA men came onto our land to carry out this order, they did not confine themselves to the eighty-six acres.

A hearing on our problem was held before the Federal Power Commission in Washington, D.C., in November of 1958. The SPA had subpoenaed a room full of "experts" to testify on their behalf. The room was so crowded that our chiefs and representatives had to stand in the back of the room, after barely having been able to squeeze in through the doorway. At recess time, our representatives went forward and cleared the briefcases off the front row of seats so they could sit down. The most absurd and false information was presented for three days to the commission. Attorney Lazarus protested this drivel, but Mr. Fraze, the examiner, told him he was accepting all testimony.

The SPA had a long list of forestry, soil, and real estate witnesses who claimed that our land was next to worthless. Pictures were taken from the air of every spot on our reservation, including every single outhouse. The SPA lawyers decided that the extent of a people's civilization was determined by the number of flush toilets they had. The whole testimony was an enormously expensive attempt on the part of the SPA to belittle our Tuscarora people and our living conditions.

Robert Moses and his henchmen very clearly demonstrated their race prejudice and contempt for Indians. What they were trying to impress upon the FPC was the assumption that since this Indian community did not amount to anything, it had no right to stand in the way of whites who wanted Indian land for their own purposes. They respected only power and wealth and might, and we had none of these. That such a seemingly insignificant people would stand up to Robert Moses and fight back was the thing that infuriated him most of all, as his hysterical press releases only too plainly revealed.

Moses, in his *Tuscarora: Fiction and Fact* pamphlet, later repeated the same nonsense that was brought out at the hearing by saying: "the bulk of the land is not used for any purpose at all. Most of the farms have been abandoned and there is only one real farm run by an Indian on the reservation." A man who had spent his career dumping concrete over the landscape would, of course, not be able to see how people could be using land unless they did likewise. The "one real farm" he was referring to on our supposedly worthless reservation was owned by Barbara and Harry Patterson. It was the extensive farmland once owned by our noted Chief John Mt. Pleasant many years ago. Harry was the biggest farmer on our reservation. The topsoil on that land was four and five feet deep. The white man had no better land than this anywhere. What Moses neglected to mention was that this farm was in the area that the SPA intended to dig up for a reservoir.

In this *Fiction and Fact* pamphlet, which was mostly fiction, Moses ridiculed us for having a small population and made it out to be even smaller than it actually was. So few people, he said, had no right to stand in the way of his project. Small minorities then must always be swept aside. We admit to being few in number as Indian nations go, but our reduced population is a result of the wholesale massacres and kidnappings that we suffered 250 years previously when white people stole our children for slaves and grabbed our lands because, then as now, we were in their way. We had come north to forget our misery and find peace. Now we knew there was to be no peace.

The SPA offered us a land exchange for the land on the western side of our reservation which they wanted, and we expressed interest in this proposition. When the owners of the basic industries in our area heard of this proposed land exchange, they took options on 1,280 acres touching the eastern edge of our reserve. Our attorney explained to us that we would have to sell our land on the western side to the SPA and then buy the eastern acreage from the industrial committee holding the options. Moses said in his *Fiction and Fact* leaflet: "In effect all we asked the Indians to do was to swap some land on the River side of the reservation which the topography made necessary for the power project for some better contiguous land to the tremendous profit of the Nation and its members." This is only a half truth. Some of that eastern land was good, but there were also many acres of swamp and one very dry, rocky area. We would have been required to pay $1,100 an acre for this land to the option holders, which was the same price we were to have received for our own land on the west end. The average option price on the eastern land was $850 an acre, and some of it as low as $500 an acre. This exchange would certainly not have been one of "tremendous profit" to us as Moses claimed. Still, we did maintain an interest if the SPA could guarantee that this land would have the protection of the Treaty of 1794, the protection of the United States government, and be tax free. The SPA turned us down flat on this demand, saying that for this proposal to go through Congress would take time, and the power project did not have the time to spare. Instead, the SPA spent nearly two and a half years taking the case through one court after another. Surely they could have seen our guarantee through Congress in that amount of time.

The real reason the SPA did not want this land exchange plan to go before Congress was revealed when the case was argued before the United States Supreme Court. One of the Justices asked Solicitor General J. Lee Rankin, who was arguing the case for the Federal Power Commission, why the land exchange arrangement had not been undertaken. Rankin explained that the SPA did not want this proposition presented to Congress because it would set a dangerous precedent and jeopardize the methods that New York State had been using for a hundred fifty years in taking Indian lands for various public purposes. Here was proof of what we had known all along, that the state was not interested in justice—only convenience.

Attorney Lazarus held a meeting with our people in January of 1959 to persuade us to enter into negotiations with the SPA to show our good faith. He said our efforts in this direction would help us in our case. William opposed him hotly, saying that this would look as though we were just holding out for big money and were not sincere when we said that our land was not for sale at any price. The debate went on until 2:00 A.M. in a room that was 12° above zero. The SPA had begun to drive a wedge into our people and already at meetings the cry "Sell out! Sell out!" had become a byword with a few members of our nation. A motion was now made and passed to allow our attorney to negotiate with the SPA. Many of us still opposed this vigorously but were overruled. We had some comfort in the fact that the attorney was authorized only to negotiate and not to bind us. A final vote was to come a week later, after Attorney Lazarus had given us his report from the SPA.

The press had been barred from this meeting, but the newsmen got the details soon after we broke up. It was in the early-morning editions that same day. The papers reported that the Tuscaroras had a price and had directed their lawyer to negotiate for it. As some of us had feared, we were pictured in a very bad light as shrewd and crafty negotiators, interested only in holding out for the largest sum of money possible.

On January 29, 1959, we were to have our decisive meeting to vote on the issue of whether to accept the SPA offer. They were now prepared to give us $3,000,000 for our lands, and some of our people were being led astray by thoughts of big money. Others were prepared to reject this offer when the SPA went back on its promise to obtain an equal amount of land for us, because we had wanted the land guaranteed to us by the United States Congress. William and I were both in despair lest our people should be divided over this issue. Anything less than a unanimous voice would be weakness and might eventually mean our downfall. William had always told our people during these many months of trial and sorrow, when some began to weaken: "Money is like water in your hands. It falls through your fingers and disappears. But the land lasts forever." Now he was discouraged for he had run out of arguments.

On the day of our meeting, William received an encouraging letter from a friend telling of the struggle of the black people in the South and asking if the Tuscaroras were not as courageous as they. William was much cheered and felt that the presentation of these thoughts in our meeting that evening would strengthen those who were wavering. It was the answer he had been looking for. He read this letter before the council of our whole nation that evening and added a few other comments of his own. Then he moved to reject the SPA offer. The motion was quickly seconded and passed unanimously. The meeting had lasted only forty-five minutes. Our people had held together and had overcome the great temptation to part with our lands for a price.

The newspapers then began carrying word that the SPA was seeking permission to build its entire reservoir off our reserve. The Power Authority had claimed all along that this would be more expensive since there would be a graveyard to move and more houses to relocate. It would seem, however, that expense was no object with Moses, since he dragged the case out for over two years and spent a tremendous amount of money on legal and other fees to beat us. He kept complaining how much we were costing the SPA by holding up work; yet he could have had white man's land immediately and held his costs down. The trouble, we feel, was mainly spite on Moses' part. It seemed to us that he could never bear for anyone to oppose him in any way whatsoever, and he would spare no expense in sweeping away all opposition.

Our case went before the United States Supreme Court, on appeal by the SPA and FPC, because we had won in the United States Court of Appeals for the District of Columbia Circuit. The Supreme Court decision was handed down March 7, 1960, and was a split decision 4 to 3 against us. Justice Whittaker, speaking for the majority, based his decision on the claim that the Tuscarora Reservation was not a reservation because the title to the land was in the Tuscarora Nation and not in the United States government. This was a very strained definition of an Indian reservation.

Justice Hugo Black wrote the dissent, in which he was joined by Chief Justice Earl Warren and Justice William O. Douglas. He said that our lands were not indispensable to the SPA project and that there was "absolutely no evidence that Congress was in any way aware that these Tuscarora lands would be required by the Niagara Power Project" when it passed the 1957 Niagara Power Act. This was true, because the SPA bosses had never made specific mention of our lands when they applied to Congress for this act. The map exhibited to Congress by the SPA did not indicate that an Indian reservation was involved. This fact was brought out in the pleading before the Supreme Court. Justice Black further stated that our reservation was truly a reservation within the meaning of Congress and the fact that we owned title to it was merely a matter of Indian policy at the time we secured the land. Congress and the Supreme Court, he said, have always given a large interpretation to Indian treaties in order to protect Indians. He warned that this narrow interpretation of what an Indian reservation was would put in jeopardy many western tribal reservations that were owned in fee simple by the Indian people.[1]

It is seldom easy for a white person to understand why our lands are dear to us. Justice Black understood our feelings perfectly when he spoke of our great attachment to our ancestral homelands. He said what we could not have said better: "Some things are worth more than money and the costs of a new enterprise." He concluded his dissent with these famous words: "I regret that this Court is to be the governmental agency that breaks faith with this dependent people. Great nations, like great men, should keep their word."

Despite all our efforts, we had lost. Injustice had triumphed. A large portion of the land that we had so carefully accumulated 180 years earlier to compensate us for the loss of our North Carolina lands and to provide a homeland for our people forever had been wrenched from us by a government that was supposed to protect us. We had only the small consolation that our long delaying fight in the courts had forced the SPA to redesign its reservoir to take a smaller portion of our lands. Now only the southwest corner of our reserve west of Garlow Road was confiscated, and the section east of Garlow Road was retained by us. We were still despondent over our great loss, for the land that was taken was a significant portion of our reservation.

The families in the reservoir area were moved by the SPA. Some chose to have their old homes moved and others had new homes built for them by the Power Authority. Those who lost land were paid for it. The rest of the enrolled Tuscaroras whose land was not taken received $800 apiece as final settlement. The SPA got its reservoir and we were left with the scars that will never heal.

10

Undefeated

OUR LONG BATTLE with the State Power Authority and our eventual
defeat had left many of my people in a state of shock, rage, and despair.
For many years, we had taken the curses and insults of the SPA representatives, and then we felt the tight noose of the white man's courts
squeezing us. When it was over, we saw some of the best portions of our
land ruined as the state began digging its reservoir. No money could
ever compensate us for this great loss.

How can we ever explain to outsiders what our lands and our homes
mean to us? Industrial expansion and progress must be served, we are
told. It was just our misfortune to settle on lands that the white man
would want. A few good white friends supported us, but the business-
men and the politicians were against us. It was our further misfortune that the white politicians had more power and influence than we did
when it came to protecting their lands from confiscation. Many of our
white friends have assured us that even though we lost the land, we
gained a moral victory. We unfortunately live in a day when moral victories count for little.

Now that we have had to live with this reservoir a number of years,
we have witnessed the further permanent damage it has done. It has
ruined the fishing on our reserve by damming up the inlet. The Northern
Pike like to lay their eggs in swampy areas, and our reservation provided several such places for them. Now they are gone, along with the
other fish that used to swim in our waters. We have never been compen-
sated by the state for this loss.

While we were losing our land, the Seneca Nation in the 1950s and
early 1960s was also fighting a losing battle with the United States
government and the Army Corps of Engineers. The Kinzua Dam was
being built to flood a great part of the Allegany Reservation and all of
the Cornplanter Reservation, even though this project would violate the
Treaty of Canandaigua of 1794, which was the oldest treaty made by

the United States yet in existence. The army was interested in building this dam for flood-control purposes in western Pennsylvania. The Senecas wanted an alternate site that would save their lands.

The Philadelphia Quakers, who had a long-time interest in the Senecas, gave them strong support in fighting to keep their land.

We also found two good friends in Senators Jacob Javits and Kenneth Keating, who both opposed this project, but the rest of the big politicians were against us. President John F. Kennedy, for instance, refused to help us, even though as commander-in-chief of the army and head of government he could have done so. When a reporter in a press conference asked him about the Kinzua Dam controversy, he just brushed the whole issue aside and said that he believed the courts had decided it. This was a most hard-hearted attitude. He did not show the least distress of conscience that the treaty with our people was being broken or that Indian lands and homes were to be destroyed. For a politician who pretended to be a friend of oppressed peoples, this attitude showed his true colors. During World War I, we kept hearing that it was an immoral act for Germany to violate the Belgian treaty and call it "a scrap of paper." But now it was thought to be all right for the United States to consider an Indian treaty "a scrap of paper" any time it wanted to. That was different. After all, we were only Indians and the government had been pushing us around for centuries.

Our Indian people are often in greatest despair to find justice. When the Europeans first came among us, we received them kindly and taught them what we knew about surviving in this country. When the settlers at Plymouth and Jamestown were starving, we gave them corn to save them. When the Europeans finally became established in this country, then they wanted our lands and fought wars with us to seize our homes. This has been our history for more than three hundred years. We have survived because we have remembered the traditions of our ancestors and have refused assimilation and have refused to bow to injustice.

It is our hope that the resistance to aggression will be carried on by every succeeding generation, that men and women will arise who will follow the leading of the Great Spirit and hold our people together in their continuing struggle for survival. I always considered it the greatest blessing that my son William was such a person as this.

William's health had been declining for many years. The emphysema was advancing and he was often in pain. All his life he would never

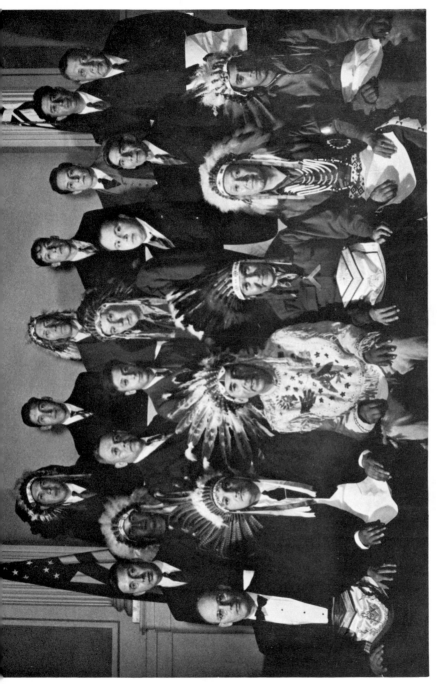

Indian Night at a Masonic Lodge. Indian Masons pose with the Master of the lodge. Front row, left to right, Master of the lodge, Roy Longboat, Clinton Rickard, W. Henry Watso, John Waterman, William Rickard. Second row, Melvin Johnson, Charles Neuman (a white man adopted by the Senecas), Noah Henry, Clark Rickard, Nelson Mt. Pleasant, Edison P. Mt. Pleasant, Wyman Jemison. Third row, David Patterson, Franklin Patterson, Harry Patterson, Titus Patterson (David, Franklin, and Titus are Harry's sons), unidentified, Carl Jemison, John Button. Photo around 1947. *Courtesy of Clinton Rickard family*

Beulah Rickard looking across Lake Bitobi on the Maniwaki Indian Reserve, July 26, 1972. It was her first trip back to Maniwaki in more than forty years, when, as a young bride on her honeymoon, she saw her husband arrested and thrown into jail in retaliation for his Indian rights work.

Officials of the Indian Defense League of America at the League's annual banquet in the Sheraton-Brock Hotel, Niagara Falls, Ontario, November 14, 1959. Left to right are Grand Chaplain Alexander J. General, President of the Niagara Falls Branch of the IDLA William Rickard, Grand President Clinton Rickard, Grand Vice-President David Hill, Grand Secretary Lehigh Antone. William is wearing his much-prized Cree jacket, given him by Lieutenant Colonel C. N. A. Ireson of Toronto. *Courtesy of* Niagara Falls Evening Review, *Niagara Falls, Ontario*

Chief Clinton Rickard in 1960. *Courtesy of Raymond V. Putt, Toronto, Ontario*

William Rickard shortly after he rose to national prominence as leader of the Tuscarora resistance against the New York State Power Authority's assault on Tuscarora land. He wears an Iroquois headdress and a Cree jacket. *Courtesy of Theodore Hetzel, Haverford, Pennsylvania*

Melvin W. Patterson, noted Indian leader, Tuscarora historian, journalist, and member of the Iroquois Temperance League. He played a major role in organizing the annual Indian Day pilgrimages held to honor Indian leaders of the past. The picture was taken at the ceremonies honoring Mohawk Captain Joseph Brant in Brantford, Ontario, September 16, 1967.

This was Clinton Rickard's favorite picture of his son William.
Courtesy of Clinton Rickard family

Flag of the Indian Defense League of America, made by Ray Fadden, director of
the Six Nations Indian Museum at Onchiota, New York, and presented to Clinton
Rickard. The name Te-ha-we-ia-he-re on the left is "Spreading Wing," or David
Hill. On the right, Ro-wa-da-ga-ra-de stands for "Loud Voice," or Clinton Rickard.
The pictorial symbolism on the flag represents various events from Indian history
and tradition. Directly underneath the title, the Plains tipi on the left and the Iroquoian bark longhouse on the right depict the ancient manner of living of these
peoples. The turtle, left center, represents the Iroquois Creation story: the world
on the turtle's back, with the sky dome overhead and the Tree of Light in the
middle of the dome. The animals on the bottom represent the seven Tuscarora
clans: Beaver, Wolf, Eel, Turtle, Snipe, Bear, and Deer. The Tuscarora tribe is in
this way especially honored because Chief Clinton Rickard, founder of the Indian
Defense League, was a Tuscarora. The wampum belt right center is a representation of a famous seventeenth-century Iroquois wampum belt, still in existence,
picturing the original union of the first five tribes of the Iroquois Confederacy. In
the center of the flag is Niagara Falls, dividing Canada and the United States, with
an Indian on each side. This symbolizes the great triumph of the Indian Defense
League in overthrowing the United States immigration law and opening the border
to Indians in 1928. The eagle, hovering above all, is an Indian emblem of watch-
fulness and protection. From his mouth proceed the Mohawk words, "Peace, Pros-
perity, Power, and Equity for all!" *Courtesy of Clinton Rickard family*

The old soldier at a ceremony honoring Tuscarora war. veterans held at the Tuscarora National Picnic, July 1968.

The two old comrades, Clinton Rickard and David Hill, stand together after more than forty years' service on behalf of their Indian people. *Photograph by Ron Roels*. Niagara Falls Evening Review, *Niagara Falls, Ontario*

Teresa Meness, who had long been prominent in Indian affairs, sits in the stands at the July 17, 1971, Border Crossing Celebration and listens to the memorial speeches honoring Chief Clinton Rickard, her friend of over forty years standing. She had lost her own husband Frank in April of the same year. It was she and Frank Meness who had entrusted the Algonquin wampum belts to Chief Rickard in 1926. With the passing of these two guardians of the wampum, she took the precious belts into her own custody, returned them to Maniwaki, and appointed a new wampum keeper from the Algonquin Nation.

marry because he did not want to be a burden to any woman. Despite his sickness, he was continually active. He worked on the farm and held jobs off the reservation and was always known as a good workman. For many years he served as my secretary. He wrote continually on Indian matters, and he traveled frequently, visiting other tribes and making valuable contacts. He never let down in his work for our people.

On September 16, 1964, the family took William to Niagara Memorial Hospital. As he lay there, he told the family that he felt this was his last trip to the hospital and that he would never come out again. At 6:15 in the morning on September 18, he passed away. The cause of his death was given as acute pulmonary edema, resulting from long-standing bronchiectasis.

Shortly after William's death, the following account of his life and work appeared in *The Native Voice,* an Indian newspaper in British Columbia:

> William Rickard, President of the League of North American Indians, died September 18, 1964, after an illness. A lifelong resident of the Tuscarora Reservation in New York State, he was also a former president of the Niagara District of the Indian Defense League of America, a post he held for 10 years. His passing at 46 takes from our midst one of the outstanding fighters for Indian rights in the United States.
>
> William "Fighting Bear" Rickard came to national prominence as a leader of his Tuscarora people in their struggle against the New York State Power Authority's attempt to appropriate a large part of the reservation for a reservoir. His writings on Indian problems and Indian values have been widely published. He was well-known in both the United States and Canada for his activities on behalf of Indians. He will always be remembered for his dedication to Indian life and his work in spreading friendship and understanding among all people.

This was a blow from which I thought I would never recover. I felt I had lost both arms when I lost William. I had suffered great grief before in my life, but now everything seemed to crumble. For a long while, I could not bear to hear his name mentioned without being overcome with grief. One night Clark came over to see me and we both sat out on the porch while he talked. He reminded me of my war experiences many years ago and recalled how I had narrowly escaped death on the battlefield. He spoke also of his own war experiences and told how he had been through the Battle of Bulge, seeing thousands of men killed on both sides, and had never received a scratch. What he had to say did console me somewhat and helped me to bear up under this great loss.

There was no one to carry on for me now that William was gone. For a long while, it was only with the utmost difficulty that I could maintain my interest in my former work. With my continued declining health, and with the loss of my son, it seemed as though there was nothing ahead anymore and that I had come to the end of the road. I had a big family, but they were all away during the day. My wife worked as a baker at the Niagara-Wheatfield High School and left the house early in the morning. My two older sons were married and living in their own homes. My daughter Onalee was also married and living in Rochester. Our other daughters, Beverly, Karen, Enid, and Lois, all worked off the reservation during the day. The only one who was home was my youngest son Norton, and he took care of the farming and was out of the house most of the day. Being in an empty house and thinking of William was more than I could stand. I stayed outdoors most of the time, even when it was raining, for that was preferable to the emptiness of the house. The family finally hired a man from the Six Nations Reservation to be a companion to me and do chores. Having some one around to talk with during the day gave a great boost to my spirits. As time passed, and as some friends continued to take an interest in me, I was able to come out of my grief and resume many of my old activities.

Our Tuscarora Nation continued to be threatened by outside forces. The SPA's taking of our land and the Supreme Court's split decision that we were not a reservation had set a bad precedent. Now any state agency that felt like it could walk in and condemn our lands and take them over. In the spring of 1966, Niagara Community College officials were considering a portion of our reservation as a new location for their expanded college. Fortunately, they chose another site instead. My people would not have stood idly by to be trampled on again. Many members of our nation were so enraged by the previous loss of our land that they had lost patience with passive resistance and the white man's courts. If the United States government would not protect us, we would have to protect ourselves. There was no point in going on living a life as humble doormats for the politicians to wipe their feet on. I myself was ready to take my gun and die defending our land, even as my ancestors had done.

All about us at every turn we continue to see the many problems facing our Indian people. Our treaties are always in danger of being undermined, our rights threatened, our reservations invaded, our way of life endangered. There comes a time when the older folks, who have fought so long and hard, will no longer be able to carry on the battle. Whoever reads these pages and is a true Indian, I pray that you may take up the struggle and carry on for and with our people. Always look to the Great Spirit for your guide, and then you can never go wrong and can never lose heart. Remember that the Indian way is a good way.

In more recent years, as I have advanced along into my eighties, I have suffered continued poor health. Progressing osteoarthritis has been most painful and has made walking difficult. Other illnesses have put me down from time to time. But I know that the Great Spirit must still have kept me here for a purpose. Since I have been active all my life, I find it very difficult to be inactive. The best way I can forget about my own problems is to become involved in something that will be of help to others. I feel that there are still ways in which I can be of benefit to my people.

For the past few years, a friend and I have been working on preserving the Tuscarora language. We have spent many hours recording both the language and the history and traditions of my people. In this way, the future generations will have our history and will not lose their knowledge of our language. On our reservation today, none of the little children can speak the Tuscarora language. In a few years, when the old folks have died off, the language will have died with them. That is why I have considered this work so important, so that eventually our young people can come back to their language. There is always much interest among our people in reviving the Tuscarora language. I believe that this extensive work we have been doing will help to make this possible.

Since 1967, I have taken an active part in pleading with the Canadian government to recognize the Jay Treaty of 1794. Article III of this treaty between the United States and Great Britain guarantees Indians special border-crossing privileges. From 1925 to 1928, we carried on the battle to get the United States to recognize this treaty protecting our rights. Canada, as a successor state of Great Britain, should, according to the British North America Act, according to international law, and in all honor, recognize this treaty. It has consistently refused to do so ever since 1867, even though the Canadian Parliament could very easily right this great wrong by simply passing legislation implementing the treaty. In 1967, which was Canada's Centennial Year, the Indian Defense League began pleading with Parliament to recognize our rights in this regard. Lehigh Antone, grand secretary of the League, wrote to every member of Parliament, and I made a personal appeal to Prime Minister Lester Pearson. Later, I made the same appeal to Prime Minister Pierre Elliot Trudeau. To implement this treaty would be a small matter to Canada but a great relief to my people. Instead, Canada has dealt harshly with Indians who have been demonstrating on the St. Regis Reservation in favor of their Jay Treaty rights, and their rights which existed long before the Jay Treaty was in effect or there were even any white men in our country. The officials have even threatened to send the Canadian army into the St. Regis Reservation if there are any more demonstrations in support of the Jay Treaty. We Indians support law and order, too. We ask only that Canada also support the law by recognizing this longstanding international treaty. We continue to maintain hope that the people of Canada will support us in securing our old rights.

Another project that has occupied my attention in recent years has been to warn my people about the shyster lawyers who are continually gaining their confidence and then bleeding them dry. These lawyers promise great things for large sums of money and then go off with the money and leave us with no results. Some will drag their "cases" out indefinitely by writing a few letters and doing a minimum amount of work while continually requesting more and more money to carry the "case" to a conclusion that never comes. Some of them live close to Indian reservations and solicit Indian cases in a way no honest lawyer would do. Others travel from reservation to reservation soliciting cases, winning the confidence of Indians by their anti-government talk, and charging far more than any honest lawyer would for their work. One of them recently came to our reservation without any invitation from the chiefs whatsoever and offered to take over a case for which we already had an attorney and which was already in progress. When asked what he would do and how much it would cost, he said he would write a letter and it would cost $500. The chiefs turned him down flat, but many of my people are taken in by him and by other lawyers just like him. Indians are not a competitive people, and therefore they are an easy mark for an aggressive and greedy person. It seems as though our people will never be free from these slick-tongued parasites.

An unexpected recognition of my life's work came to me from Niagara University in the summer of 1969. A university citation was presented to me at our annual Border Crossing Celebration on July 19 by President Kenneth F. Slattery. It read as follows:

> You have been honest, resolute, and forthright in standing firmly for justice and equality throughout your entire career. By your efforts, important international treaties were honored, many persons falsely accused were set free, and the values and contributions of Indian culture were preserved. You have worked tirelessly to build bridges of friendship and understanding between all peoples. In recognition of your more than half century of dedicated service in behalf of human rights, the Board of Trustees of Niagara University present to you this citation so honorably earned and nobly deserved.

I was gravely sick in Veterans Hospital in Buffalo at the time and not so sure that I would ever recover. My family asked Dave Hill to accept this citation for me at the celebration. I was glad that Dave could share the honor with me in this way, because he has always stood by my side and has never let our people down.

Since the Great Spirit has preserved me thus far, beyond the usual span of years, and has carried me safely through all sickness, I know it is for a purpose. He still has work for me to do, and as long as I have breath in me, I will continue this work in whatever way I can to benefit our people.

The latest thing I have been able to do for our people is to enter a protest on a violation of their border-crossing rights. Every once in a while we hear of American immigration officials at Niagara Falls and other places along the border forcing Indians coming across the border to show an Indian identification card that the Canadian Indian Department issues on request to registered Indians. Many registered Indians never bother to apply for one, and the many thousand nonregistered Indians cannot get one at all. Some of these immigration officials will not let our people across the border into the United States without one of these cards, which is the equivalent of making Indians have passports—

something that is not required of white Canadians. It is also a direct violation of the immigration laws, of the Jay Treaty, the Treaty of Ghent, the court decisions in our favor, and the historic rights we had as original inhabitants of this land.

In December of 1970, there came to my attention an especially bad series of violations of the treaties, immigration laws, and Indian rights by certain immigration stations in Minnesota. This situation had existed for a number of years before I heard of it. There is an Indian school in that state that has a number of Ojibway and other Indian students from across the border. The United States immigration agents, particularly at Emerson and Rainy River, were being harsh toward Indians and not permitting them into Minnesota without showing Indian identification cards, which they did not have, even though they were obviously full-blooded Indians. They finally did let one girl across because, although she did not have a card, she could present a Canadian treaty number and she also had the school's dean of women along to plead for her. One young man who was a treaty Indian but who had no Indian identification card was required to report back to the port of entry periodically, just because he lacked this card.[1]

I got to work on this problem immediately. Senator Walter F. Mondale of Minnesota is well known as a good friend of the Indian people. I therefore sent him proofs of this racial prejudice and violation of laws that were occurring in his state. I also sent him copies of the old legal cases that supported our border-crossing rights. Senator Mondale gave this matter his prompt attention and sent me periodic reports on its progress.

The ruling of Immigration Commissioner Raymond F. Farrell on this problem was set forth in a letter to Senator Mondale dated March 17, 1971, and completely vindicated the Indians' right to cross the border without hindrance. Because of its historic importance, the letter is quoted below in its entirety. Although the commissioner claims, obviously in good faith, that identification cards were not required of Indians entering the United States, it is evident that he was not given the complete facts by his subordinates.[2]

Dear Senator Mondale:

Further reference is made to your letter of January 7, 1971, concerning the entry of persons of the American Indian race into the United States.

American Indians born in Canada possess historic treaty rights to enter this country without hindrance. These rights are safeguarded by section 289 of the Immigration and Nationality Act, a copy of which is attached. The effect of that section is that an American Indian born in Canada with at least fifty percent of blood of the American Indian race is not subject to any impediment in entering across the border.

The Regional Commissioners of this Service at both Twin Cities, Minnesota, and Burlington, Vermont, have conducted a thorough inquiry of our Canadian border offices and it has been determined that no officers have required the presentation of Indian identification cards or other documentation by Indians seeking entry into the United States. Some questioning is, of course, necessary to establish the eligibility of the applicant for classification as an American Indian born in Canada. Once established, however, the questioning is terminated and the individual allowed to proceed.

It must also be recognized that some individuals not entitled to Indian classification will attempt to fraudulently claim Indian classification or even use Indian documentation as a means of accomplishing their entry into this country. Such individuals can be detected only by careful questioning and we are aware that it is possible to involve a person who actually is a North American Indian. However, we believe that it is rare that a bona fide Indian would be so mistaken.

We wish to emphasize that there is no requirement now, nor has there been one in the past, that for the purpose of this Service a North American Indian need apply for or present documentation of any kind.

> Sincerely,
> Raymond F. Farrell
> Commissioner

This ruling should stop the harassment of Indians by American immigration officials.

The one message I wish to leave with all my people everywhere is to work for unity. If we do not all work together, if we are divided, then eventually we face the danger of being destroyed. I have always considered all Indians everywhere to be one people. We speak different languages, but we are of one blood and we have the same problems throughout the country. I want to see Indians help themselves, carry on their own affairs, and be independent. This we can do if we all pull together.

While we are working to advance ourselves, we should also spread peace wherever we go. This has been the teaching our ancestors handed down to us. It is the lesson I have tried to teach throughout my life. I have continually sought to build a bridge of peace between peoples of different races. The Great Spirit did not create men to destroy each other. My jacket carries in beadwork the symbol of universal friendship. A white hand and a red hand hold fast to the Covenant Chain, signifying a perpetual link from ancient times to the present. Our hand is open in friendship. We do not seek hostility. We do not want to be forced into it. But we are determined to protect our rights. My experience through more than eighty years has taught me that people of good will of all races can work together to bring about justice for all and the betterment of mankind. May the Great Spirit help us all.

Editor's Afterword

WHEN I FIRST BEGAN the task of compiling this autobiography, my hope was to be able personally to present the final printed copy to Clinton Rickard as a memento of our many years' work together. Such was not to be. Although Chief Rickard saw the typescript and knew that "the history," as he called it, was nearing its completion, he took the long trail before the book could be published.

At 5:45 in the morning of June 14, 1971, Chief Clinton Rickard passed away in the Veterans Administration Hospital in Buffalo, not quite a month past his eighty-ninth birthday. The cause of death was given as right middle cerebral artery thrombosis.

As one reads over Clinton Rickard's autobiography, one can see very plainly that his life was one of repeated tragedy—his unhappy childhood, the deaths of his first two wives, the deaths of four of his children, the bitter opposition to him from among his own people and the deep and lasting hurt it caused him, the unjust jail sentence that nearly killed him. He never permitted these sorrows to crush his spirit or to distort his personality. He was sustained both by his deeply religious nature and by the conviction that he had been predestined "to spread peace" wherever he went. It was this belief that carried him through the most difficult of times and gave him a personal spiritual victory over the forces that sought to defeat him.

This world and the next were always very close to Clinton Rickard, as they are to all Indians who have not been totally assimilated to the white man's ways and thinking. Glenn B. Coykendall, an Episcopal missionary to the Senecas and close friend of Rickard, recalled an occasion when they were in Washington attending a congressional hearing on Indian affairs. Clinton Rickard took time out to escort some Indians, dressed in full regalia, and a few white friends to the Washington Monument. There, in a quiet ceremony, Rickard communed with the spirit of George Washington, telling him about Indian troubles, confident that

163

the first president would understand and sympathize. In a brief ten minutes, the meeting between this world and the next was over. Rickard, having unburdened himself, quietly left with his little group of friends.[1]

The old cooperative spirit of the Indian people comes to the fore when a family has suffered bereavement. People began stopping by the Rickard home to leave dishes of food so that the family would not have to be bothered with cooking during their time of sorrow just prior to the funeral. Some of the women of the community came by to help with the meals and to wash dishes to relieve the grieving family of these chores.

With the decline of the role of the clan in Tuscarora society, and the complete abandonment of the concept of phratry, or moiety, the modern funeral practice considerably modifies the older custom, as described by J. N. B. Hewitt in 1882:

> At the present time, the Tuscaroras observe the following custom in regard to the disposal of their dead. When any one dies, the body is dressed for burial by brothers, or sisters, of the clan of which the dead person was a member. The dead is then given a wake, or wakes if necessary, at which there is continual singing and a midnight feast which is free from indecent levity. The family of the dead person are requested to retire to sleep and are not allowed to do anything toward making arrangements for the funeral which is conducted after the manner of Christians. The watchers, singers, grave-diggers and cooks, etc. must be from clans different from that of the deceased and must be from clans composing the phratry to which the clan of the dead belongs.[2]

Today, this older arrangement is no longer followed. Instead, the Tuscaroras follow the white practice of seeking the services of a professional undertaker, and the preliminary services and watching usually take place at the funeral parlor, with the funeral service being held later in the church. Those friends who assist the family in their bereavement are not necessarily from the clan or moiety of the departed. It is, in fact, doubtful that any present-day Tuscarora remembers the proper division of clans into moieties—or phratries, to use Hewitt's terminology.

The Tuscaroras still follow the old Indian custom of not leaving the house vacant for ten days after a death. It is the belief that the spirit of the departed stays around for that period and might want company before its final departure. The home is therefore always kept occupied during this time. A neighbor woman kept the house and took care of the small grandchildren during the hours the Rickard family was watching at the funeral parlor and attending the funeral service and burial.

A large company of mourners—both the obscure and the prominent —was present from near and far to pay their last respects to a great man. Friends from as far away as Ohio, Chicago, New York City, Grand River, St. Regis, Maniwaki, Allegany, and Cattaraugus came to spend a last few moments with their departed friend. There were also mourners from the nearby Tonawanda Reservation, and many from his own Tuscarora Reservation. People whose admiration and respect had never been suspected appeared at one or more of the services. Only one of two individuals came to be seen rather than to mourn. The others were all sincere in their presence.

Mrs. Frank Meness, who had lost her own husband on April 18, made the eight-hour trip from Maniwaki with one of her sons to be at the grieving family's side and to mourn her good friend of forty-six years' standing. He was clothed in the Indian costume she had made for him in 1925. As she commented approvingly to Mrs. Rickard on the fact that he was to be buried in his costume, Mrs. Rickard explained: "His most precious possession!"

About twelve years before his death, Chief Rickard had chosen the hymns he wanted sung at his funeral. A group of five Mohawks from the Grand River Reservation used to practice hymn singing in their own language at his house. The chief loved to listen to them and indicated several of the hymns that he especially liked for his funeral service. At the time of his death, two of the original five—Chester Bomberry and Harry A. Hill—were still available. They were joined by Jesse Porter of Grand River and Tuscarora Pine Tree Chief Edison P. Mt. Pleasant, who had learned to sing in Mohawk and had often sung with Harry and Chester.

The opening hymn was "The Lord Is My Shepherd," followed by the chief's favorite, "Send the Light." The other selections were "The Narrow Road," "The Beautiful Beyond," and "Will You Seek To Save the Lost." During the singing of the last hymn, "Alone with God," the members of the Indian Defense League of America arose and remained standing, out of respect for their departed leader.

He was given a military burial on June 16 in the Mt. Hope Cemetery on the Tuscarora Reservation. As the Tuscarora Honor Guard fired the final salute and the bugler played taps, the old warrior was laid to his final rest.

It has long been the custom among the Tuscaroras to bury the dead in special areas according to their clan affiliation rather than according to nuclear family affiliation. With the large number of "out" marriages and with the decline of clan functions in modern times, this custom has often fallen into abeyance as the Indians follow the white practice of burying in family plots. Clinton Rickard, according to Tuscarora tradition, would have been buried in the Beaver clan section, next to his mother. His son Norton, however, picked out a spot for his father's burial next to William, who was a member of the Bear clan. The entire family approved, believing that it would be the wish of the two men to be buried side by side.

After the burial, according to Tuscarora custom, the mourners came to the Rickard home to visit with and to console the family. At such a time, the bereaved family always provides a meal for those who come by the house to pay their respects. The Ransomville Chapter of the Order of the Eastern Star, which contains both white and Indian members and to which both Beulah Rickard and her daughter Beverly belong, volunteered to take over the responsibilities of the luncheon, as they had done when William died. Indian neighbors also brought extra food to the Rickard home for the occasion.

The house could not contain all the people who came by after the funeral, and the overflow went out into the yard to eat and to visit.

There was an added note of sadness among those mourners who had been involved in Indian rights work. Not only had they lost a friend and a leader, but they recognized that, with his passing, they had come to the end of an era. "There is no one to take his place" and "No one now can do the work he did" were typical of the comments. A few began reminiscing how some rivals over the years had tried jumping into Clinton Rickard's moccasins while he yet lived, by ridiculing him and trying to shove him aside. None of these rivals could measure up to the man they tried to replace. Some of the men shook their heads and wondered who would have the strength, the personal prestige, and the vision now to hold Indians together and to lead not only the Indian people but whites as well. They had no answer to these questions but merely became more deeply convinced of the seriousness of their loss.

The many letters of condolence that came to the Rickard family showed the esteem in which this elder Indian statesman was held by those who knew him. One of the most feeling tributes was written by Congressman Henry P. Smith III, from Niagara County's 40th Congressional District: "Chief Rickard was a mighty oak which has now fallen in the forest when its time had come. His life was one of leadership and courage and integrity. He was a pillar among his people and among the white man too. His accomplishments for his people will constantly furbish and brighten his memory, and his name will remain glorious to his descendants."

The Indian Defense League's Border Crossing Celebration on July 17, 1971, was turned into a memorial ceremony in honor of Chief Rickard. A riderless horse representing the fallen leader led the parade. Behind him came Indian horsemen in full regalia, Indian and white dignitaries in colorful Indian costumes, the Oneida band, and several floats representing Indian organizations. At Oakes Park in Niagara Falls, Ontario, farewell speeches recounting the grand president's achievements over the years were given by both Indian and white friends of the chief.

The founder and grand president was gone, but those he had trained and who were inspired by his example were determined to carry on both the organization he had established and the continuing struggle for Indian rights.

Clinton Rickard was an Indian patriot. More than that, he was a great humanitarian. He had the knack of drawing not only all tribes but all races together in the common cause of humanity and justice. He built bridges of friendship wherever he went, overcame evil with good, and conquered injustice with honesty and perseverance in the right. Among those who did not agree with him in all respects, there were always a number who admired him and were willing to work with him to advance justice. His enemies were able to hurt him but not conquer him. He was essentially a man of good will and was therefore far more interested in converting his enemies and making them his friends than he was in crushing or humiliating them. Most remarkable was his ability to overcome the jealousy that often plagues Indian groups and to hold the Indian Defense League together for over forty years through numerous tribulations and financial stringencies. As one devoted Indian member said after Clinton Rickard's death: "Chief always had the right words to say to smoothe over our difficulties." He taught Indians to be proud of being Indian, to honor their traditions, and to appreciate their culture. A man of tremendous courage and dedication to high purpose, he was able to overcome the personal tragedy in his own life and to live a life of service to others.

Notes

EDITOR'S INTRODUCTION

1. Black Hawk's autobiography has been reprinted many times since it first appeared in 1833 and has become an American classic. The best edition is Donald Jackson, ed., *Black Hawk: An Autobiography* (Urbana: University of Illinois Press, 1955). Wooden Leg's narrative contains much valuable historical and ethnological information on both his own tribe, the Cheyenne, and also on the Sioux. See Thomas Marquis, ed., *Wooden Leg: A Warrior Who Fought Custer* (Lincoln: University of Nebraska Press, 1962; originally published in Minneapolis by The Midwest Company, 1931). Paul Radin was the first trained anthropologist to elicit and edit an Indian autobiography, and his *Crashing Thunder: The Autobiography of an American Indian* (New York: D. Appleton and Company, 1926), is accordingly an anthropological landmark. Many years later, anthropologist Nancy O. Lurie persuaded Crashing Thunder's sister to dictate her life story: Nancy Oestreich Lurie, ed., *Mountain Wolf Woman, Sister of Crashing Thunder: The Autiobiography of a Winnebago Indian* (Ann Arbor: University of Michigan Press, 1961).

2. A careful discussion of the disastrous effects of termination on Indian tribes can be found in William A. Brophy and Sophie D. Aberle, *The Indian: America's Unfinished Business* (Norman: University of Oklahoma Press, 1966), Chapter 7.

3. The Buffalo Creek Reservation was disbanded as a result of the Treaty of Buffalo Creek in 1838; its inhabitants moved to the Cattaraugus Reservation.

4. Annemarie A. Shimony, *Conservatism among the Iroquois at the Six Nations Reserve,* Yale University Publications in Anthropology No. 65 (New Haven: Department of Anthropology Yale University, 1961), p. 53.

5. Lewis Henry Morgan, *League of the Ho-De-No-Sau-Nee or Iroquois,* 2 vols. (New Haven: Human Relations Area Files, 1954; originally published in 1851 and 1901), I, 93.

6. For a discussion of Iroquois secret societies, see Shimony, *Conservatism among the Iroquois,* pp. 281–85; and William N. Fenton, *Masked Medicine Societies of the Iroquois,* Annual Report of the Board of Regents of the Smithsonian Institution, Publication 3624 (Washington: Government Printing Office, 1940), pp. 397–430.

7. Jack O. Waddell and O. Michael Watson, eds., *The American Indian in Urban Society* (Boston: Little, Brown and Company, 1971), is a recent study dealing with problems faced by urban Indians of various tribes in the United States.

CHAPTER ONE—EARLY YEARS

1. This is a reference to the legendary Iroquois Tree of Peace, which was planted at the time of the founding of the Five Nations Confederacy. All weapons of war were thrown into a cavern beneath the tree, where they were carried away by an underground stream. The formerly warring nations were then joined together in a perpetual league of peace.

2. Clinton's paternal grandmother was born in November 1822, the daughter of Abigail and Harry Patterson. This Harry Patterson had a great grandson of the same name who figures later in the book. Register of Deaths, Town of Lewiston Records.

3. When William Garlow died, March 25, 1917, his daughter, Lucy Rickard, gave his birthdate as "unknown" and his age as "about 90." Tuscarora tribal census rolls, which, however, are frequently inaccurate, list him as being ninety-two at time of death. Clinton believed he might even have been ninety-four. Register of Deaths, Town of Lewiston Records.

4. These were Warren Curtiss (joined Ransomville Lodge in 1866), Elton E. Ransom (joined 1867), and probably William N. Burmaster (joined 1901). Personal communication from Neil C. Robinson of Lockport, New York, Secretary of Ransomville Lodge No. 551, April 23, 1972.

5. It was originally a Congregational church, but when the American Board of Commissioners for Foreign Missions withdrew its support from the church in 1860, deeming it capable of self-support after more than fifty years of nurture, the mission associated with the Niagara Presbytery in 1861. At the present writing, it is nondenominational.

6. Although there was a longstanding belief on the Tuscarora Reservation that Edgar did undertake formal study for the ministry, letters from the Registrars of both Dickinson College and Moody Bible Institute indicate that he never attended either institution and was never enrolled in the Moody Correspondence School.

7. There have always been a few whites living on the Tuscarora Reservation, as there have been on many reservations throughout the United States. Occasionally these are white families renting land from Indians. More frequently, they are whites married to Indians. Intermarriage of Tuscaroras with Indians from other tribes is also common. Although individual Tuscaroras have frequently rented or leased different portions of their land to whites, they can never alienate their land by selling it to whites. Ultimate sovereignty over the lands of the Tuscarora Reservation resides in the Tuscarora Indian Nation.

CHAPTER TWO—ARMY LIFE

1. Both Clinton Rickard and Charles Helenbrook, of Troop F, have this date in their "Soldier's Handbook." The Monthly Returns for the Eleventh Cavalry state that the ship arrived on February 4, 1902. The discrepancy can undoubtedly be attributed to confusion in dates after crossing the International Date Line. Monthly Returns of the Eleventh Cavalry, February 1902, Records Group 94, Records of the Adjutant General's Office, Microcopy 744, Roll 103, National Archives.

2. Approximately five thousand Filipinos, representing various Filipino ethnic groups, fought on the side of the Americans. According to an official army report in 1902: "This force consists of 11 companies Macabebes, 13 companies Ilocanos, 4 companies Cagayans (Northern Luzon), 4 companies Tagolos, 2 companies Bicols, 6 companies Visayans, and are serving as any other regular company organization." United States War Department, *Annual Reports of the War Department for the Fiscal Year Ended June 30, 1902* (Washington: Government Printing Office, 1902), IX, 204. The Igorotes were also friendly to the Americans.

3. Lieutenant Colonel Argalus G. Hennisee was actually transferred to the Island of Samar, where the First Squadron of the Eleventh Cavalry was operating. After a very lengthy illness, he was sent back to the United States in August 1902 for further hospitalization. That the loss of the pack train and his unpopularity as a commander did not affect his career adversely is noted in his transfer to the Fifth Cavalry with promotion to full colonel on September 13, 1902. He was retired from the service on January 16, 1903. Monthly Returns of Eleventh Cavalry, April–August 1902, Microcopy 744, Roll 103, National Archives; Francis B. Heitman, *Historical Register and Dictionary of the United States Army from Its Organization, September 29, 1789, to March 2, 1903,* 2 vols. (Washington: Government Printing Office, 1903), I, 523.

4. According to Charles Helenbrook, who served with Rickard in the Philippines, the Filipinos carried their bolos in a two-piece bamboo scabbard, held together with bamboo fibers. The boloman could thus put his weapon to use very quickly, without having to draw it from the scabbard, for the sharp edge would cut right through the fibers holding the scabbard together when the user struck an opponent. On the effectiveness of these bolomen, Helenbrook commented: "They could lay you away quick!"

5. General Miguel Malvar surrendered to General J. Franklin Bell at Lipa, Batangas, April 16, 1902, and gave the following reasons for his capitulation. The letter is found in Captain John M. R. Taylor, *The Philippine Insurrection Against the United States. A Compilation of Documents with Notes and Introduction,* 6 vols. in galley proofs (1906, National Archives Microfilm Publication M-719, Roll 9), V, Galley No. 89 GV F-M.

THE REASONS FOR MY CHANGE OF ATTITUDE

April 16, 1902

The desertion of my most trusted officers.

The knowledge that the people in all the towns were looking for me, to induce me to surrender.

Lack of food in the field, owing to the concentration in the zone, apart from the increased activity of the American troops; because of the adherence of the towns, to the American troops on account of the concentration and the measures taken by General Bell.

Compassion for the prisoners and the exiles.

Because I believe that if the planting of rice in the month of May was prevented by a continuation of the war, the non-combatants, as well as the men in the field would die of hunger.

Because the American forces kept me constantly on the move from the month of February down to the last moment, when I found myself without a single gun or clerk, as what little escort I had became separated from me in a sudden attack made on us by the American forces near the town of Rosario; and because all my staff officers had already fallen into the hands of the Americans.

Also on account of a letter from Pedro Paterno.

The government I wanted to ask for was independence under a protectorate; a government of our own, with a flag of our own, under the protection of the American government.

MIGUEL MALVAR

6. There is no indication throughout his military career of Rickard's ever having displayed cowardice. He, in fact, received an excellent commendation from his officers and was even remembered years later by Captain Tompkins for his great spirit and loyalty as a soldier. Rickard is probably referring to a fear or apprehension upon going into battle—a common emotion among soldiers which many of them do not like to admit.

7. It is a common Indian belief that a spirit that is about to depart, or one that has already departed, will occasionally appear to a living person. In this instance, it was a cherished grandmother taking farewell of her favorite grandson.

8. Companies I, K, L, and M of the Thirtieth Infantry were stationed at Malahi (Malagi) Island. The prisoners sent to this island were men sentenced to hard labor, one of their tasks being to quarry and crush rock for use in laying roads. United States War Department, *Annual Reports of the War Department for the Fiscal Year Ended June 30, 1903* (Washington: Government Printing Office, 1903), III, 165, 458.

CHAPTER 3—MARRIAGE AND FAMILY

1. The judgment of the Court of Claims to compensate the original New York tribes for the Kansas Claim was made on November 22, 1898, and payments to the Six Nations and allied tribes were begun in 1906. Payments were made to the Tuscaroras in 1906, 1907, 1908, and 1909. Out of the total award of $1,733,-267.72 for the Kansas lands, the Tuscaroras received $68,862.72 as their share. The tribes who participated in this award were: Brotherton, Cayuga, Oneida, Oneidas of the Thames, Onondaga, Seneca, St. Regis, Stockbridge-Munsee, and Tuscarora. A small final payment of $179.33 was made to the Stockbridge-Munsee in 1924. See 33C.Cl.521 and *United States General Accounting Office Report: Re Petitions of the Cayuga Nation, Emigrant New York Indians, Munsee Tribe, Oneida Nation, Oneida Nation of New York, Oneida Tribe of Wisconsin, Seneca Nation, Seneca-Cayuga Tribe of Oklahoma, Six Nations, Stockbridge Munsee Community, Stockbridge Tribe, Tonawanda Band of Senecas, and Tuscarora Nation. Indian Claims Commission Nos. 75, 84, 300, 321, 340, 342-A, 341-1, and 368-A* (Washington: United States General Accounting Office, June 29, 1962), pp. 99–108.

2. Clinton Rickard's land was also known in the Tuscarora language as *Miahgyageha'*. That is, "the late Miah's place"—Miah being the common diminutive of Jeremiah. Who this Jeremiah was, or whether he was the same person as Chief Black Nose, could not be ascertained.

CHAPTER 4—INDIAN LEADERSHIP

1. When a person becomes a chief, he is said to be a member of the silver circle.

2. This is the way Chief Rickard generally wrote the name. The phonemic rendering of the name is *Ruwedogoradi*.

3. The determination to maintain their status as a sovereign confederacy, separate from the United States, had been traditional with the Six Nations Indians. Many other Indians in the United States worked for and accepted United States citizenship. Traditionalist Indians generally saw the offer of United States citizenship as a means of assimilating them and destroying their government and culture.

4. Theron M. Ripley to Clinton Rickard, February 19, 1925, Fifth Division, New York State Department of Public Works, Personal Papers of Clinton Rickard.

5. This controversy between Mt. Pleasant and Rickard dragged on for many months and was faithfully reported in the western New York newspapers. *The Buffalo Courier,* November 18, 1923, pp. 89–90, gave a detailed account of the trial, and also a list of the Tuscarora chiefs as taken from the court testimony. The chiefs were listed as follows: Deer clan, George D. Rickard, sachem chief, and Dr. P. T. Johnson, chief warrior; Beaver clan, Clinton Rickard, sachem chief, and Edgar Rickard, chief warrior; Bear clan, Thomas Williams, sachem chief, and William Chew, chief warrior; Snipe clan, Lucius Williams, sachem chief, and George Williams, chief warrior; Wolf clan, Luther Jack, sachem chief, and Warren J. Brayley (J. Warren Brayley), chief warrior; Eel clan, Thomas Isaac, sachem chief; Turtle clan, William Johnson, sachem chief, and Grant Mt. Pleasant, chief warrior.

6. "Indians enfranchised in the 1920s were entitled to enfranchisement funds calculated on the same basis as present-day enfranchisement payments. On enfranchisement an individual is entitled to receive one per capita share of the funds of his band and, if his band receives treaty annuity annually, he is also entitled to 20 times the annual per capita treaty payment from departmental funds." Personal communication from the Office of the Registrar, Community Affairs Branch, Department of Indian Affairs and Northern Development, Ottawa, Canada, January 27, 1972.

7. Anti-Oriental sentiment had been strong in the United States for more than forty years before the passage of the restrictive Immigration Act of 1924. The most intense prejudice against Orientals centered in California, which had the largest Oriental population of any of the states. The Chinese Exclusion Act of 1882 prohibited the entry of Chinese laborers into the United States for a period of ten years. This limitation was ultimately extended and then made permanent. Section 14 of this act denied Chinese the right of obtaining United States citizenship. The Root-Takahira Agreement, or Gentlemen's Agreement, of 1907 permitting Japanese immigration was abrogated by the Immigration Act of 1924, with California again leading the way in calling for complete exclusion. United States naturalization policy had permitted naturalization only to "white persons." Under this restriction, in 1922 in the Ozawa case the United States Supreme Court

denied naturalization to Japanese persons. In 1923 the Supreme Court overturned the Oregon-granted naturalization of a high-caste Hindu, born in India, on the grounds that he was not a "white person" within the meaning of United States naturalization law. It was against this background that the United States Immigration Service excluded North American Indians from Canada from entry into the United States under Section 13 (c) of the new immigration law.

8. John C. Plain, M.D., the white physician who attended Deskaheh, gave the cause of his death as "pulmonary hemorrhage." Deskaheh was the son of William and Lydia General. Register of Deaths, Town of Lewiston Records.

9. The belief that there was an "extra-limital" Masonry among American Indians was held by other Indian Masons such as the noted Seneca anthropologist Arthur C. Parker, who had written a pamphlet on the subject. For Parker, the essence of Freemasonry lay in its "spiritual impulse," and "the practice of its moral and philosophical teachings." There was, then, "an *inherent* Masonry in men capable of becoming Masons and . . . an *inductive* Masonry into which inherent Masons are led. . . ." "A thorough examination," said Parker, "will reveal that the Indians had indeed a Freemasonry but not the Accepted Masonry." Arthur C. Parker, 32°, *American Indian Freemasonry* (Buffalo: Buffalo Consistory, A.A.S.R.N.M.J.U.S.A., 1919), pp. 8–10. Parker and Clinton Rickard were frequent correspondents and this pamphlet is preserved in the latter's personal papers.

10. This ceremony is held among the Longhouse people ten days after the death of a person to give comfort to those who are grieving and to bring the mourning period to a close.

CHAPTER 5—THE BORDER CROSSING

1. Henry Hull, Commissioner General, Bureau of Immigration, to Clinton Rickard, September 11, 1925, Bureau of Immigration File No. 55442/383, Personal Papers of Clinton Rickard.

2. The moose-hide costume was made by Mrs. Meness and the yoke was beaded by Mrs. Elizabeth Brazeau of the Maniwaki Reserve.

3. *Amikonini* is the Algonquin word for *Beaverman*.

4. The name was originally *Tentensee* or *Tentensi,* meaning Blue Jay. White people, who had difficulty pronouncing it, made it *Tenasco.*

5. The tribes represented may possibly be the so-called Seven Nations of Canada. This alliance was formed by the French during the French and Indian War to aid them in their imperial struggles with the British. The tribes of the Seven Nations were the three Lake of Two Mountain groups—Algonquin, Nipissing, and Mohawk—Abnaki of St. Francis, Caughnawaga Mohawk, Huron of Lorette, and Cayuga and Onondaga of Oswegatchie. The Oswegatchies later joined the émigré Caughnawagas who settled at St. Regis and were absorbed by them.

6. 18 F. (2d) 282.

7. 25 F. (2d) 71.

8. Public, No. 234, April 2, 1928. 45 Stat. 401.

CHAPTER 6—TRAGEDY AND TURMOIL

1. The United States and Great Britain had submitted the Cayuga Claim to international arbitration. For the United States argument in this case, see *American and British Claims Arbitration, Cayuga Indians. Oral Argument by Fred K. Nielsen, Agent and Counsel for the United States* (Washington: Government Printing Office, 1926).

2. According to informants from the Tuscarora Reservation, Robert Anderson's bitter hostility against Clinton Rickard and against Indians from Canada stemmed largely from the fact that a married woman whose husband was related to Anderson had a Canadian lover. He accused Rickard of "bringing Canucks over to be lovers to our women while we are away at work." Anderson felt that had it not been for Rickard's work in opening the border, this situation affecting his family would not have happened. Clinton Rickard was completely unaware of the Andersons' personal problem in this regard and believed the trouble in the council was largely the result of his brother Edgar's resentment over having lost the election as secretary. Anderson, however, merely exploited Edgar's longstanding jealousy of his brother for the purpose of recruiting a potent ally in his feud with Clinton.

3. The Shawnee Beaver clan are the descendants of a group of Shawnees adopted by the Tuscarora Beaver clan. Clinton Rickard said that his clan adopted them "about a hundred years ago" and that "they came in from Pennsylvania." They might have joined with the Tuscaroras during the latter's northward journey through Pennsylvania in the eighteenth century, but they were probably adopted sometime around 1832, when the Tuscaroras received payment for the sale of their North Carolina lands. According to some Tuscarora informants, adoptions took place "when the Tuscaroras got their money." These adoptees and their descendants are not supposed to hold office in the Tuscarora Indian Nation while there is a living member of the Tuscarora Beaver clan. The old Tuscarora Wolf clan has now died out and the present Wolf clan members on the Tuscarora Reservation are from an adopted Oneida line. The clan is small, but provides clan mothers and chiefs for the Tuscaroras. Luther Jack and J. Warren Brayley were the last of the old Tuscarora Wolf clan chiefs.

4. Lila Jimerson afterwards married a white man named Wallace H. Hilliker and lived quietly near Perrysburg, New York. She died January 18, 1972, in her seventies. Nancy Bowen died many years before.

5. It was Rickard himself who, at a time when public interest in Indians was high, seized the opportunity to publicize the inadequate educational facilities for Indians. This had been a problem that had worried him for many years, and now, through speeches and newspaper interviews, he was able to arouse whites to help his people. On June 2, 1956, at a ceremony in Buffalo, New York, the Peter Doctor Memorial Scholarship Fund, an all-Indian organization, honored Chief Rickard for his part in securing equality of education for reservation Indians. Calling him a "Door Opener," the citation stated that he had "helped to open in 1930 the doors of New York's high schools for the first time to all reservation Indian pupils. This was accomplished by telling well and truthfully the story of Indian needs to the public, with result that the New York Legislature enacted the law of April 22, 1930, providing transportation and tuition costs for such pupils."

State Senator Nelson W. Cheyney of Eden, New York, who sponsored this legislation, was honored at the same ceremony.

CHAPTER 7—LEGALIZED TREACHERY

1. The following letter from Alex Nattoway of Barriere, dated July 15, 1931, gives definite proof that, despite the Canadian government's contention that Rickard solicited money at Barriere, he had never been there and was known to Indians north of Maniwaki by reputation only. The letter is preserved in Rickard's personal papers. It is presented exactly as Nattoway wrote it.

Barriere Post
July 15/31

Dear Chief, Clinton, Rickard,

We are writing to you to let you no some news.

We had a meeting July 9th their were some Grand lake indians and also Simon lake indians and all our band barriere indians.

And we were talking about to ask you to come and see us. If you could come up you would make all you indians glad and happy lots of us never seen you yet.

We would like if you could come right here at barriere, and at Grand lake indians and also the Simon lake indians want to see you very bad.

You could use a car 60 miles from Maniwaki and from their we could meet you by canoe, 55 miles to reach Barriere.

And from barriere to Grand lake distant 60 miles and other 45 miles to reach Simon Lake indian and Simon lake to Semnettere 25 all by canoe. And we will take you back from where we meet you.

I wad [was] down at Maniwaki June 6th and I seen Moses Odjick.

He told me that they were to have a meeting Sept 15th and I heard that you were coming up at that time. I told the Grand lake indian and Simon lake indian for that time Sept 15th and rally can not afford to go because it is to much expence for the gang, the people is poor this year it would be all right For three men[.] If you could come up we could help you for your fair.

We could wait on you all the month of August because later some indian is going up for in the bush. Answer soon this letter let us No if you could come up or not.

If we get you letter soon and saying that your coming up, Some indians want to get some Moose hides and Moccison and Mitts and we like to get the answer soon.

Simon lake indian want you to answer one letter to Chief Inyas Papate, Simon lake, Senneter, P. Quebec.

Well this is all the best wishes and luck for you from all our indians And answer one lette[r] here

Your very faithful

Alex Nattoway,
Barriere Post,
Hudson Bay, Co.
Via Maniwaki, Quebec

2. During a visit to Maniwaki in July of 1972, I found it stated by both Indian and white informants that Xavier Fafard, the priest to the Indians, had pressured

Indian Agent Gauthier into issuing the warrant for Rickard's arrest. Rickard had suspected all along that his arrest was connected with his role in reforming the Indian school the year before. Editor.

3. The entire letter of complaint of the Algonquin Indians, of which this is only a portion, was printed in full in *Niagara Falls Gazette,* October 13, 1931.

4. Seth T. Cole to Clinton Rickard, December 16, 1931. Personal Papers of Clinton Rickard.

5. The Canadian report is quoted at length in Henry L. Stimson to Royal S. Copeland, December 7, 1931, United States Department of State, State Department File No. WE 342.1121 Rickard, Clinton/21. Copy in Personal Papers of Clinton Rickard.

CHAPTER 8—DEPRESSION AND OPPRESSION

1. "His spirit is not here," is a direct translation from the Tuscarora. It means that the child will not live to grow up.

2. Report to Clinton Rickard from J. William O'Brien, Supervisor of Census, Niagara Falls, New York, May 12, 1930, Fifteenth Census of the United States, Department of Commerce, Bureau of the Census, Personal Papers of Clinton Rickard.

3. In his reply to Rickard, Agent Harrison made the following defense: "When I was asked to submit road projects for the different reservations and had a meeting with the Council of your reservation to get the information the same as I did with the Councils for all the other reservations, my report and recommendations were made and personally presented to the Commissioner. At that time I was told that the road projects on these reservations could not be carried out for the reason that the reservations in this state belonged to the Indians and not to the Government and no funds have ever been appropriated under those projects for any reservation in this State." W. K. Harrison, Special Agent, New York Agency, to Clinton Rickard, May 21, 1936, Personal Papers of Clinton Rickard.

4. *United States ex rel. Goodwin* v. *Karnuth,* 74 F. Supp. 660.

5. The first pageant, entitled "The League of Peace," was presented on both August 11 and 12, 1949, and portrayed the founding of the Iroquois Confederacy.

6. Chief Rickard came in late, as the guests were already in the midst of the meal. As he entered the hall, walking with slight difficulty because of arthritis, the guests arose and gave him a spontaneous ovation and remained standing until he was seated at the head table. Nothing could have better demonstrated the affection and esteem with which these friends regarded their aged leader.

CHAPTER 9—THE STATE POWER AUTHORITY

1. The decision rested very largely on the grammar and interpretation of Section 3(2) of the Federal Power Act, 16 U.S.C. Sect 2796(2): "'reservations' means national forests, tribal lands embraced within Indian reservations, military reservations, and other lands and interests in lands owned by the United States, and withdrawn, reserved, or withheld from private appropriation and disposal under the public land laws; also lands and interests in lands acquired and held for

any public purpose; but shall not include national monuments or national parks."

Justice Whittaker emphasized, "and *other* lands and interests in *lands owned by the United States,*" exempting Indian tribal lands owned in fee simple by Indian nations from the designation of "reservation." Justice Black emphasized the phrase, "*tribal lands embraced within Indian reservations,*" claiming that since the Senate had specifically included this as an amendment to the House version of the act, it had meant it to include such lands as the Tuscarora and Pueblo reservations, which were owned in fee simple; otherwise, there would have been no point in adding the phrase, for the House bill already covered lands "title to which was held by the United States Government." He denied that the phrase "tribal lands embraced within Indian reservations" was in any way limited or qualified by the following phrase, "other . . . lands owned by the United States." Supreme Court of the United States, Nos. 63 and 66. October Term, 1959. *Federal Power Commission* v. *Tuscarora Indian Nation. Power Authority of the State of New York* v. *Tuscarora Indian Nation,* March 7, 1960.

CHAPTER 10—UNDEFEATED

1. Canadian Indian law divides the aborginal people into status Indians, nonstatus Indians, and Eskimos. Status Indians are further divided into treaty Indians and nontreaty Indians. According to Section 2(1) of the Canadian Indian Act (R.S.C. 1970, c. I–6), an "Indian" is "a person who pursuant to this Act is registered as an Indian or is entitled to be registered as an Indian." Just who is "entitled to be registered" is largely determined by a statute of May 26, 1874, which considered who was eligible "to use and enjoy the lands belonging to the various tribes and bands of Indians in Canada," or who belonged to a band for whom land had been set apart by the government or by treaty. A declaration of the Governor-in-Council was also sufficient to designate an Indian band to come under the terms of the act. A descendant of any one of these persons is also entitled to be registered. Legal status as an Indian is thus achieved by being registered according to the terms of the Indian Act. A treaty Indian is one whose tribe had at one time entered into treaty relations with the government.

2. Raymond F. Farrell, Commissioner, to Senator Walter F. Mondale, March 17, 1971, United States Department of Justice, Immigration and Naturalization Service, File No. CO 703.821. Copy in Personal Papers of Clinton Rickard.

EDITOR'S AFTERWORD

1. Personal communication from Glenn B. Coykendall, October 30, 1969.

2. This differs from the practice of other Iroquoian tribes, where members of the opposite phratry, or moiety, perform these functions. Hewitt MS 372–a, Bureau of American Ethnology, Smithsonian Institution, p. 187; William N. Fenton, *An Outline of Seneca Ceremonies at Coldspring Longhouse,* Yale University Publication in Anthropology No. 9 (New Haven: Department of Anthropology, Yale University, 1936), p. 19; Annemarie A. Shimony, *Conservatism among the Iroquois at the Six Nations Reserve,* Yale University Publications in Anthropology No. 65 (New Haven: Department of Anthropology, Yale University, 1961), p. 236.

Index

Aguinaldo, Emilio, 17, 33
Algonquin Indians, 66, 70–71, 73–75
Alien Registration Act, 127
American Revolution, xix–xx

Barriere Post, Indian settlement, Quebec, 104–105, 112
Bell, J. Franklin: reconcentration policy, 17; conquest of General Malvar, 23–27
Bennett, Robert B., 110
Black, Hugo, 151
Bonnelly, Adrian, 85
Border Crossing Celebration. *See* Indian Defense League of America and illustrations
Bowen, Nancy: 98–100; *see also* illustrations
Boy Scouts, 132
Brayley, J. Warren, 79–80, 97
Burmaster, William N., 7
Bussell, Frank P., 119

Camp Wallace, Luzon, 29
Caughnawaga Reserve, 83, 127
Cayuga claim: 93–94; *see also* illustrations
Chabot, John, 66
Chaffee, Adna R., 17
Chew, Leah, xxi, 45
Chew, William, 95–97
Cheyney, Nelson W., 101
Citizenship, Indian, 52–53
Clans: Iroquoian, xx; matrilineal, xx, 1; marriage exogamy, xxi, 102; Onondaga Eel clan, xxi, 45, 102; Tuscarora, xxi; chiefs, xxi–xxii

Claus, Huron, 75
Codd, Robert M., Jr., 78–79, 82, 85–87
Cole, Seth T., 110–113
Collier, John, 125
Conscription, 126–27
Coolidge, Calvin, 87
Copeland, Royal S., 110
Cornplanter Reservation, 153
Cotton, James, 106–107, 109
Coykendall, Glenn B., 99–100, 163
Crouse, Elon, 141
Curtis, Charles, 78, 110, 117
Curtiss, Warren, 7
Cusick, Nicholas, 14

Douglas, William O., 151
Decker, George P., 60–61, 63, 67–68, 70, 88
Dempsey, S. Wallace, 73, 78–80
Deskaheh. *See* Levi General
Diabo, Paul K., 83, 85
Dickinson, Oliver B., 84–85

Eisenhower, Dwight D., 134, 140
Everett, Edward A.: 49; *see also* illustrations
Everett Report, 49–50

Farrell, Raymond F., 160–61
Fort Des Moines, 34–35
Fort Ethan Allen, Vermont, 14
Fort Myer, Virginia, 14, 134
Fort Niagara, 13–14
Fort Porter, Buffalo, 14
Franchot, Edward E., 130–31
Frazier, Lynn J., 110

179

Freemasonry: xxiv, xxvi–xxviii, 7, 41–42, 65, 77, 97–98, 105, 134; *see also* illustrations

Gamble, John G., 143–44
Gansworth, Nellie, 91, 109
Gansworth, Willard: 91, 109; *see also* illustrations
Garlow, Andrew, 52, 95
Garlow, Chauncey, 68, 86–87
Garlow, Emeline, 54
Garlow, William: 3–4, 8; *see also* illustrations
Gauthier, E. S., 104, 110
General, Alexander J.: 66–67, 68; succeeds brother Levi as Deskaheh, 71; *see also* illustrations
General, Emily, 132
General, Levi (Deskaheh): 58–65, death, 65; *see also* illustrations
Goodwin, Dorothy, 129, 130–31
Grand River Reserve. *See* Six Nations Reserve
Green, Eldreth, 127
Greene, Elton, 141
Gurley, William F. E., 91, 117

Harriman, Averell, 142–43
Harrison, W. K., 67, 122–23
Hennisee, Argalus G., 15, 19
Henry, Job, 71–73, 79–80
Hewitt, Alvis: 71, 82, 141; *see also* illustrations
Hewitt, James, 12–13
Hewitt, John, 141
Hewitt, John N. B.: 81–82, 92; *see also* illustrations
Hill, David: 75–76, 85–86, 88, 91–92, 127–30, 159; *see also* illustrations
Hill, Thomas S., 45
Huggins, W. I., 11, 39
Husband, W. W.: 78, 87; *see also* illustrations

Immigration Act of 1924, 64–65
Immigration problems, 64–65, 69–73, 75–88, 129–31, 159–61
Indian Defense League of America: formation, xxiv–xxxv, 76–77; social and cultural activities, xxv, 85; wins immigration victory, 87; Border Crossing Celebration, 88–89; opposes Alien Registration Act, 127; bogus IDLA, 128; founds Six Nations pageant, 132; and United Nations, 132; opposes termination, 136, 137; Rickard memorial service, 167; *see also* illustrations
Indian Reorganization Act, 125–26
Iroquois. *See* Six Nations

Jack, Luther, 1, 7
Javits, Jacob K., 154
Jay Treaty, 67, 69, 80–81, 119, 129, 157–58, 160
Jimerson, Lila: 98–100; *see also* illustrations
Johnson, Elias, 9, 80
Johnson, Philip T., 1, 80, 95, 97
Johnson, Tamar: 9; *see also* illustrations
Johnson, William J., 95

Keating, Kenneth, 154
Kennedy, John F., 154
King, William, 78, 85, 87
Kinzua Dam, 153–54
Kocsis, Emery J.: 132; *see also* illustrations

Latham, William, 139, 146
Lazarus, Arthur Jr., 141, 144, 147, 149
League of Nations, and Six Nations membership, 62

MacArthur, Arthur, 17
McCandless v. *U.S. ex rel. Diabo*, 84–85
MacGregor, Clarence, 78, 85, 87
Malvar, Miguel, 17, 27
Marchand, Clothilde, 98–100
Marchand, Henri, 98–99
Martin, Leslie, 76
Martin, Sophie: 76; *see also* illustrations
Masons. *See* Freemasonry
Meness, Frank: 73–74, 165; *see also* illustrations

Meness, Teresa: 73, 165; *see also* illustrations
Menominees, 137
Moieties, Tuscarora, xxi
Mondale, Walter F., 160
Mt. Pleasant, Beulah: 102; *see also* Beulah Rickard
Mt. Pleasant, Franklin, 42–43
Mt. Pleasant, Grant: 42–44; controversy with Rickard, 54–57
Mt. Pleasant, Hamilton, 139
Mt. Pleasant, John, 148
Mt. Pleasant, Margaret, 102
Mt. Pleasant, Nelson: 13, 102; *see also* illustrations
Moore, Guy B., 99–100
Moorehead, Warren K., 55–56
Moses, Robert, 142, 145, 147–49

Nash, George: 47, 94; *see also* illustrations
National Congress of American Indians, xxv–xxvi
Nattoway, Alex, 105–106
Nattoway, Philip, 74
New York State, Indian Land purchases, xix
New York State Power Authority, and Tuscaroras, xxvii, 138–52 *passim*
Niagara University, 146, 159
Nitzberg, William N., 83–84

Oka Reserve, 73
Oneida Indians: sell lands to New York State, xix; migration to Canada in 1849, xx
Onondaga Eel clan, xxi, 45, 102
Onstott, Ivy Leona: 34–35; *see also* Ivy Rickard

Parker, Arthur C.: and Freemasonry, xxiv, 174n, 66, 99–100
Parker, C. C., 103, 107
Parker, Ely S., xxii, 98, 134
Patterson, Barbara, 148
Patterson, Elizabeth (wife of Clinton Rickard): 44–45; *see also* Elizabeth Rickard and illustrations
Patterson, Elizabeth (grandmother of Clinton Rickard). *See* Elizabeth Patterson Jack Rickard
Patterson, Ely, 5
Patterson, Harry: 55, 95, 122, 127, 141, 148; *see also* illustrations
Patterson, Holland, 42
Patterson, Homer, 39
Patterson, John Wesley: 51; *see also* illustrations
Patterson, Julia Garlow: 44–45, 51, 54–55; *see also* illustrations
Patterson, Titus: 44–45, 50–51; *see also* illustrations
Patterson, William H.: 42–43; *see also* illustrations
Pearson, Lester, 158
Pembleton, Harriet, 139
Peters, Jeremiah, 4
Peters, Marcus: 39, 50, 97, 116; *see also* illustrations

Rankin, J. Lee, 149
Ransom, Elton E., 7
Reed, May, 41
Rickard, Beulah: xxviii, 102, 108, 116–17, 156, 165–66; *see also* illustrations
Rickard, Charles Curtis: 117–18; *see also* illustrations
Rickard, Chester: 1, 55, 107–109, 116; *see also* illustrations
Rickard, Clark: 4, 6, 45, 109, 117–19, 126, 155–56; *see also* illustrations
Rickard, Clinton: birth, xvii, 1, 4; influence of, xvii–xix, xxvi, xxviii; death, xvii, 163; education, xxiii, 8–10; Indian regalia, xxiii, 70–71, 78; Indian sovereignty, xxiii–xxiv, 125; religion, xxvii–xxviii, 8; boyhood, 5–6, 10–11; enlists in army, 13; army training, 14; leaves for Philippines, 14–15; arrival in Philippines, 17; war experiences, 19–29; contracts malaria, 27–29; return from Philippines, 33–34; at Fort Des Moines, 34–35; discharged from army, 35; marriage to Ivy Onstott, 37; army pension, 39, 115; buys land for home, 39; employment, 37–38; Freemasons, 41–42, 134; refuses chief-

Rickard, Clinton (*cont.*)
tainship, 42; veterans' activities, 44, 133; marriage to Elizabeth Patterson, 45; becomes a chief, 50; Tuscarora gymnasium, 50–51; opposes Indian citizenship, 52–53; controversy with Grant Mt. Pleasant, 54–57; works with Levi General (Deskaheh), 58, 60, 63–67; continues Deskaheh's work, 68; becomes wampum keeper, 73; immigration and Tuscarora chiefs, 79–80; Cayuga claim, 93–94; split in Tuscarora council, 95–97; Marchand murder trial, 98–100; improves Indian education, 100–101; marriage to Beulah Mt. Pleasant, 102; arrested, 103–108; barred from Canada, 113–14; at United Nations, 131–32; Boy Scout work, 132; opposes termination, 134–37; phone tapped, 145; Tuscarora language project, 157; Niagara University citation, 159; funeral, 164–66; memorial service, 167; *see also* illustrations

Rickard, Edgar H.: 1; attends Carlisle, 12, 80, 95; opposition to Clinton, 96–97, 126; *see also* illustrations

Rickard, Edith Leona: 40, 45; *see also* illustrations

Rickard, Eli, 91, 117–18

Rickard, Elizabeth, 44–45, 47–48, 87, 90–91

Rickard, Elizabeth Patterson Jack (grandmother): 2–3, 7, 27, 30–31; *see also* illustrations

Rickard, Frederick: 1, 45; *see also* illustrations

Rickard, George D.: 1–2, 4–6, 7, 11–13, 55, 95, 97, 110, 117; *see also* illustrations

Rickard, Herald: 40–41; *see also* illustrations

Rickard, Ivy: 34–35, 40–41; *see also* illustrations

Rickard, Lucy: 1, 4–5, 7–8, 43–44, 50, 66–67; *see also* illustrations

Rickard, Ralph, 45

Rickard, William: Indian leader, xxvi, xxvii; religion, differs with his father, xxvii, 45; beaten by schoolmates, 81, 97, 109, 115–17; breeds Indian corn, 118–20, 129, 135–36; fights to save Indian land, 139–41, 143, 145–46, 150; death, 154–56; *see also* illustrations

Roosevelt, Eleanor, 94

Roosevelt, Franklin D., 94

Ross, James H., 83–84

St. Regis Reservation, 158

Schifter, Richard, 141

Seneca Nation, 153–54

Six Nations: formation of confederacy, xix; opposes Indian citizenship, 52

Six Nations Defense League. *See* Indian Defense League of America

Six Nations Pageant, 132

Six Nations Reserve, xx, 58–66 *passim*, 84, 127

Smith, William: 119, 132; *see also* illustrations

Snell Bill, 95–96

State Power Authority, New York, and Tuscaroras, xxvii, 138–52 *passim*

Stillman, Lulu G.: 49; *see also* illustrations

Stimson, Henry L., 113

Tompkins, Frank: 20, 27, 33, 35; *see also* illustrations

Treaty of Canandaigua, 121, 153–54

Treaty of Ghent, 67, 69, 160

Trudeau, Pierre Elliot, 158

Truman, Harry S, 134

Tuscarora Indians, xvii, xxix–xxiii, 1–3, 8–9, 38, 50–51, 95–97, 120–27, 138–52 passim, 164, 172n

Wadsworth, James W. Jr., 70, 78, 80

Warren, Earl, 151

Wheeler-Howard Act. *See* Indian Reorganization Act

Wilson, Edmund, 145